I0819091

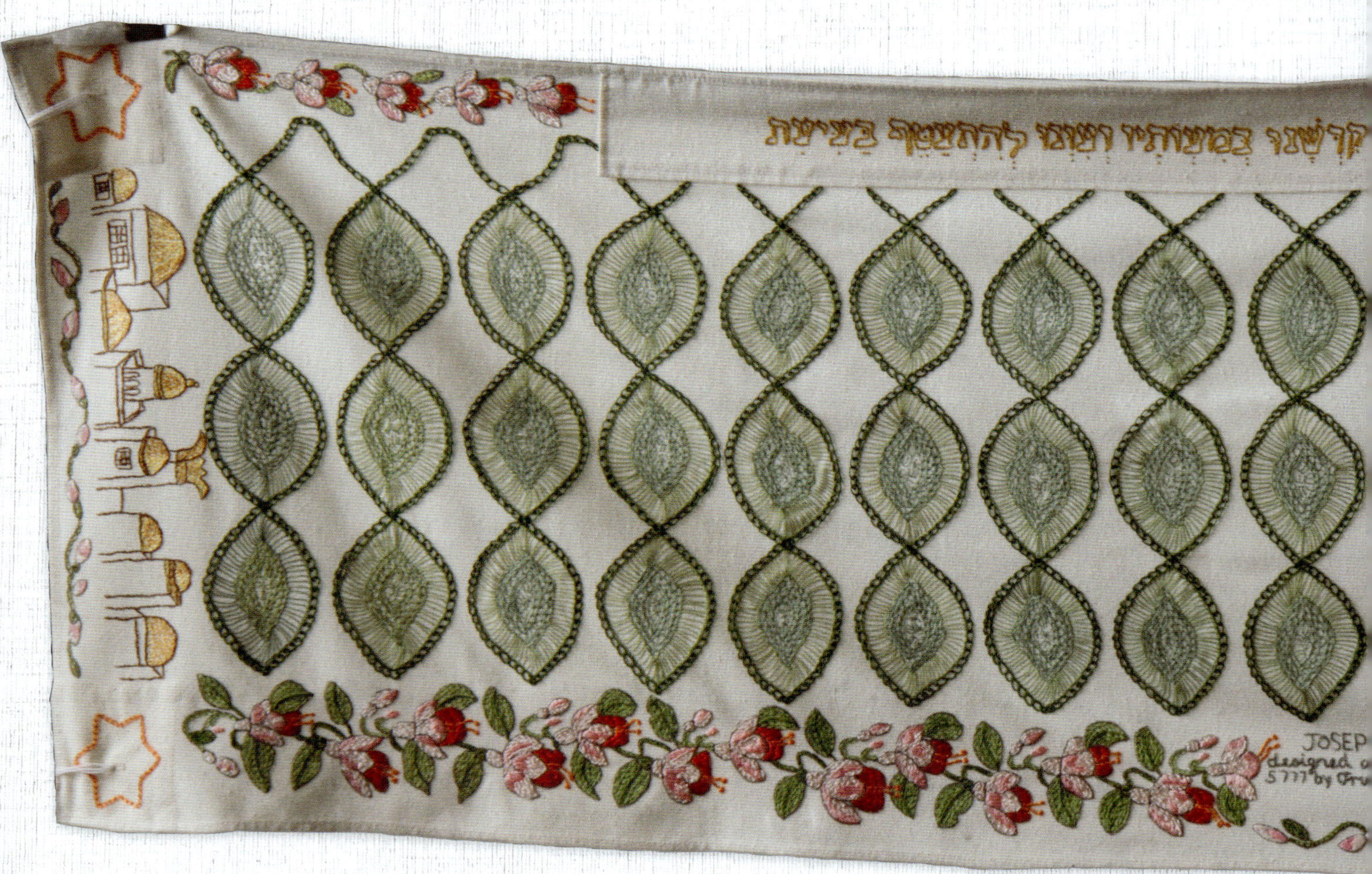

Joseph Ariel's tallit, completed 2018

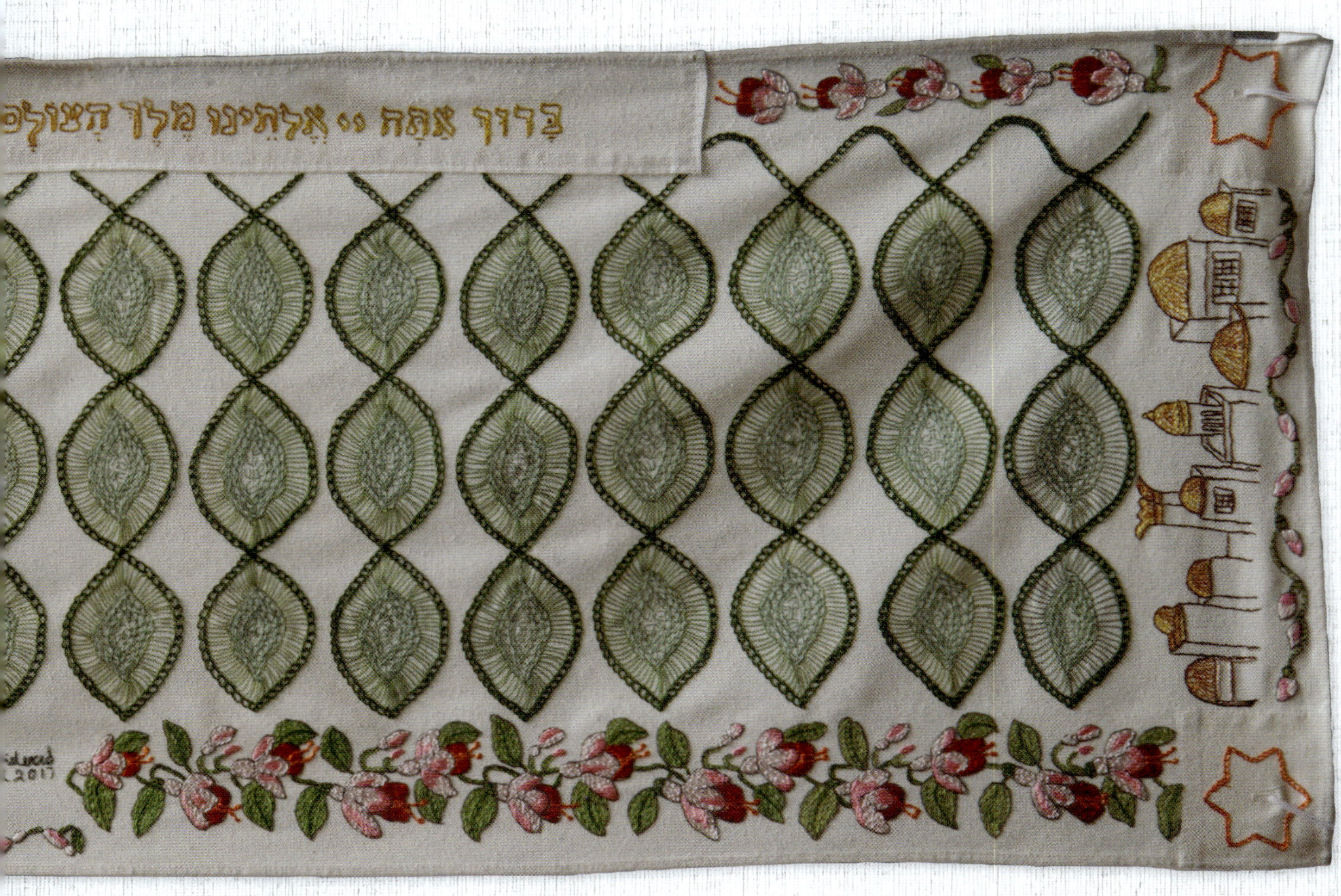
ברוך אתה •• אלהינו מלך העול

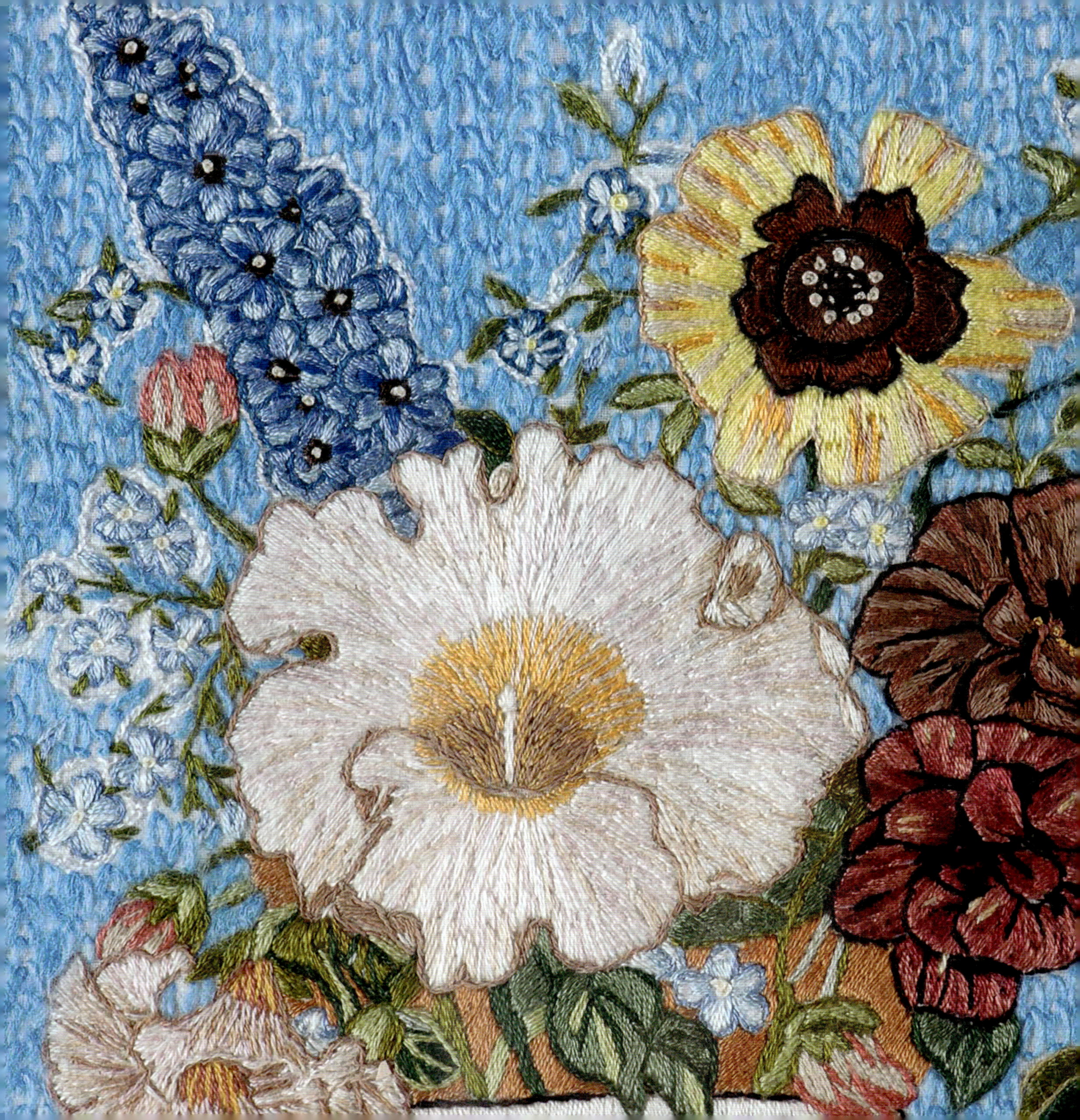

STITCHED & SEWN

The Life-Saving Art of Holocaust Survivor Trudie Strobel

Advance Praise

"A work of beauty: breathtaking tapestries, combined with a sensitive, poignant narrative of how art prevailed over suffering in the life and work of one survivor. *Stitched & Sewn* is medicine for one's eyes and heart."

— David Fishman, author of *The Book Smugglers* and professor of history at the Jewish Theological Seminary of America

"Eli Wiesel once told me that some survivors were cursed with a perfect and total recall of the worst moment they had witnessed during the Holocaust. Dr. Elizabeth Loftus has confirmed that traumatic memory does exist. As if frozen in time, survivors can literally count the stitches on an SS guard's name tag at the moment he shot the parent next to them.

"Too many memories of seeing just such unspeakable stitches eventually rendered one survivor mute. Trudie Strobel learned to speak again by preserving what she had seen, stitch by stitch, through the ancient art of monumental tapestry. Her renowned masterworks have been scattered to museums and private collections around the world. For the first time, Strobel's tapestries are curated in this little masterpiece of a book, which combines art, art history, and biography. Author Jody Savin cleverly intertwines photographs of the tapestries with the story of how these glorious works came to be. The artist speaks poignantly to Savin about how each piece helped stitch the shredded tapestry of her life back together. *Stitched & Sewn* is a remarkable story and a very important book."

— John Loftus, former president of the Florida Holocaust Museum and author of *The Secret War Against the Jews*

"For creative artists the great question had been: Can there be art after Auschwitz? The work of Trudie Strobel makes the question seem academic. *Stitched & Sewn* tells a terrifying and wondrous story."

— Joseph Koerner, Thomas Professor of History of Art, Harvard University

"*Stitched & Sewn* is truly an extraordinary book. It is a rare combination of beautifully blended text and illustration that turns pain and anguish into beauty and hope."

— Rabbi Daniel Sperber, author of *Minhagei Yisrael: Origins and History* and the Milan Roven professor of Talmud at Bar-Ilan University in Israel

"*Stitched & Sewn* is a testament to the profound power of the human experience; the ability to endure the worst atrocities and then create meaning and indelible beauty is a buoying, wondrous thing. That three artists from different media—writer Jody Savin, photographer Ann Elliott Cutting, and tapestry artist Trudie Strobel—came together to realize this book reminds us that all of our life's work, including that of survival, is autobiography. You won't soon forget the stories captured here, in words and images."

— Alison Singh Gee, author of *Where the Peacocks Sing*

"Trudie Strobel is a master storyteller who weaves her tales with needle and thread. Her work—whether embroidered or sewn—lays out a history of Jewish resilience in the face of repression and genocide. Using vibrant colors and images drawn from legend, tradition, and memory, Strobel has created stunning, detailed testaments to her own brave reckoning with her history as a child of the Holocaust."

— Michal Lemberger, author of *After Abel and Other Stories*

"*Stitched & Sewn* is a cautionary tale of what happens when a society loses its humanity. Trudie Strobel's story reveals the emotional carnage of surviving the Holocaust and the cost of silence, and it's a testament to the healing properties of art and documenting impossible pain. Strobel literally stitches together tapestries of memory and Jewish life, and in so doing implores us to face the ugliest chapters of history, and to never forget them."

— Michelle Brafman, author of *Washing the Dead* and *Bertrand Court*

"When there are no words, art is the storyteller, each stitch a story. *Stitched & Sewn* is an incredibly beautiful, haunting journey, showing the power of art to integrate us and cultivate healing."

— Tina Payne Bryson, PhD, LCSW, co-author of *The Whole-Brain Child* and *The Power of Showing Up*, and the author of *Bottom Line for Baby*

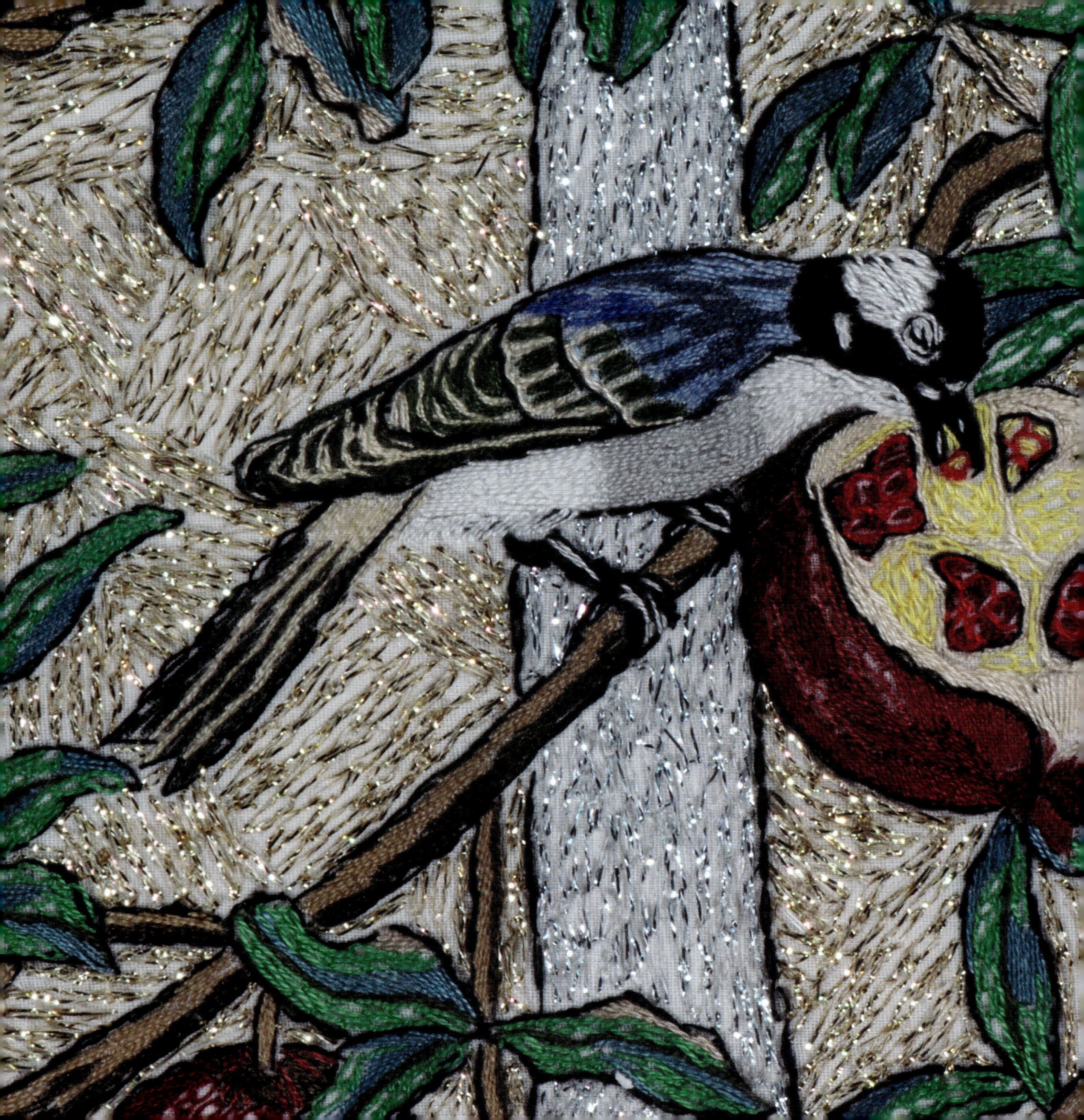

STITCHED & SEWN

The Life-Saving Art of Holocaust Survivor Trudie Strobel

Jody Savin • Photographs by Ann Elliott Cutting

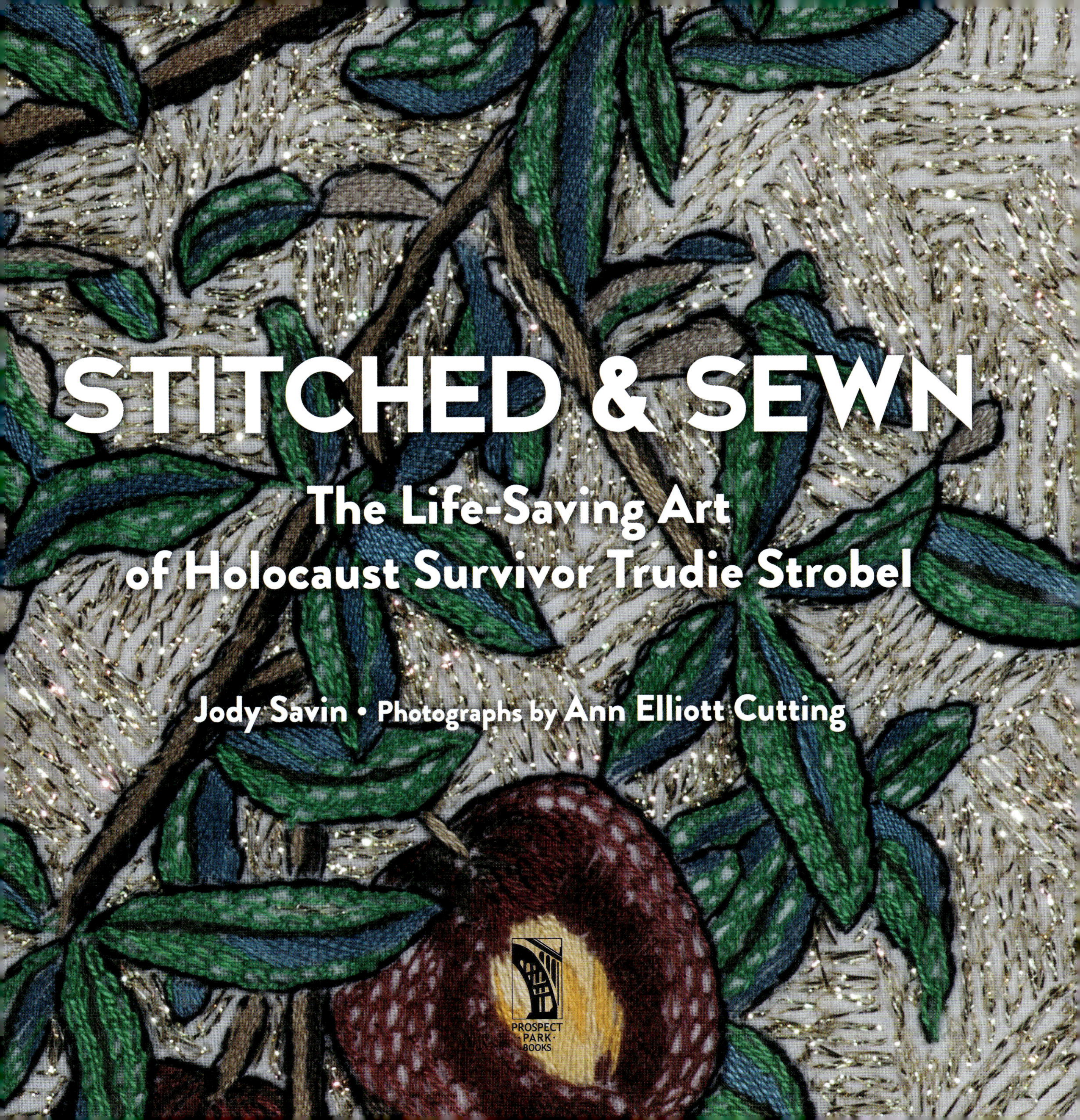

PROSPECT PARK BOOKS

The writing of this book was generously supported by a grant from the Memorial Foundation for Jewish Culture.

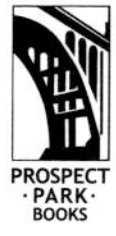

Published by Prospect Park Books
An imprint of Turner Publishing Company
Nashville, Tennessee
www.turnerbookstore.com

Library of Congress Cataloging in Publication Data
Names: Savin, Jody, author. | Cutting, Ann, photographer (expression).
Title: Stitched & sewn : the life-saving art of Holocaust survivor Trudie Strobel / Jody Savin ; photographs by Ann Elliott Cutting.
Other titles: Stitched and sewn
Identifiers: LCCN 2019034480 (print) | LCCN 2019034481 (ebook) | ISBN 9781945551765 (hardcover) | ISBN 9798887980348 (paperback) | ISBN 9781945551772 (epub)
Subjects: LCSH: Strobel, Trudie, 1938---Themes, motives. | Jewish embroidery--United States. | Holocaust, Jewish (1939-1945), in art.
Classification: LCC NK9298.S77 A4 2020 (print) | LCC NK9298.S77 (ebook) | DDC 700/.458405318--dc23
LC record available at https://lccn.loc.gov/2019034480
LC ebook record available at https://lccn.loc.gov/2019034481

Photography by Ann Elliott Cutting
Designed by Amy Inouye, Future Studio

Printed in the United States of America

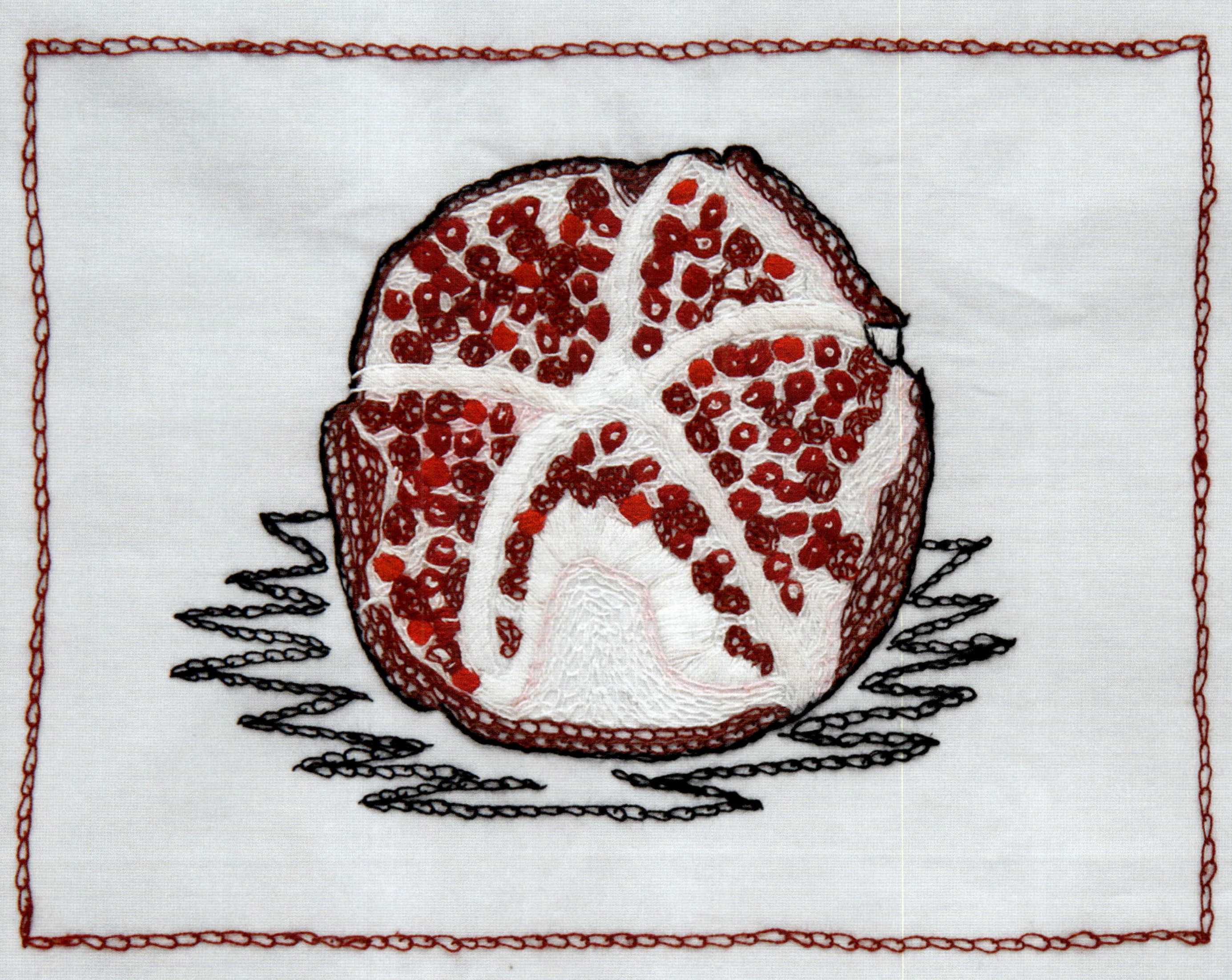

Pomegranate · 2017 · 8″ × 10″

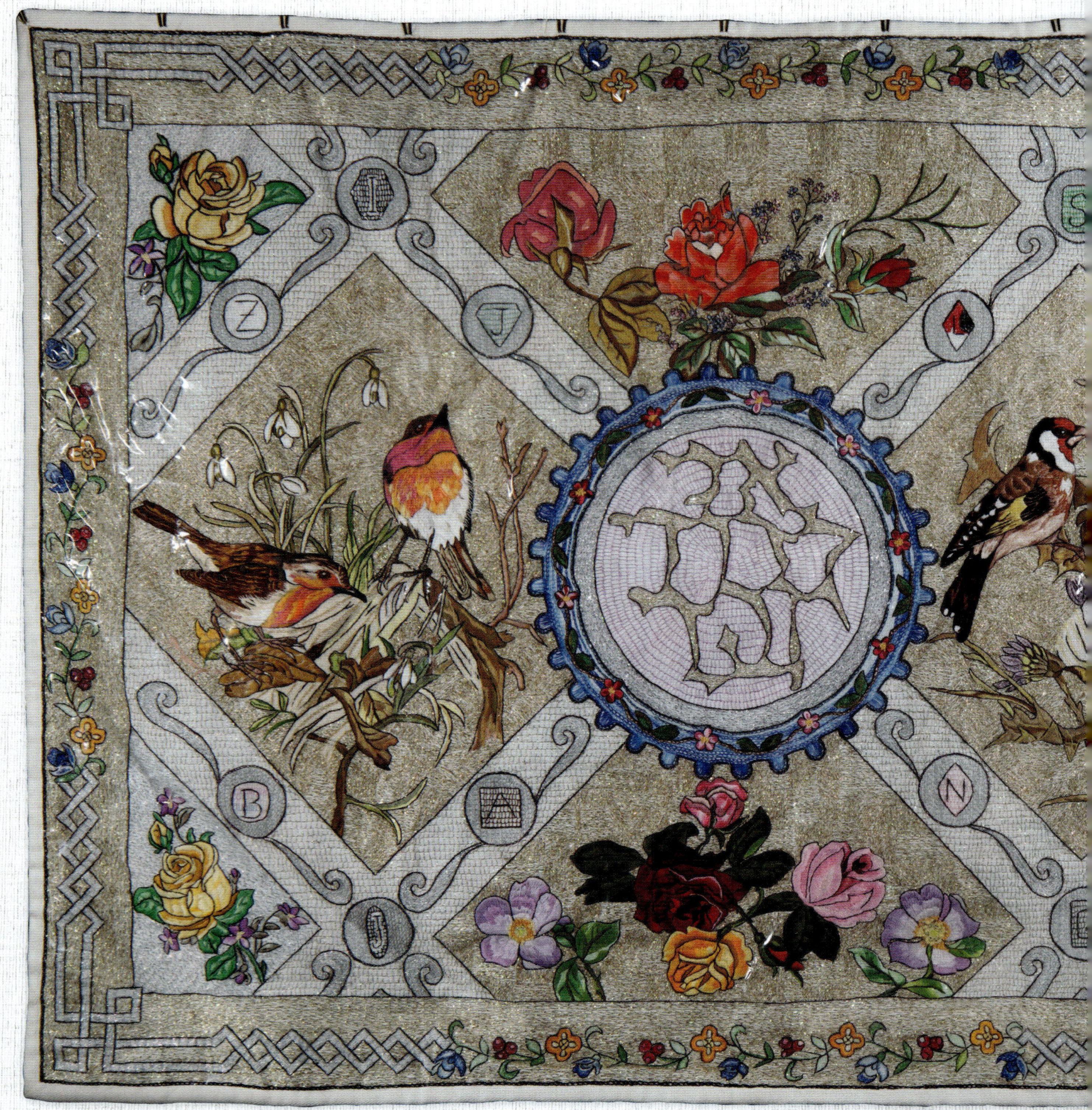

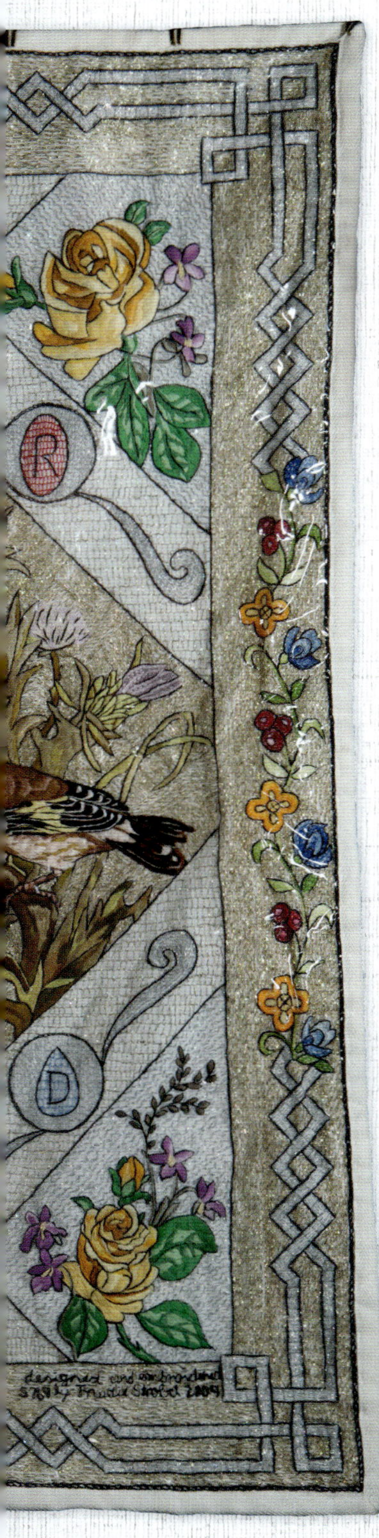

CONTENTS

Foreword Michael Berenbaum 10
But First (Introduction) 13

One: **Masha** 17
Two: **Trudie** 29
Three: **The Second Knock** 39
Shoah Series 46
Four: **The Walk** 55
Five: **Łódź** 63
Six: ***Shnell*!** 69
Seven: **Freedom?** 75
Eight: **Displaced Persons** 81
Nine: **America** 89
Ten: **Badges of Shame** 99
Eleven: **Tapestorian** 109

Stitches 159
Afterword 169
Art Notes 173
Index 190

Fantasy in Roses · 2004 · 36″ × 48″
This was a gift of gratitude to Randol Schoenberg, a legal champion of Jews whose artworks were confiscated by the Nazis. After his victory against the Austrian government in the recovery of five Gustav Klimt paintings, Schoenberg donated the funds to build the Los Angeles Museum of the Holocaust.

FOREWORD

Bashert is a Yiddish word meaning destined, or perhaps graced. Most often it is invoked by a bride and groom who are touched by passionate love and by the sense that they are meant for each other.

How does this relate to this foreword? Permit me to write of this week and then of this work.

A few days before I sat to write this, we dedicated the Dallas Holocaust and Human Rights Museum, a project that I have been working on for several years. Our assignment was to tell the story of the Holocaust as it relates to genocide and the quest for human rights. The first part of the museum is devoted to the history of Holocaust, concluding not with liberation but with the Nuremberg Trials, the attempt to rebuild the scaffolding of justice. The next part is dedicated to the Universal Declaration of Human Rights, passed by the United Nations in 1948. Finally, visitors enter a gallery focused on genocide, which showcases the ten stages of genocide, each illustrated by ten sculptures that create a sacred memorial space.

To convey the complicated information about these stages, a colleague developed ten graphic novels, each telling the story of one person who lived through a genocide. One of them addresses the stage of polarization via the composite character of a six-year-old girl in Rwanda, where the Tutsi murdered nearly 800,000 Hutu in 1994. The little girl was too young to put into words what she had seen, but under the tutelage of a Belgian psychologist, she began to draw it.

For the opening, the museum invited a survivor to speak: Lydia Nimbeshaho, a six-year-old orphaned during the slaughter, now a mother of three. When she read the graphic novel at the museum, she gasped, “That was my teacher—I drew those pictures.” When I saw Lydia’s reaction, I thought of Trudie Strobel and the foreword I had committed to write. Just like Lydia, Trudie was so young. She could have never put what she experienced into words. Much later in life, Trudie stitched her experience into tapestries and told her story, stitch by stitch, tapestry by tapestry. And the harder she worked, the more stitches she made, the more she realized that she was stitching her life back together.

Today, after I write this, I will have lunch with my friend Father Ron Schmidt, SJ, who directed a majestic film called The Labyrinth, which features the artwork of prisoner 432 at Auschwitz, Marian Kołodziej. For many years, Kołodziej, a prominent set designer in Poland, could not speak of his experience. To heal himself after a major stroke, he began to draw. The result was a magnificent series of drawings and art installations at the Maximilian Kolbe Center next to the Auschwitz Birkenau death camp. And so, as I prepare for lunch with Ron, I am brought back to Trudie Strobel, who, like Lydia and Marian, took to her art to heal herself.

Trudie could not have given voice to her experience without the brilliant and loving assistance of Jody Savin, who used words to stitch together Trudie’s life, memory by memory. We get the essence of the story powerfully, poignantly, movingly. Hers is a stark, almost minimalist, narration of a complex tale of the survival of a mother and daughter through the catastrophe now known as the Holocaust.

Everything this week was pointing to this splendid effort to join the written word and the visual arts to tell the story of one child survivor who was perhaps too young to understand the details of her experience but not too young to feel—and who, many years later, learned to express it in the craft she knew best. Word and art are joined to transmit the story.

This too was Bashert, destined.

— **Michael Berenbaum**, American Jewish University, Los Angeles

Michael Berenbaum is a scholar, writer, rabbi, and filmmaker who helped create the United States Holocaust Memorial Museum and the Dallas Holocaust and Human Rights Museum. He is the author of eighteen books and the co-producer of the Academy Award–winning film One Survivor Remembers.

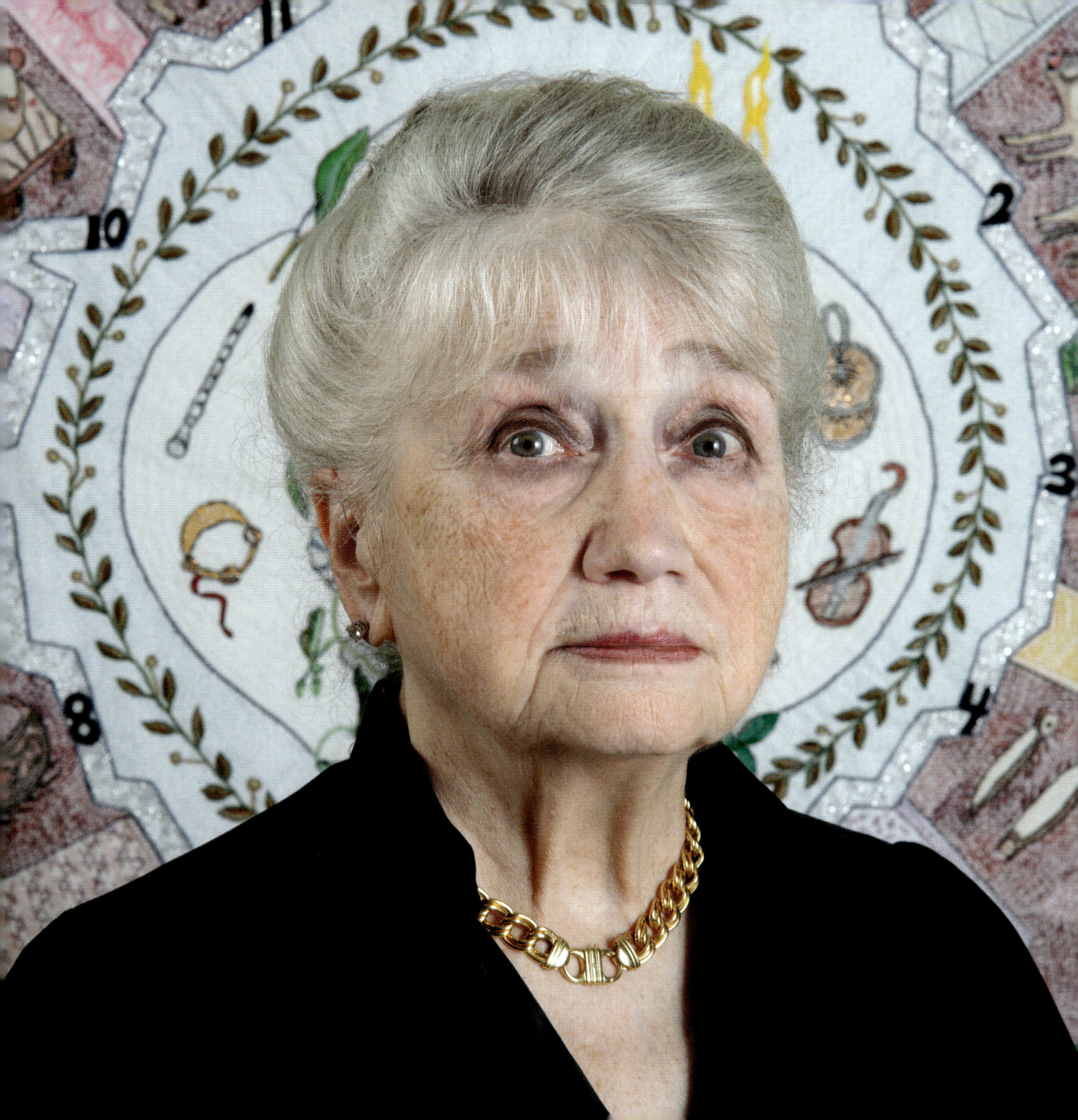
11
10
2
3
8
4

BUT FIRST. . .

There is a breathlessness to Trudie Strobel's voice that conveys at once a warmth and wariness, an invitation and a hesitation. But it is in Trudie's eyes that the treasures and the mysteries are kept. Eyes that have seen untold atrocity, as well as love and kindness. Eyes that locked memory inside for decades, like storm shutters battened for hurricane. Eyes that one day learned to open and release memory in picture-perfect detail. Moist eyes. Tired eyes. Brilliant eyes.

As a Jew, when I am told someone is a survivor, especially someone of a certain age, it means that person survived the Nazis. While one might survive a car crash, a bee sting, or a punishing math teacher, to be called a survivor implies both suffering and persevering through prolonged and horrific atrocity. One could be a survivor of chronic child abuse, of devastating infectious disease, of torture in captivity, of the byzantine US prison system, of a terrorist attack, of the Khmer Rouge. Trudie Strobel is a survivor of the Holocaust. She is a survivor of a genocide, perhaps the best known and the best planned, but only one of many throughout the history of mankind.

Trudie is considered a child survivor because she was so young when the Nazis seized her. But the challenge to survive did not end with the collapse of the Third Reich, because there was no home to go back to, no family left but her beloved mother, no money and not enough aid to do much more than to keep surviving. Moving from the concentration camp to a displacement camp was an improvement. There was bread, soup, and soap, but they remained trapped. Certainly, one could come and go, but there was nowhere to go to, and no money to finance any going. Thus, while the gates were open and some of the barbed wire removed, the displaced survivors were prisoners of situation—of poverty, of illness, of bureaucracy, of isolation, of shell shock, and of continued anti-Semitism and xenophobia. The raging fires of Nazi racism might have been choked, but the embers still smoldered malignantly inside Germany and out.

Years later, after Trudie and her mother had finally made their way to the United States, after Trudie had married, after she had raised two boys, the trauma of her childhood came flooding back and consumed her in a paralyzing depression. She was haunted by memory—the teeth of the Nazi hounds, feral and snarling in her face; the lethal boots of the Gestapo, glistening threateningly at her; the dying, the sickness, the death. She stopped speaking. And as she was retreating into that dark hall of memory, a doctor beseeched her to draw what she could not say. She had not known that she could draw. She had never really tried to draw. Life had been so populated with necessities, responsibilities, and emergencies that she could never have justified something so intimate and personal; it would have felt indulgent.

Sewing. Stitching. Mending. Not just mending but reinventing with needle and thread. This had been how Trudie and her mother had survived the Holocaust. Sewing for Nazis. Masha Labuhn, Trudie's mother, had been a seamstress. In times when wool was scarce, Masha could take apart an old coat, reverse the panels of fabric, and reassemble it to look new. She did her work diligently, and her work was valued, and thus she was allowed to keep her daughter by her side, even in the most oppressive moments in the camp. Stitching had saved Trudie's life then, and stitching would save it again.

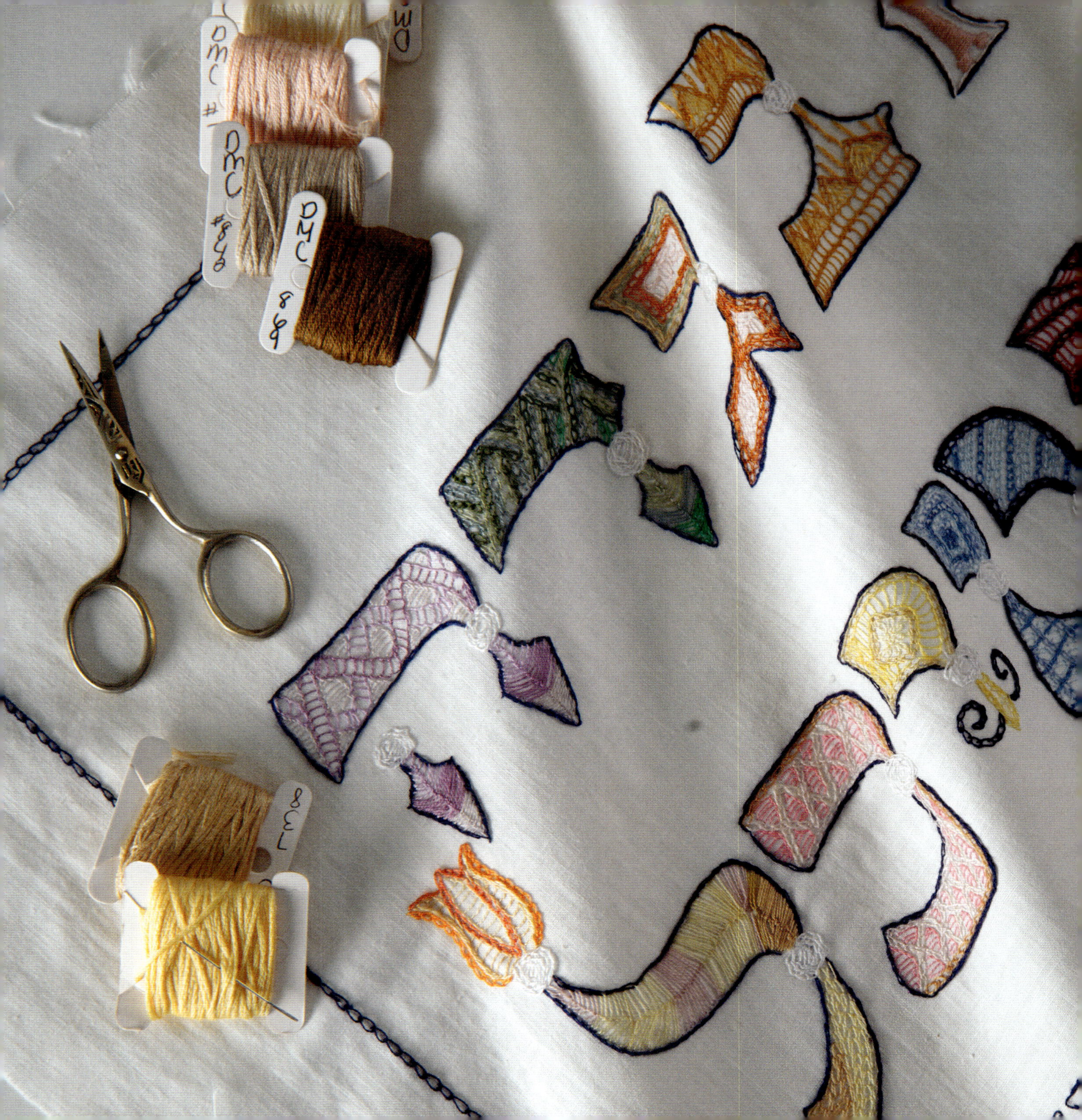
DMC
DMC
DMC

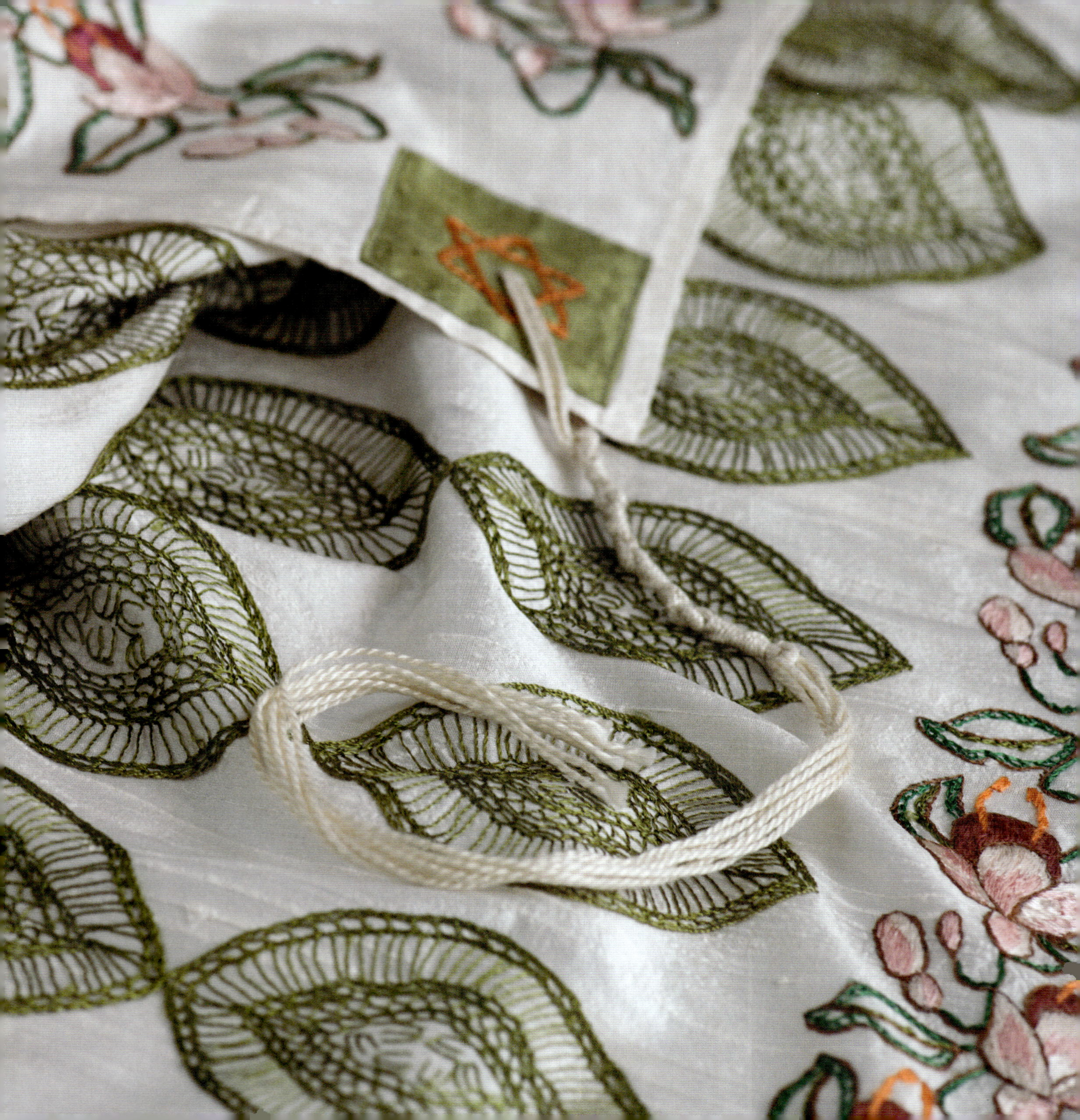

CHAPTER ONE

MASHA

Those who do not have power over the story that dominates their lives, power to retell it, rethink it, deconstruct it, joke about it, and change it as times change, truly are powerless, because they cannot think new thoughts.

—SALMAN RUSHDIE

Masha Gansky Labuhn was pregnant. It was winter on the kolkhoz,[1] and it was cold in the modest home she shared with her husband, Vasilliy. They lived in the Dnipropetrovsk region of what was then the Soviet Union and what is now Ukraine, due west of the Dnieper River.

Masha wrapped the worn shawl tighter around her shoulders and leaned to put one more log in the *pripitchok* (stove) as she sang the traditional Yiddish song "Oyfn Pripitchok" to the baby growing inside her.

A fire burns on the hearth
and it is warm in the little house
And the rabbi is teaching little children
the alphabet.

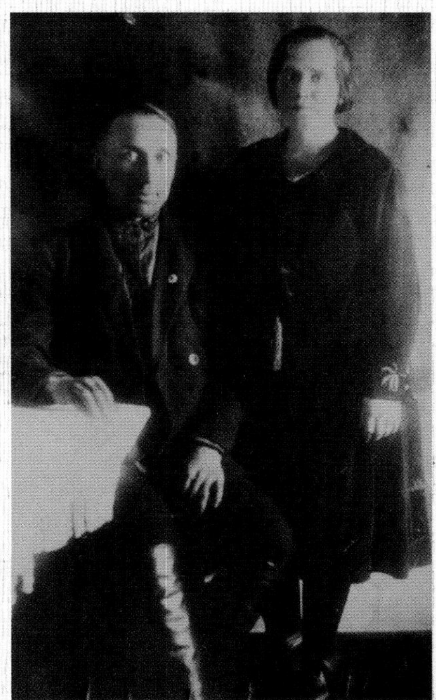

Vasilliy and Masha Labuhn, in Russia, 1937

Left: Joseph Ariel's tallit, 2018

1 A kolkhoz was a collective farm in the Soviet Union. However, make no mistake: Forced collectivization under Stalin was far from an actual cooperative.

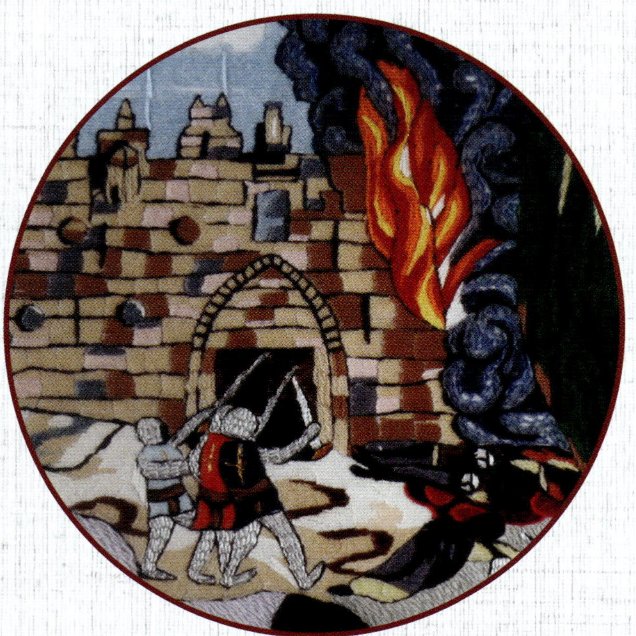

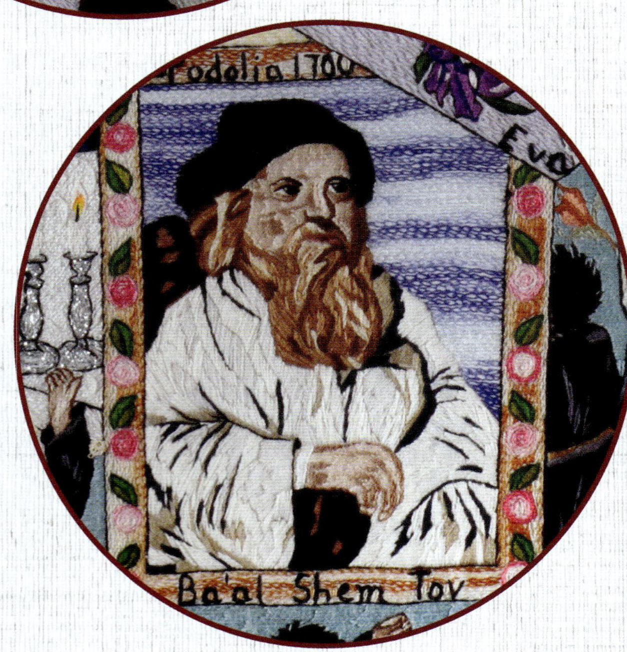

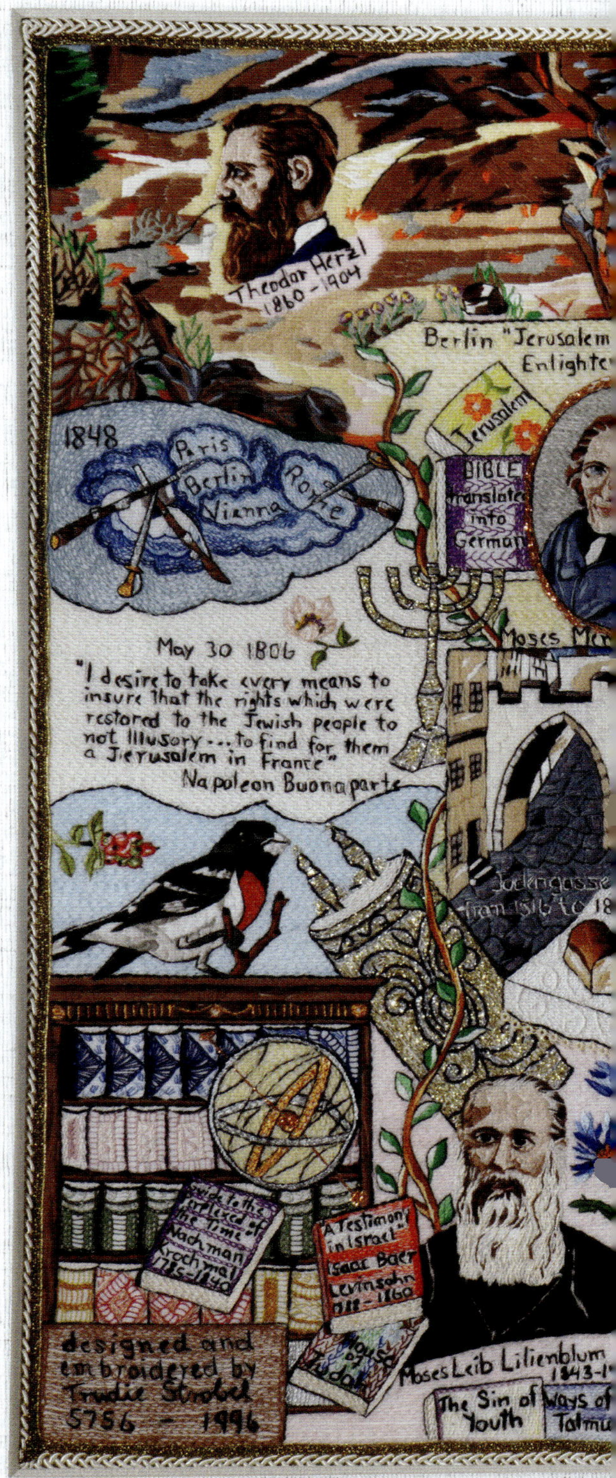

European Ashkenazi History · 1996 · 30″×41″
Read more about this work in Art Notes, page 183

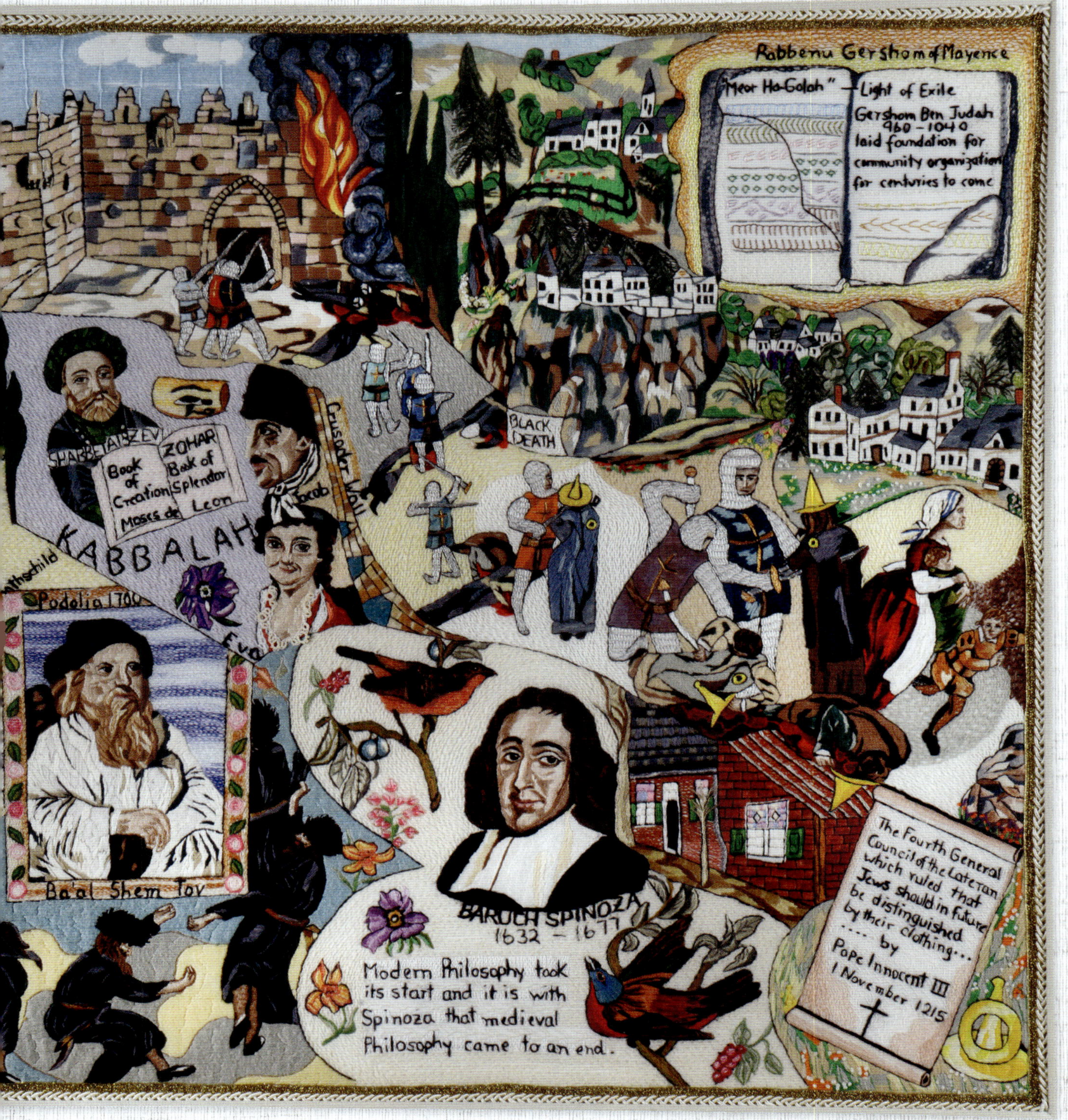

Rabbenu Gershom of Mayence
"Meor Ha-Golah" — Light of Exile
Gershom Ben Judah
960 - 1040
laid foundation for
community organization
for centuries to come
BLACK DEATH
SHABBETAI ZEV
Book of Creation
ZOHAR
Book of Splendor
Moses de Leon
KABBALAH
Jacob
Crusader Wall
Eva
Podolia 1700
Ba'al Shem Tov
BARUCH SPINOZA
1632 - 1677
Modern Philosophy took
its start and it is with
Spinoza that medieval
Philosophy came to an end.
The Fourth General
Council of the Lateran
which ruled that
Jews should in future
be distinguished
by their clothing...
.... by
Pope Innocent III
1 November 1215

Remember, children
remember, dear ones
what you learn here.
Repeat and repeat yet again
komets alef-o.

Masha's last four pregnancies had been difficult, and if she were to be honest, she had experienced mixed feelings when she found out she was pregnant again. But this time was different. She felt strong this time, and healthy, and filled with possibility. This time, Masha loved being pregnant. She never felt alone. When Vasilliy went off to work, she sang to the baby growing inside her; she told the baby stories of her ancestors, always in whispers, because being Jewish made them a target. But she wanted her baby to know her heritage, to emerge into the world with an identity and with pride.

Masha knew she was carrying a girl. And she was certain this child would be born healthy. Early in her pregnancy, Vasilliy had doubted her ability to predict, but even he was convinced now. Masha had named her daughter Gertrude but called her Trudie for short, and whenever Masha addressed her baby by name, baby Trudie kicked or moved, and so Masha knew.

Vasilliy was excited about the prospect of another chance at fatherhood, and he accepted Masha's conviction that if this baby were a girl, she would survive. There had been four boys born to Vasilliy and Masha, and all had suffered the same twisted spine that could not support their little lives for more than one year. The heartbreak of those losses had been devastating, but things were going to be different this time. Masha knew, and he knew too. When he had first felt the baby moving inside of Masha's body, he had gasped, and tears had sprung from his eyes. The way this baby moved was somehow different from the others. This baby seemed to be reaching out to him. And after that, he looked at Masha differently, as if she were the bearer of miracles, as if she were the beacon of hope in a world that seemed so vulnerable to the incomprehensible politics and hostilities of men.

It was winter of 1937. A new year was just around the corner. One had to hope that a new year might bring new tidings, winds of change, a kinder world. One thing it would certainly bring was baby Gertrude Labuhn. Trudie. Trudela in the Yiddish of affection. And with the impending birth came a certain hope.

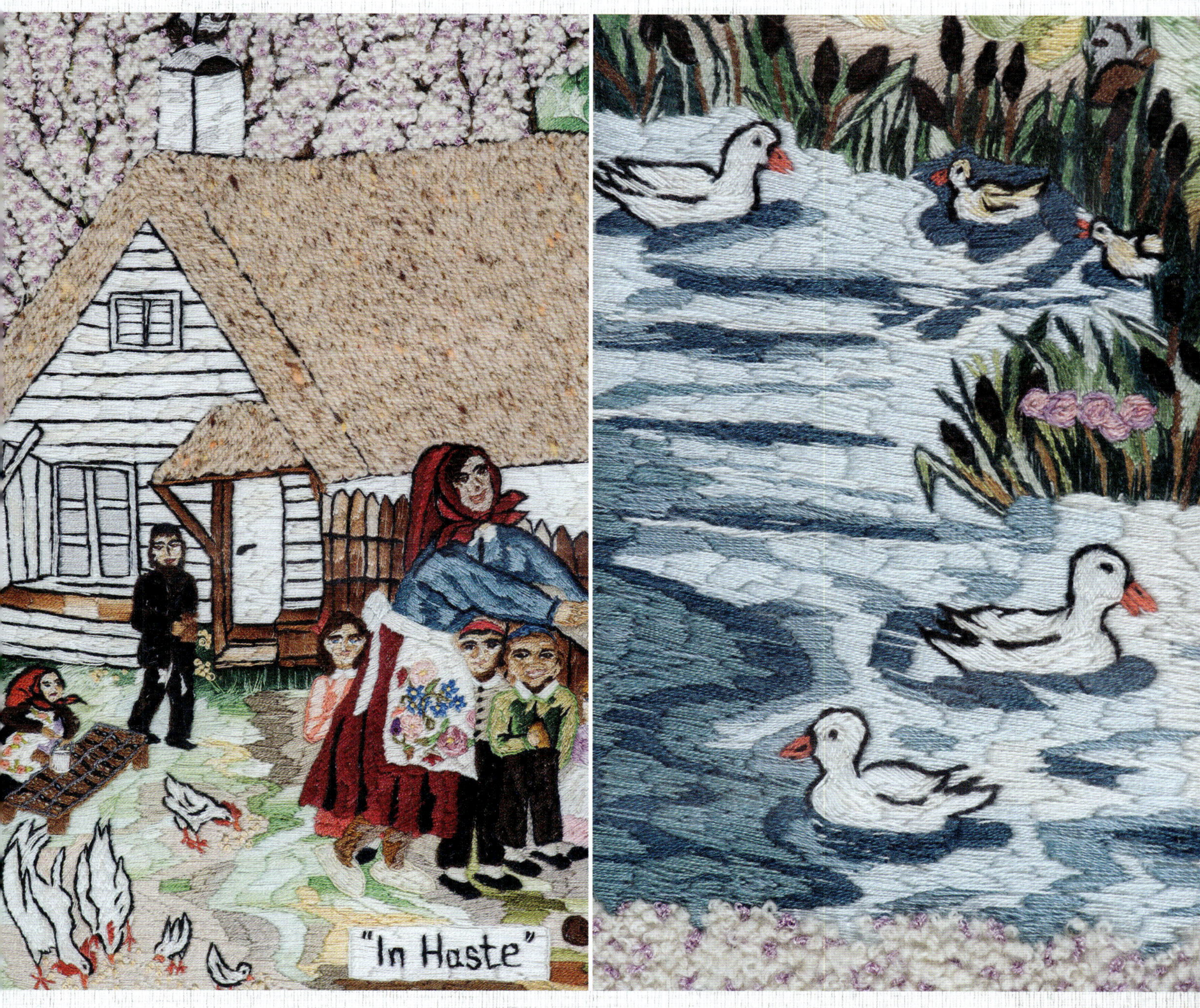

Details from ***A Tribute to Sholem Aleichem*** · 1990 · 44″ × 57″

It was a hope that was hard to sustain. People were disappearing around them. Especially Jewish people. Mostly the men. The Labuhn family was Jewish, but Vasilliy did his best to keep a low profile about his religion. Keeping a low profile on all matters political and religious had been a good tactic, although at times he felt like he might be betraying his fathers and their fathers before him. Yet there was no time for guilt. There was no time for philosophizing. Keeping to one's own business was necessary to survive. He knew it, and he had seen it countless times before: When human beings get trapped in a corner where Life smells Death, where the chance to persevere is dependent on the demise of a neighbor or fellow worker, man's atavistic impulses are unleashed, and the result tends to be a devastation from which there is no return. Literally no return: So many had been taken, none had returned.[2]

The soldiers usually came in the evening, just after sundown, when men would be at home and their identities easily verified, when there would be no constellation of friends, relatives, or coworkers to protest or interfere, when the greatest obstacle would merely be a hysterical wife. They took them from the kolkhoz in Neu Chortitza to Krivoy Rog, the closest city with a *gefängnis*, a prison.

Vasilliy Labuhn was not a laborer at the kolkhoz. Although still young, he had risen to the position of director and was responsible for the merchandise coming into and going out of the community. He was good at his job. He was efficient and conscientious and professional. This position of authority had insulated him in many ways. He was not so easy to replace. There were the logistics of commerce in the labyrinthine Soviet economy. There was quality control to be managed and trade relationships to be maintained in a culture of personality and often lawlessness. He had navigated these challenges well, and his aptitude had made him less of a target for Stalin's police.

On one of his buying trips, Vasilliy had seen a doll, a perfect little girl doll with a bow in her silken hair. This was no small doll made of rags like the ones he had seen little girls coo over on the kolkhoz. This was a treasure and bigger than Baby Trudie would be when she

---

2 "People belonging to national minorities 'should be forced to their knees and shot like mad dogs.' It was not an SS officer speaking (SS stands for Schutzstaffel, Hitler's paramilitary organization, administrators of the "Final Solution"); it was a Communist party leader, in the spirit of the national operations of Stalin's Great Terror. In 1937 and 1938, a quarter of a million Soviet citizens were shot on essentially ethnic grounds."
Bloodlands: Europe Between Hitler and Stalin, by Timothy D. Snyder, Basic Books, 2010, p. 89.

was born. This was a doll that he must have, that he must take home as a gift to the baby girl that would be born in less than three months' time. The merchant was amused as Vasilliy stood there, transfixed by the doll. Vasilliy was a virile man, not tall, but muscular, with large, strong hands and typically, when not at home, an inscrutable visage. Today the incongruous look on his face was something akin to romantic.

When Vasilliy arrived home that night with the doll, Masha could not believe how much she herself delighted in this gift, the innocence of its acquisition and the extravagance of its purchase. Her husband was a cautious man, never prone to indulgence, so this was a wondrous and unexpected departure. Masha accepted the doll, an elegantly manufactured and sturdy simulacrum of their baby-to-be. It was another sign, Masha believed, that her baby would be healthy, "elegantly manufactured," and strong. Masha smiled. The omens were all lining up. She hugged her rarely impulsive husband and reminded him how much she loved him. He was a good man, a smart man, a good provider, normally quite stoic these days, but occasionally—and this was one of those occasions—the romantic in him awoke. When he was younger, Vasilliy had been a pianist. He'd been raised in a more affluent family than Masha's, in Felsengut, and he had received music lessons. Vasilliy Labuhn had played for his temple's congregation during services and celebrations, but he also played Mussorgsky, Balakirev, and Tchaikovsky. And so, in the corner of Masha and Vasilliy's small home there was a piano, but these days it was mostly silent. Masha held the doll and sighed: Moments like this were tiny diamonds of joy offered from the all too stingy pockets of life—the most precious kind of diamonds, ones that could never be seized.

Vasilliy was touched by Masha's delight with the doll. For all of her intrepid optimism about the coming baby and her certainty that it would be a healthy girl, he knew she worried. The heartbreak and guilt over the deceased babies lingered, an impossible accounting, never to be reconciled. Tonight, her happiness made him happy and he felt a certain pride that he had been the engineer of mirth. Tonight, they would lie together and talk to Baby Trudie and she would kick in response. And yet, what Vasilliy did not want to admit to himself or to Masha was the other reason he had purchased this extravagant doll. That was the terrible reason, and acknowledging it could do no good. In his heart, Vasilliy knew that the Soviet soldiers would come for him, too, just as they had come for the other Jews, and that no amount

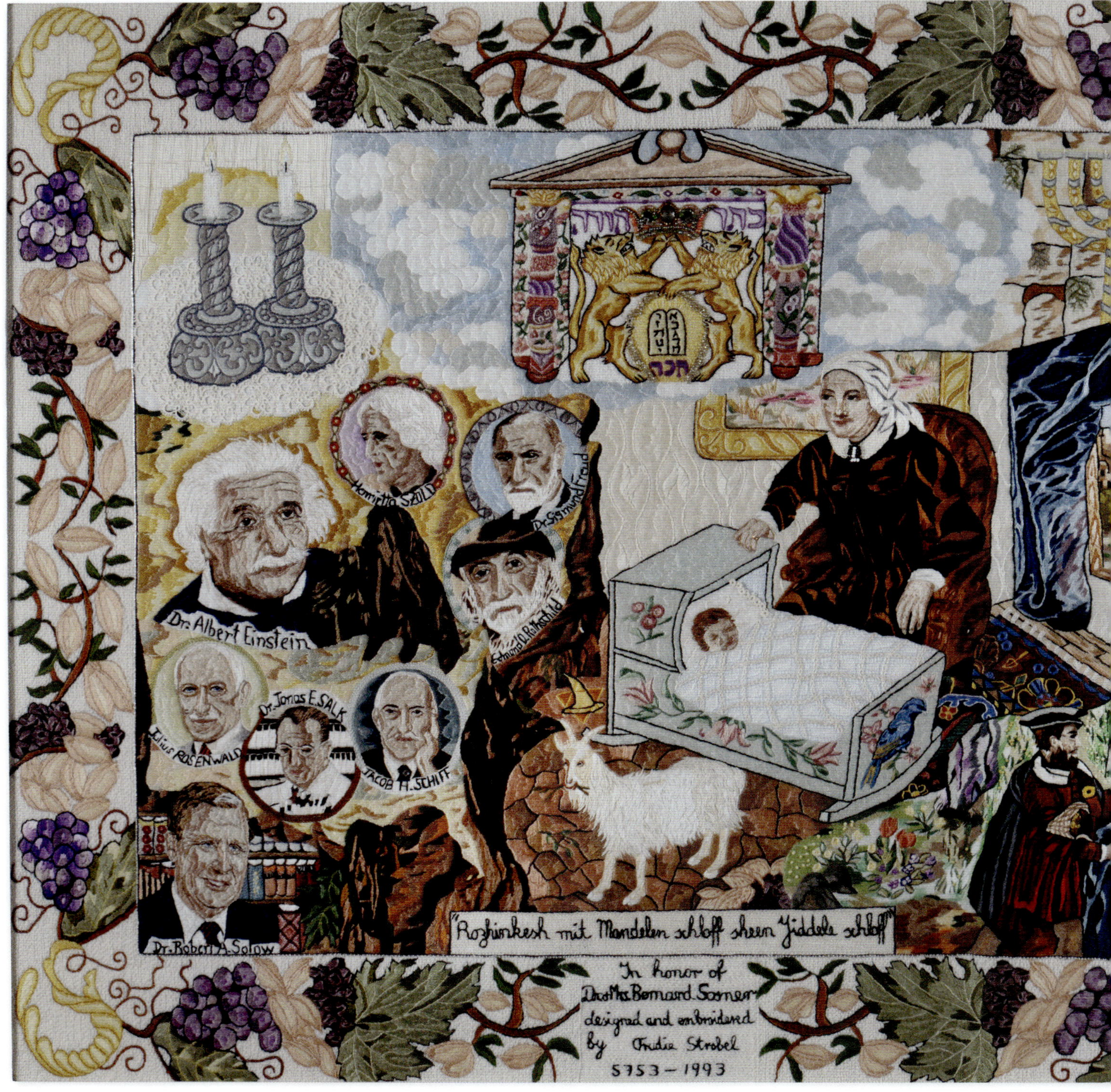
Dr. Albert Einstein
Henrietta SZOLD
Dr. Sigmund Freud
Edmond D. Rothschild
Julius ROSENWALD
Dr. Jonas E. SALK
JACOB H. SCHIFF
Dr. Robert A. Solow
"Rozhinkesh mit Mandelen schloff sheen Yiddele schloff"
In honor of
Dr.&Mrs. Bernard Sosner
designed and embroidered
by Trudie Strobel
5753 – 1993

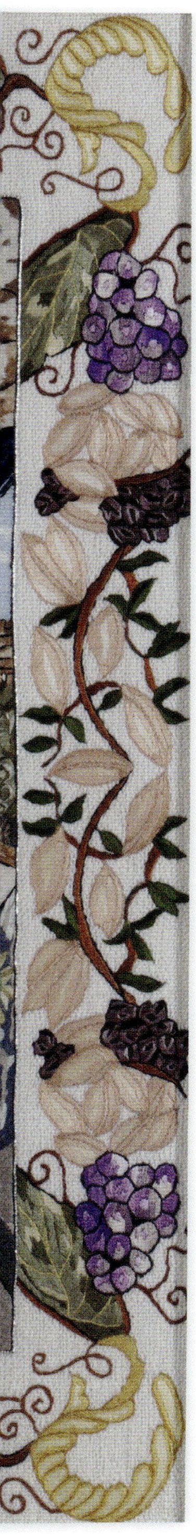

of communal responsibility, not even his position as director, no amount of expressed allegiance to Stalin, no amount of assimilation and deferential acquiescence to authority, would ultimately spare him. Of course, he hoped he was wrong. How else could he function day in and day out? And he would never put words to his fears, but they were there. They were always there. And so, if what he dreaded came to fruition, if they came and took him away, he would have left this precious doll for his newborn daughter, something of him to hug when she could not hug him. It had seemed like such a good idea when he first laid eyes on the doll, but now when he thought about it more, it seemed woefully inadequate. And he could not help but hope, again, that he was wrong. How he wanted to be wrong.

In the kolkhoz, no one seemed to know anything about what happened to the men who were taken to the *gefängnis*, the prison in Krivoy Rog. And if they did, they would never dare discuss it, not even in whispers. But in his dealings with vendors outside of the community, Vasilliy had heard stories. He had no confirmation of the information, and for the most part, he, like the others, tried to believe that there was some justification for what was going on. Because if there were justice of any kind, he would never be taken. He had done nothing wrong. He had made sure to offend no one. Granted, there were those who resented his

Rozhinkesh mit Mandelen (Raisins and Almonds) · 1993 · 30″ × 36″
Read more about this work in Art Notes, page 183

ascendency to the position of director, and at such a young age, but although he had more responsibility than the laborers, it had brought little extra reward. He had access to the world outside the community—though many of the others did not consider that a particular reward—and of course he had access to a little more information, although Stalin had long ago stopped the flow of any true information. So, whether inside the kolkhoz or in the towns to which he traveled, the people, the workers, and probably, he thought, the greater population of the entire country knew very little of what was really happening. They were only informed of the party's narrative on the state of affairs in their country, a whitewashed, propagandistic story that fueled Stalin's national machine. And Vasilliy's position had certainly not brought him financial reward, for this was a communist country that fiercely enforced the notion of equality, especially economic and material equality among all men. Thus, his position did not often inspire envy among other kolkhoznik; if anything, they were happy the added responsibility was not theirs.

What Vasilliy had heard in the scant whispers to which he was privy outside the kolkhoz was that the Jews, and some Mennonites, who had been seized from their homes were viciously beaten and whipped, until they broke down and confessed to some crime they had likely never contemplated, much less committed. And then they would disappear. He had heard they were sent to labor camps, reeducation camps, gulags in Siberia. So far, none had returned. He wondered, as he lay awake at night, if they were really sent to Siberia or if they were just summarily killed. He wondered if any of them would ever come home. He watched his pregnant wife sleep and tried to conceive of a way out, a way to protect her and their unborn child, and he realized they would need a miracle. He sighed and hoped that the baby would be that miracle.

During the days, while Vasilliy was away at work, Masha sewed. She mended, she altered, she tailored, and once she made a wedding dress. This work brought them a little extra income, though some customers paid by barter, but every little bit helped. In her spare time and with leftover bits and pieces of very soft cloth she had saved, Masha was making clothes for the baby. Perhaps one day, when baby Trudie was old enough, Masha would teach her daughter to sew clothes for her Papa Doll; this is what Masha called the spectacular doll that Vasilliy had bought for his as yet unborn daughter. Yes, thought Masha, the Papa Doll could have a wonderful hand-sewn wardrobe someday, a project she and her daughter could do together proudly. Masha smiled at the thought of it, and baby Trudie kicked in response. "My Trudela," said Masha as she gently rubbed her belly where a tiny baby foot seemed to be tapping out a code.

And then, one night, there was a knock on the door. The knock they had been dreading. Masha had been expecting a terrifying pounding that would rattle the whole structure they called home. But it was an extraordinarily normal knock. An almost neighborly rat-tat-tat. That this moment of familial doom could be advertised by such a casual knock was the most egregious insult. This is what ran through Masha's mind as she studied the face of her husband, this suddenly terrified man who was her other half. How she wanted to comfort him, he who had always comforted her. How she wanted to not be hearing this scandalously unremarkable knock on the door.

"Vasilliy Labuhn, you will be coming with us."

"Where?" Masha heard herself ask, though she knew full well there would be no answer. "But it is late. And he is tired. He has been working all day. Dutifully. For the State." Vasilliy said nothing. Not one word. He stared at Masha, and he nodded ever so slightly, and then he was gone. "What kind of stupid knock was that?" Masha thought she had yelled at the door that closed behind them, but in reality, she had just stood there, holding her swollen belly, tears streaming down her face, trying to get enough air.

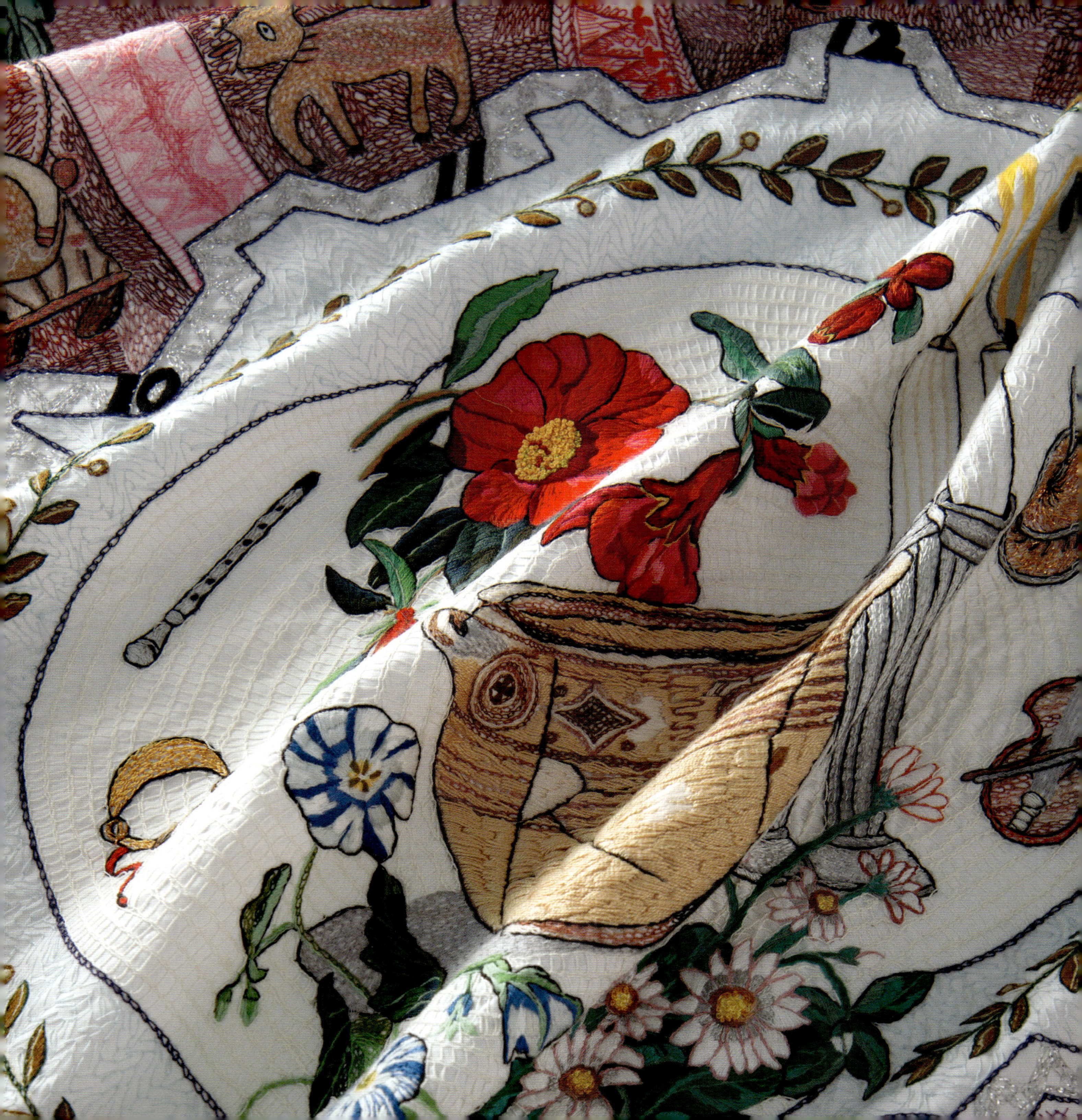
12
11
10

CHAPTER TWO

TRUDIE

The highest form of wisdom is kindness.

—THE TALMUD

Several weeks later, on a frigid day, the 10th of March, 1938, Trudie Labuhn was born. A girl. Her spine was not twisted like that of the boys who had preceded her. She was a tiny pink miracle. Masha wept with both sadness and joy. She knew in her heart that this beautiful baby girl was a sign that good things would come. Maybe none of the other men who had been seized by the Soviet soldiers had returned, but Masha now knew that the Labuhn family's luck had changed. And Masha vowed that once she had the strength, once baby Trudie was a few days old, she would take this precious life to meet her father. And they would bring him home. That is what they would do. Somehow.

The Papa Doll sat in the corner lording over the room, like a beacon of strength, and the presence of the doll steeled Masha's resolve. They were three girls now in the home—Masha, Trudie, and her Papa Doll—and somehow that brought Masha a modicum of comfort.

As soon as Masha felt strong enough, she wrapped her baby girl in the magnificent new shawl, meticulously stitched, that Masha had made expressly for carrying her baby. It was an intricate design of brilliant pieces of fabric that seemed to dance in a tempestuous harmony. Masha wound the shawl tightly around her own body in a sling and, early in the morning, they set off on foot for Krivoy Rog. It was a very long walk and Masha grew weary, but she pushed on, determined to reach Vasilliy. What Masha could not have known then was how

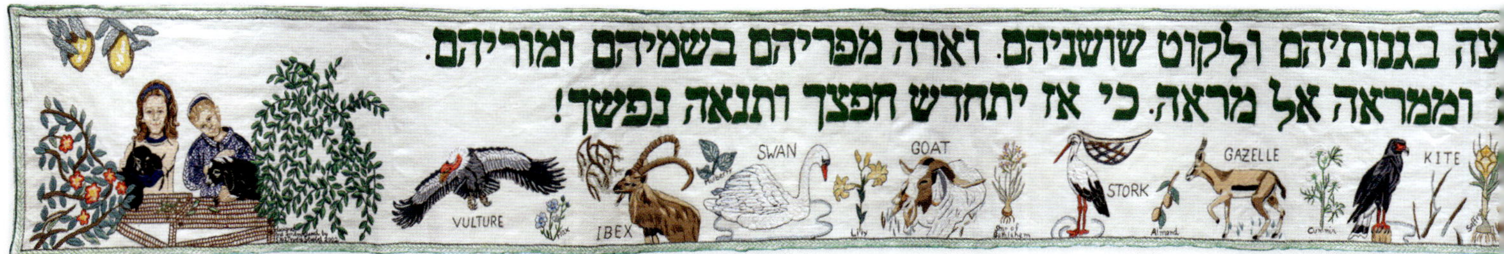

Banner for Peter Kahn Library

this walk was minuscule in comparison to the brutal marathon she and Trudie would be forced to endure in just a few years' time. It was early afternoon when they reached the prison at Krivoy Rog, where a long line spat forward from the entrance. In the line were mostly women and children, hungry, tired, distraught, and fearful of their own forbidden anger. Those who cursed the prison and its guards did not do so overtly, but furtively between grinding teeth. Masha refused herself anger; she was determined that her healthy baby girl would meet her father on this day. And it would be a special day that they would all three remember for the rest of their lives. So, she waited. The line did not move much, and the frustration of the families around her mounted, but Masha was steadfast in her resolve to will something good to happen. Hour after hour, they waited. Bit by bit, the line inched forward. And with each inch, Masha's hope was renewed.

As Masha got closer to the prison, it became harder and harder to ignore the frigid chill that emanated from this stalwart edifice of detention and the undulating waves of repressed grief. She marveled at the softness of such a tiny cheek, at the precious crinkles in the flesh of Trudie's little wrist, at the miraculous warmth of her well-protected neck.

"Yes?" asked the guard. She had expected a brute—a tiger at the gate, its fangs bared, its growl menacing—but here was a thin, gray man. Gray hair, gray complexion, even the white of his eyes had gone gray.

"I am here to see my husband, Vasilliy Labuhn, so that he might meet his newborn girl." She looked down at Trudie. "Right, Trudela? We are here for you to meet Papa."

The man had a list. "Spell the name for me."

"L-A-B-U-H-N" Masha peered down at the names. "The child needs her father. Can he come home with us, please? He has done nothing wrong. He is a good man. He works hard.

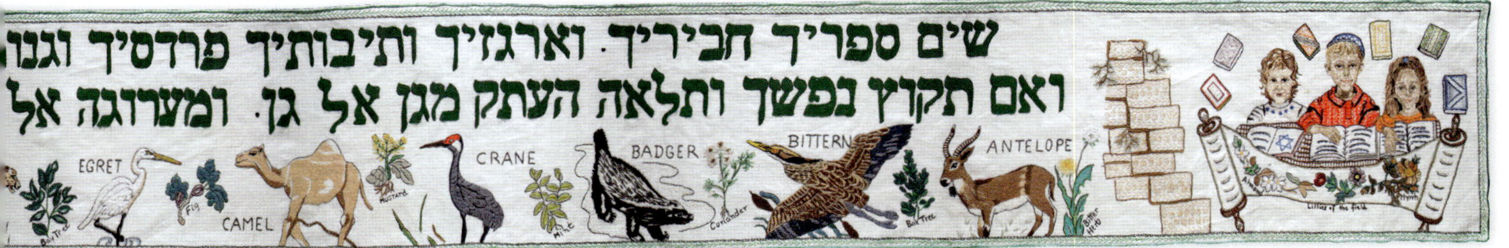

He has committed no crime. This is his baby girl. He will want to hold his baby girl and watch her grow."

"He is not here," said the gray man.

This is not something Masha had contemplated. How could he not be here? This is where they had taken him. "Where is he then?"

"He is not here," repeated the man.

"Please. Please tell me where he is," Masha begged quietly, tears streaming down her face. "Trudie must see her father. I will go to him. Where is he? Please." But the man just stared at his list. He was neither frustrated nor impatient; he was neither wistful nor hostile. He was just gray. "Please," she pleaded one last time, knowing her words would be consumed in the cacophony of deafness that imbued this place.

Masha walked out of the jail slowly but deliberately, determined to stay one small foot ahead of the avalanche of grief cascading down around her. Trudie was crying now. With good reason. Her tears were a proxy for the tears Masha could not afford to shed. Unconsoled, Trudie's cries escalated into wailing. "They took them to Siberia," said a whisper in the wind. Masha turned and there was a fist of a woman sweeping the walkway, her eyes turned away, her head bowed. "The men. All of them." Had the woman even spoken? Masha was confused. "Don't look at me," reprimanded the woman. And Masha obeyed, studying the other women waiting in line to receive devastating news of their loved ones. "Glavnoe Upravlenie ispravitel'no-trudovykh LAGerei."[3]

"Gulag," Masha heard herself say before the world went black.

---

3 Main Office of Forced Labor Camps.

The woman had caught her as she fainted, which was kind. But then she had slapped her, which felt unkind but was actually, once perspective had been restored, more than kind. The slap had startled Masha back to consciousness. And face to stinging face with this incongruous fist of a woman, Masha had been forced to absorb the message: Vasilliy had been exiled. As had this woman's husband. As had, most likely, the husbands and sons and brothers and fathers of all the women standing in line, clinging to a hope that would shortly be dashed by an affectless gray man. "Go home," said the woman, who was back at her sweeping and who seemed once again acutely unaware of Masha's existence.

It was a long walk home. Longer now as each step was leaden with dread. There were others walking too, women and children mostly. Broken families, all, returning to homes that would reek of absence. As the road lengthened and became more remote, there were fewer people. And then a tall woman walking alone ahead of Masha began to sing. Softly. Tenderly. Masha clung to the sound of her voice, lifted by its beauty, buoyed by the suggestion of harmony in such a discordant universe. Trying to get closer to the singing, which wafted through the air like wings propelling her forward, Masha walked faster.

Masha caught up to the woman and realized that she, too, was carrying a baby. Masha noticed that the shawl the singer wore had been torn and clumsily restitched. The two mothers regarded each other with unspoken understanding—two husbandless women; two fatherless babies. And they walked on, side by side, for miles. Her name, Masha learned, was Alyona, and her singing was a gift to both of the children—Trudie and Alyona's daughter Eva—and to Masha. Indeed, it was a gift Masha would cherish forever. After a few miles, when the others had split off or hurried ahead or lagged behind, when they were all alone on the road, Alyona finished her song.

"Thank you," said Masha.

"I saw you with the sweeper," Alyona said quietly.

"Siberia," said Masha.

Alyona swallowed this information slowly. And then she said, "Your husband was a kind man." Alyona's use of the past tense turned Masha cold. "He was the director."

"Yes," Masha whispered.

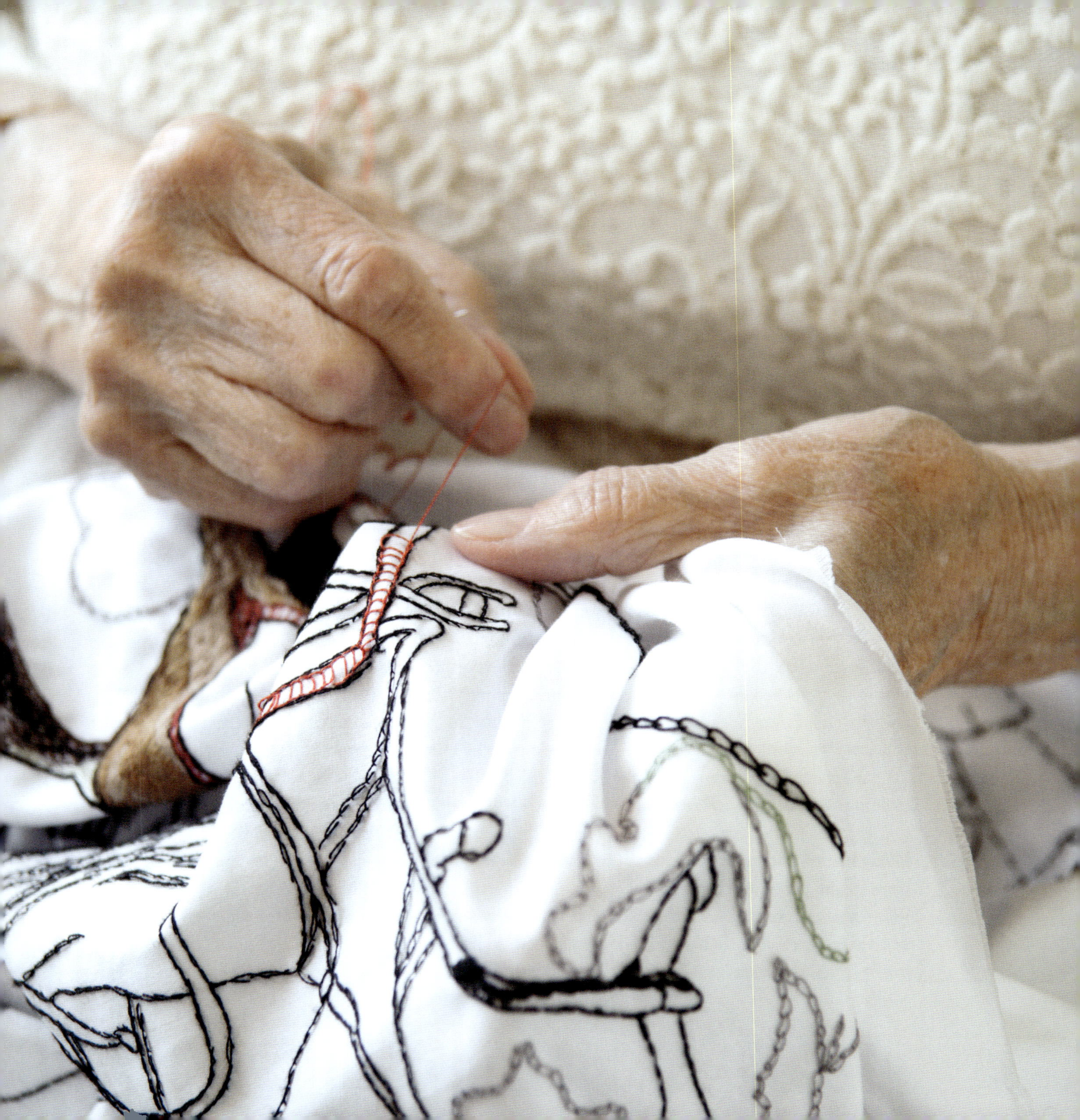

"My husband worked under him. He warned my husband. He knew," said Alyona. Deep in her heart, Masha had known that Vasilliy had expected his own arrest, but it was a fear he had never expressed to her, a fear that would have consumed the act of living, and thus a fear that had to be denied purchase. Alyona was speaking: "But what could we do?"

"What could we do," repeated Masha.

"Where could we go," said Alyona. It was a statement more than a question. "What will we do now?"

"We will carry on," said Masha. "We will. We will carry on. For Trudie and for Eva and for your husband and for Vasilliy. We will do it for them. We must do it for them." Alyona nodded, but without conviction. "Tomorrow, bring me your shawl and I will fix it for you."

Alyona said, "No, you don't need to do that."

"I want to do it. You sing; I sew. Bring it to me. And perhaps now you would sing some more?"

It took Alyona a couple of days, but she came to the house with the shawl. And Masha set to work on it. She deftly disassembled all the frayed seams and removed the compromised portions of fabric. From her boxes of bits and pieces of material, she stitched together a magnificent mosaic of fabrics, saving the softest for the panel that Eva would rest her tiny head against. Masha worked to reinforce all the weight-bearing seams. She worked on it in between Trudie's feedings and diaper changes. She worked on it between other sewing jobs that she now desperately needed. She worked on it late into the night. What evolved in her expert hands and with her fantastic eye was a shawl of such beauty that Alyona wept when she lifted it for the first time. And Masha wept too. The weeping of the mothers triggered the weeping of the baby girls, which, in turn, caused the mothers to laugh—to laugh and weep at the same time. Laughter had become a scarce commodity in the kolkhoz, so this was treasure in a moment.

Alyona's shawl attracted quite a bit of attention, even in the humble activities of her lonely life. The shawl was masterful in its execution, but not showy or gaudy. When Alyona wore it, she felt as if she were swathed in a hug of artistry and kindness, and it soothed her. Women in the kolkhoz admired it so much that they wanted something like it for themselves, and they searched their meager belongings for a coat or shawl or cape or dress that Masha might be able to transform for them. They collected odds and ends of fabric, thread, lace, and even beads to bring to Masha, and they paid her in fits and spurts with what little money they could put together, but they did pay her. Masha, they discovered, was not simply a seamstress, but she could weave and embroider and bead. She wove gorgeous lace by hand, items the women in the kolkhoz could ill afford but that they coveted.

With so many men gone, the women now worked the farms and the fields. This was an agrarian community, and it required laborers. Masha sometimes worked in the fields, but mostly she milked the cows and cleaned their stalls, which had its perks, as she could always bring some fresh milk to Trudie to make her bones grow healthy and strong. The women of the kolkhoz, who had long been wary of one another in a culture of suspicion and betrayal, now found ways to communicate in a kind of code, where words had different meanings from traditional usage and where any shred of information—about the husbands and fathers and sons, about illness and death, about punishments and shortages—could be shared. But there was so little information that mostly the days were spent caring for their children, working, and dreaming, either ambitiously, of better times to come, or more realistically, of the beautiful item of apparel that Masha might be able to craft for them. And so, Masha became known in the community as an artist and a mensch, and she had many visitors.

All visits to Masha's home were short, cordial, and professional. Only Alyona came for longer visits. Alyona would bring Eva, and the two mothers would nurse their daughters, share their cabbage soup, brew tea in the samovar, and compare the girls' development. Often Alyona sang to the girls, which brought Masha so much peace. Alyona was not Jewish, and so the songs she sang were different from the songs Masha had learned as a girl, before she had married Vasilliy and before the young couple had been sent away to this farming collective west of the Dnieper River. They were beautiful songs, wistful and plaintive. Alyona's lush intonation was how Masha imagined that the famous Nadezhda Plevitskaya once sang.[4]

Life was hard, work was grueling, but Masha loved her precious little daughter, who was healthy and inquisitive and who introduced daily wonders to Masha's life. Spring was coming, and the geese were returning to breed and nest. Masha and Trudie loved to watch the geese,

---

4 Little did she know that the exiled chanteuse, Nadezhda Plevitskaya, had come full circle, enlisting as a Soviet agent. At the time of this story, she was caught by the French police and sentenced to twenty years in a French prison, where she would die.

with their fierce attitudes and their dignity, and nothing made Trudie happier than to hear Alyona sing "Two Merry Geese," a traditional Russian folk song. "Two merry geese lived with Granny. One gray, the other white, two merry geese." Trudie was so small, but Masha would swear that she kicked along to the tune. "The geese washed their feet in a pool. One gray, the other white, in a pool," sang Alyona in a voice so beautiful that Masha was certain it cleared clouds from the sky. "When they were finished, they hid from Granny. One gray, the other white, hid from Granny. 'Oh', Granny cries, 'Oh, my geese are gone!' One gray, the other white. The geese are gone! The geese went out and bowed to Granny. One gray, the other white, bowed to Granny." In the brutal years ahead, Masha would try to conjure the sound of Alyona's voice singing about the mischievous geese and think back to Trudie's wide-eyed rapture.

The other thing that brought Masha contentment was the sewing work she did late into the night and the excitement of the women who wore her work proudly. One day she would have to sew a goose for Trudie, Masha thought to herself. Or perhaps she would teach the girl to sew a goose for herself. The thought of that made Masha smile.

Weeks became months and months became years. The absence of Vasilliy was a constant, painful bewilderment. And although the bewilderment never dissipated, somehow the ringing

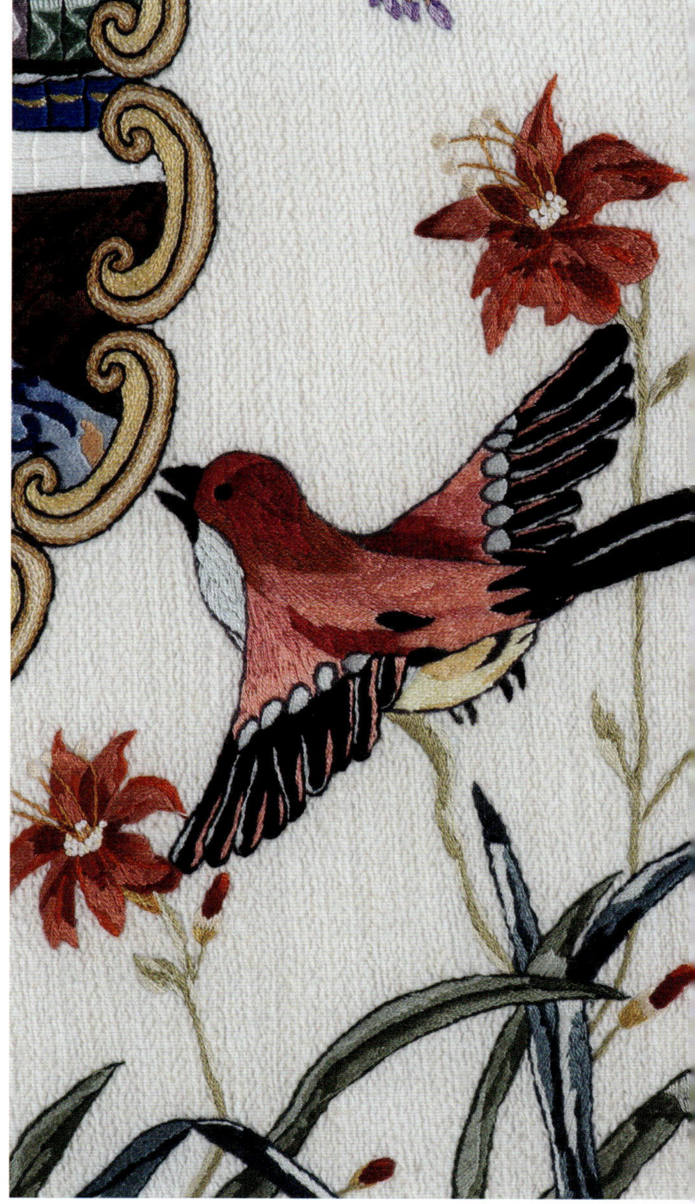

pain melded into the fabric that was life and became familiar, and in that familiarity the unbearable became routine, and the routine eventually fostered adaptation. Thus, the unspeakable loss of her beloved husband and the father of her precious child became normalized.

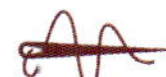

By the time she was four years old, Trudie had become so attached to Papa Doll that she carried it with her wherever she went. Trudie ate with Papa Doll, napped with Papa Doll, played games with Papa Doll, and learned her letters by teaching them to Papa Doll. Every day she combed Papa Doll's hair and wiped Papa Doll's face and straightened Papa Doll's clothes. Trudie was learning to sew so Papa Doll could have another outfit to change into. No one was allowed to touch Papa Doll without Trudie's permission. And despite her normally even temperament, any violation of the sanctity of her relationship with her doll would send young Trudie into fits. Masha honored the imperative of Papa Doll; indeed, Masha was touched by it, for Papa Doll was all her daughter had left of Vasilliy.

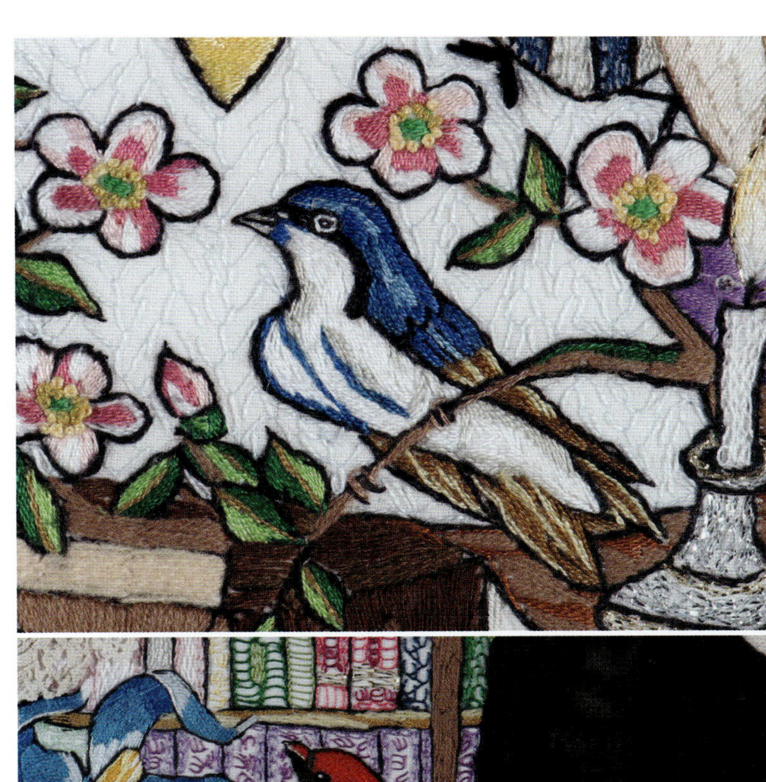

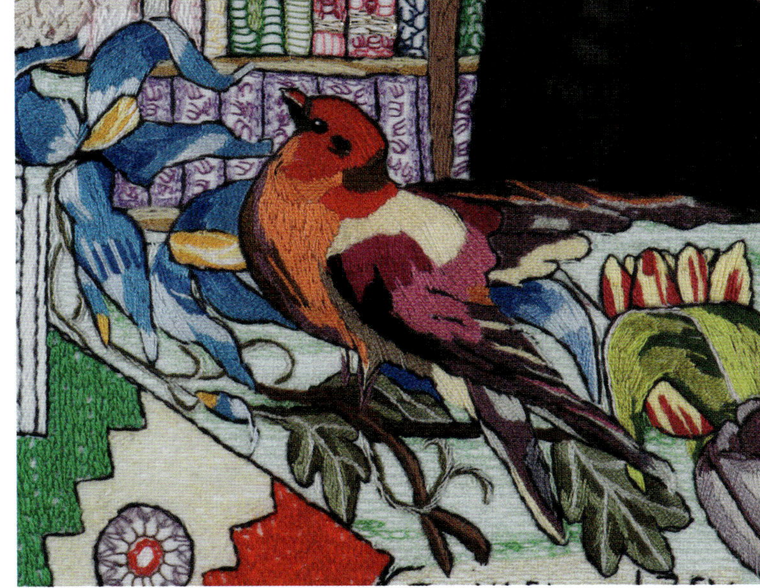

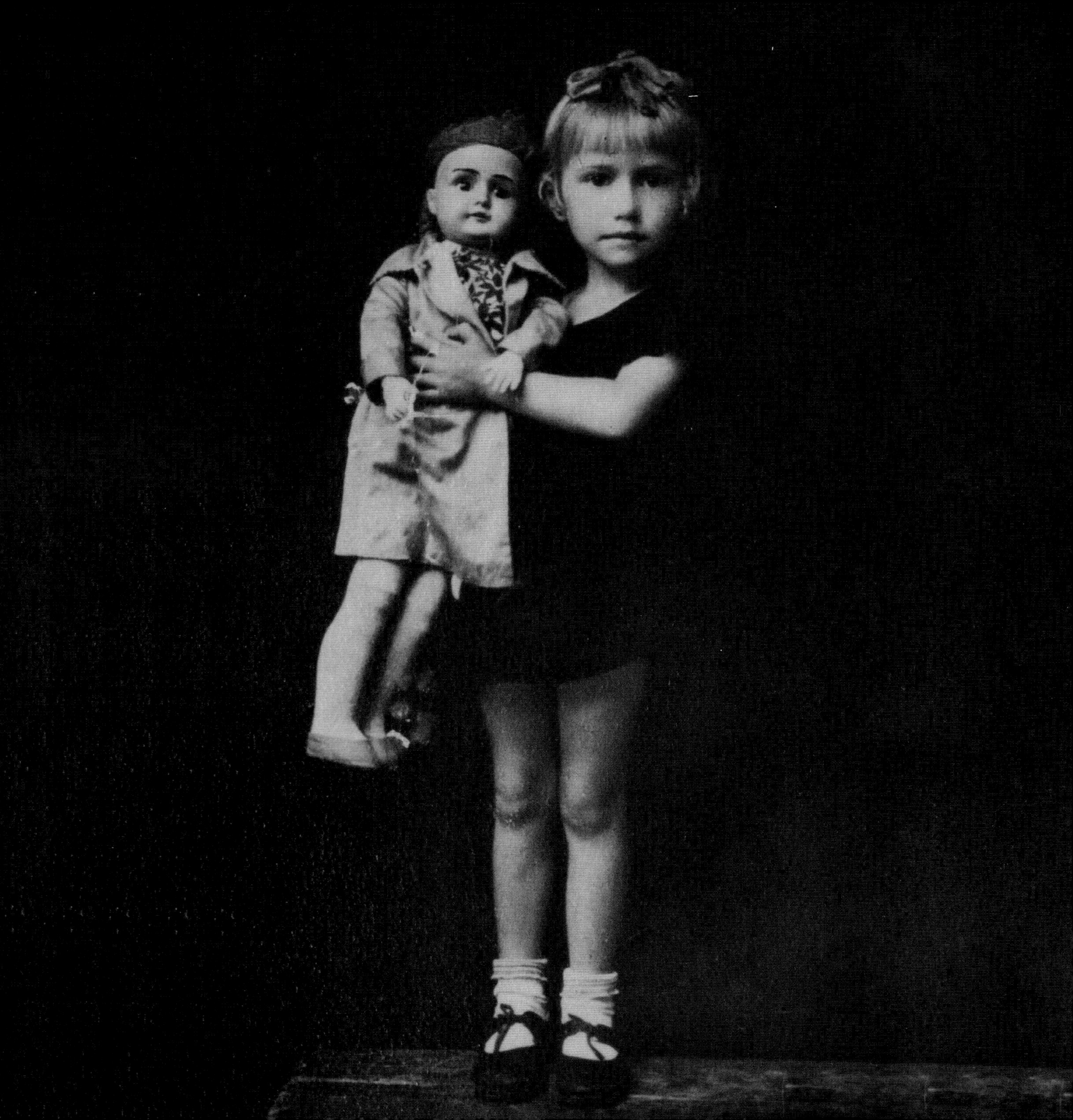

CHAPTER THREE

THE SECOND KNOCK

deracinate [dih-ras-uh-neyt], verb
1. to pull up by the roots; uproot; extirpate; eradicate.
2. to isolate or alienate (a person) from a native or customary culture or environment.

—DICTIONARY.COM

There was nothing normal about this knock. Indeed, nothing about it would qualify as a knock, because a knock implies some degree of solicitation. Even the offensively casual rat-tat-tat that had heralded the seizure and imprisonment of Vasilliy had been an engagement—a hostile engagement, a terminal engagement, but an engagement nonetheless. That time, there had been the rapping entreaty, Vasilliy's responsive opening of the door, the troop's intransigent order, which was, for all intents and purposes, an arrest, and then Vasilliy's forced departure. But what was happening now in the kolkhoz was an upheaval, a tsunami of aggression. This was an uprooting—a seizure. This was war.

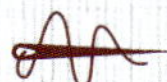

They must have known it was coming. Even in such an isolated community, news trickled in. Merchants peddled it in whispers on the side. Couriers left behind murmurings of gossip, rumors, and bona fide reconnaissance picked up along the way. As much as they were served a regular meal of state-spun narratives and outright propaganda, the people of the kolkhoz

Left: Trudie, age three, with Papa Doll, taken by a traveling photographer. All that Masha was able to preserve from life before the Nazis were a few photographs, the most precious of possessions.

knew to look under rocks for news that had not been Stalinized. It was 1941. Aiming to conquer and repopulate large areas of the western Soviet Union with Germans, to enslave the former occupants, to eliminate the "communist threat," and to seize Soviet oil reserves and agricultural resources, German forces had been invading the Soviet Union for months. And of course, of tantamount importance to the Third Reich was the elimination of all Jews.

It was too hard to drink from the huge lake of worry all day, every day, so Alyona and Masha, much like the others in the community, mostly went about the incremental business of living, with its endless tasks and challenges and the exquisite rewards of parenting even under such formidable circumstances. It took tremendous resolve and courage, although neither of them recognized that. There was no time for introspection or analysis; there was nothing to be gained by dreaming or yearning. Memory hurt. During the fleeting moments when Masha allowed herself to think about the past, to indulge her aching need to nest her head in the warm embrace of her husband, she would feel her strength recede and her determination ebb, and she would have to reprimand herself harshly. This is how one lost one's mind. Masha had seen it happen. After the soldiers had taken Dotnara Andrusyshyn's husband and two sons, Dotnara sat down in her chair and pulled out her hair, strand by strand, until her eyes retreated deeply into her skull, until the gray flesh of her face hung like the skin of a desiccated chicken. Sometimes, when the embers of her memory would flare, she would howl in pain. And then she would go back to pulling out her hair, until she was completely bald. She stopped eating and drinking. She stopped sleeping and never spoke another word. Planted in her chair, the eviscerated human being that once was Dotnara Andrusyshyn pulled down the shades and shuttered the doors of her life. Unlike Dotnara, who had been robbed of all she loved, Masha possessed this miracle that was Trudie. Masha had responsibilities, and she had purpose, and for this she was lucky.

There were times when the two mothers shared their concerns. Alyona had no religion. To avoid persecution, Alyona's parents, like most Russian families, had renounced the Russian Orthodox church during the revolution. Alyona was young when the communists mandated this forced conversion to atheism. So was Masha. But Masha's family, indeed the entire Jewish community in which she was raised, could not abandon the religion that so thoroughly defined their lives. In their remote community, far to the east and north of where Masha now lived, in the abject poverty of their village in Ufa, Masha's family had gone about their religion unobtrusively, managing to avoid the brutal forces for religious compliance and only suffering the occasional pogrom. Masha identified as Jewish first, Russian second. Being Jewish had been a constant throughout generations. It was the bedrock of Masha's being, the mainspring of her existential coherence. On the other hand, Masha often thought, being Russian was something fungible that kept undergoing redefinition.

As much as they did not want to express the fear in words and thus birth it into a shared consciousness, both Masha and Alyona acknowledged that the Nazis might come, and that if they came, all the Jews would be taken. While the Soviets were opposed to all religion, including Judaism, this Nazi hatred was laser targeted at Jews.

In the event the Nazis were to come, Alyona had offered to take Trudie and to raise her as a state atheist, just like she was raising Eva. They were hard words to share, but both mothers knew that the grim alternative was most likely a death sentence, perhaps swift, perhaps prolonged—either way terminal for both mother and daughter. Alyona's offer was the life raft that allowed both women to sleep at night.

There are many wrong ways, dead ends, and perilous yields at the fragile intersection of hope and fear.

The Germans took Dnipropetrovsk in early September. It was a gray September. Day after day offered flat, opaque skies and a monotonous chill. The day the Nazis came to Neu Chortitza would be no different.

It was still dark out when Masha and Trudie awoke to a cacophony. It started with the shrill shrieking of the geese, prescient harbingers of the trouble to come. Trudie held tight to Papa Doll and listened to the terrifying onslaught of rumbling jeeps and their blaring horns. "Mama?" she asked. Masha was already out of bed, getting dressed and handing warm clothes to Trudie.

"Put these on, Trudela," Masha said in the calmest, gentlest voice she could muster. Masha stuffed food into a satchel while from outside they could hear the rumble of motorized vehicles, the clacking and clanking of wagons, and the rush of horse hooves and heavy-booted men.

"Mama, I'm scared," said Trudie.

"It's okay to be scared, Trudie, but put on your shoes. We must get ready quickly."

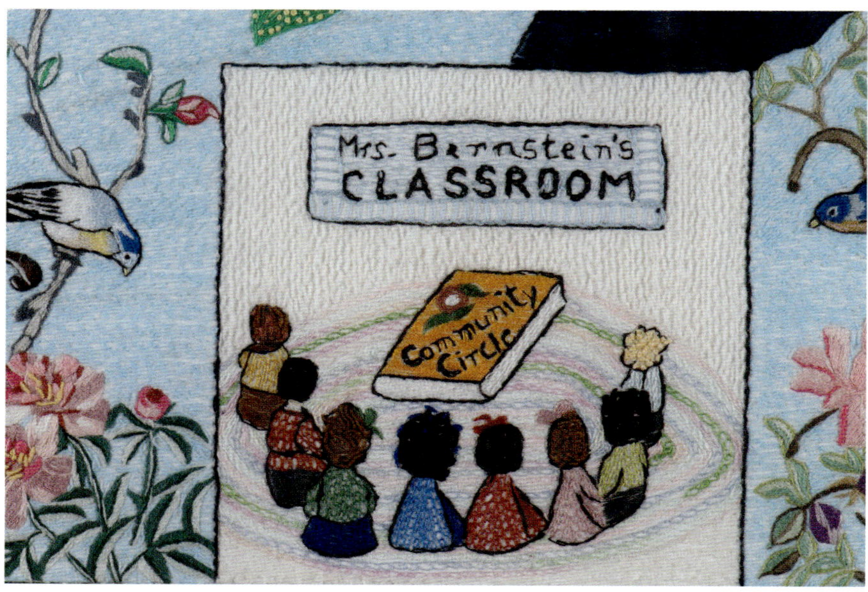

"Ready for what?"

"I'm not sure, but we have to be ready."

Outside there was much shouting amid the squall of amplified orders in German, the calling of names, and batons beating the doors of houses.

Trudie was dressed now, clutching Papa Doll and staring at the front door in terror. Masha was packing up necessities, or at least the things she thought they would need. How could one know? How could one plan? What was going to happen to them? Masha wrapped her beautiful shawl around her shoulders. She wrapped another around Trudie's shoulders.

The darkness was filled with the anguished protests of women being dragged from their homes, babies crying, children screaming. A shot rang out. It was followed by silence. The silence was almost more terrifying than the hellish commotion, which soon returned, augmented by the vicious barking of dogs and the snarling commands of soldiers.

The pounding of a baton on their door rattled the house. The ceramic kneading bowl fell off the stove and shattered. Masha froze. Trudie took her hand. "Mama," was all Trudie said.

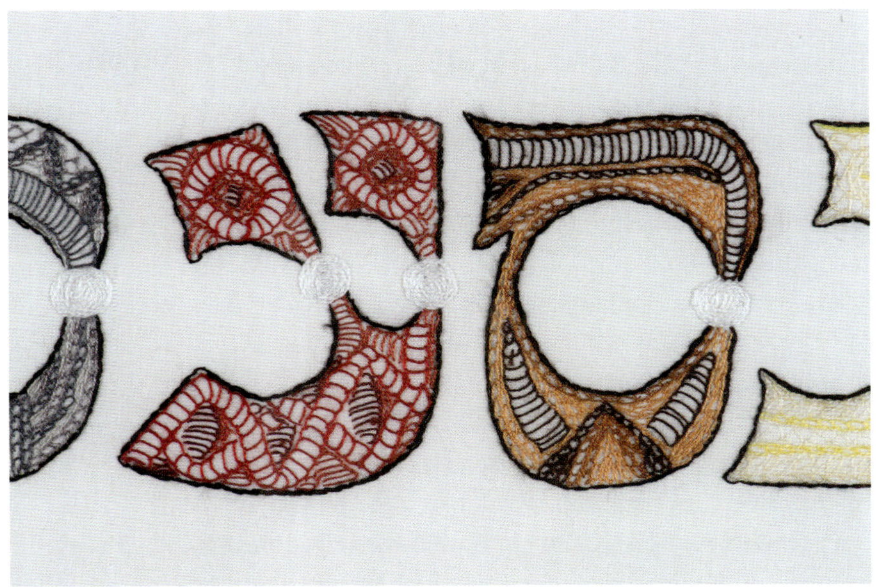

"Papa Doll must be brave. Just like you and me. Okay, my child?" said Masha. Trudie nodded. Masha gripped her daughter's hand firmly and opened the door to a blinding light.

"Masha Labuhn?" She could not see him with the bright light suffocating her vision.

She could only hear him. His accent was strong. She thought how peculiar her name sounded in this German tongue. How foreign. How wrong. "And child," the voice added.

Someone grabbed Masha by the arm and yanked her out of the light, shoving her toward a crowd of women and children. She clutched Trudie tightly until she was released from the wrenching grip of the Nazi soldier. As Masha's eyes began to adjust, she stared transfixed at the German soldier. He was just a boy, really. In shiny black boots and a big combat helmet, wielding a large rifle, he looked both vulnerable and lethal. He was someone's little boy and someone else's executioner, she thought to herself.

And then Masha saw the sweeper—the woman who had caught Masha when she fainted outside the prison in Krivoy Rog, who had slapped Masha into consciousness and ordered her to go home, who had let Masha know about Vasilliy's exile, who had been so gruff and yet so generous. The sweeper was on the ground, her face bloodied from a bullet wound through the head. The sweeper was dead. It must have been the gunshot Trudie and Masha had heard when they were still inside. Masha stared at the lifeless body and her thoughts came rushing in on her: The Russians took the sweeper's husband; the Germans took her life. In her head, Masha was screaming and crying and pounding her fists. It was so loud and chaotic in her head that she became disoriented. And then, somehow, through all the roaring in her brain, Masha suddenly imagined the slap of the sweeper. The hunched older woman who would have snapped Masha back to reality had she been alive and nearby. And then Masha felt a tug on her hand, and the reality of her situation came rushing back. She swept Trudie up in her arms and hugged her tightly.

When she looked up again, Masha saw Alyona across the square, in the perimeter, in shadows, fear scratched across her face. The two friends locked eyes, their silent goodbye. "Two merry geese, one gray, the other white, two merry geese," thought Masha. It was the last time she would ever see Alyona. Masha thought how ill-conceived their plan had been. There was no way to leave Trudie in Alyona's care, not now, not here with such public proceedings, not even if they were to shoot Masha dead right here, right now. And Masha knew in her heart that she could never leave her precious child. She would never leave Trudie. Trudie was her life.

Sometimes in the months and years ahead, when things got desperately hard, Masha would wonder if her maternal possessiveness was simply selfish—if she had held on to Trudie because doing so was the best thing for Masha, if leaving Trudie with Alyona would have been better for the child—even though this was a futile line of thinking because the opportunity had never presented itself and because there were too many unknowns. But for her part, Trudie never once wished to have been separated from her mother. Not for a second. Not for the rest of her life.

Masha glanced at the women and children who had been herded together alongside herself and Trudie: the Jews. Many of the women were wearing the shawl or coat that Masha had fabricated or overhauled for them, their most treasured and incorruptible item of attire. So many fabrics, so many materials, so many hues of hope were assembled here in this terrified group. In some small, impotent way, the wearing of these meticulously crafted garments was an act of defiance, a last grasp at self-respect, even a kind of tacit communion among the women.

"Is Papa Doll okay?" Masha whispered to Trudie. And Trudie nodded, but she was staring at the snarling dogs, beasts much larger than herself.

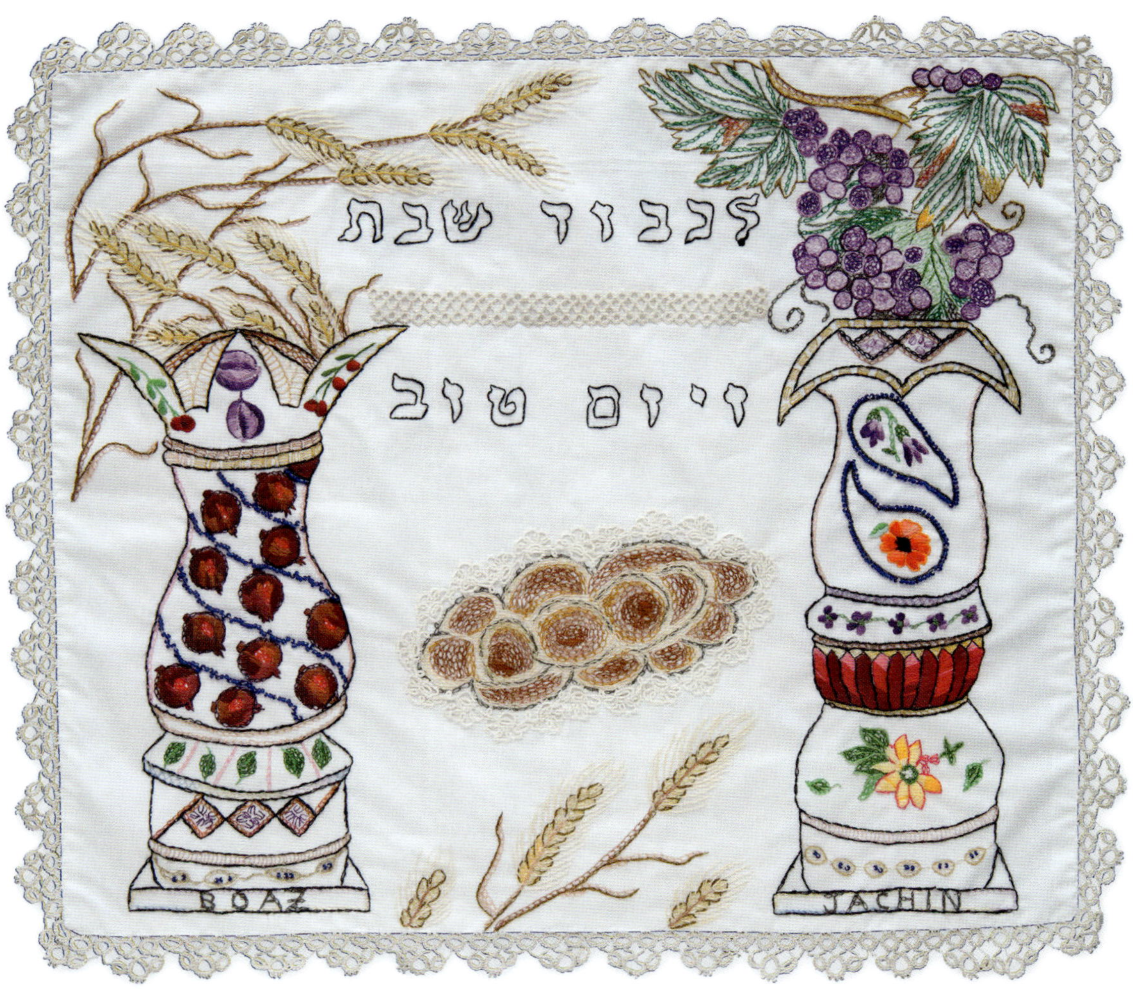

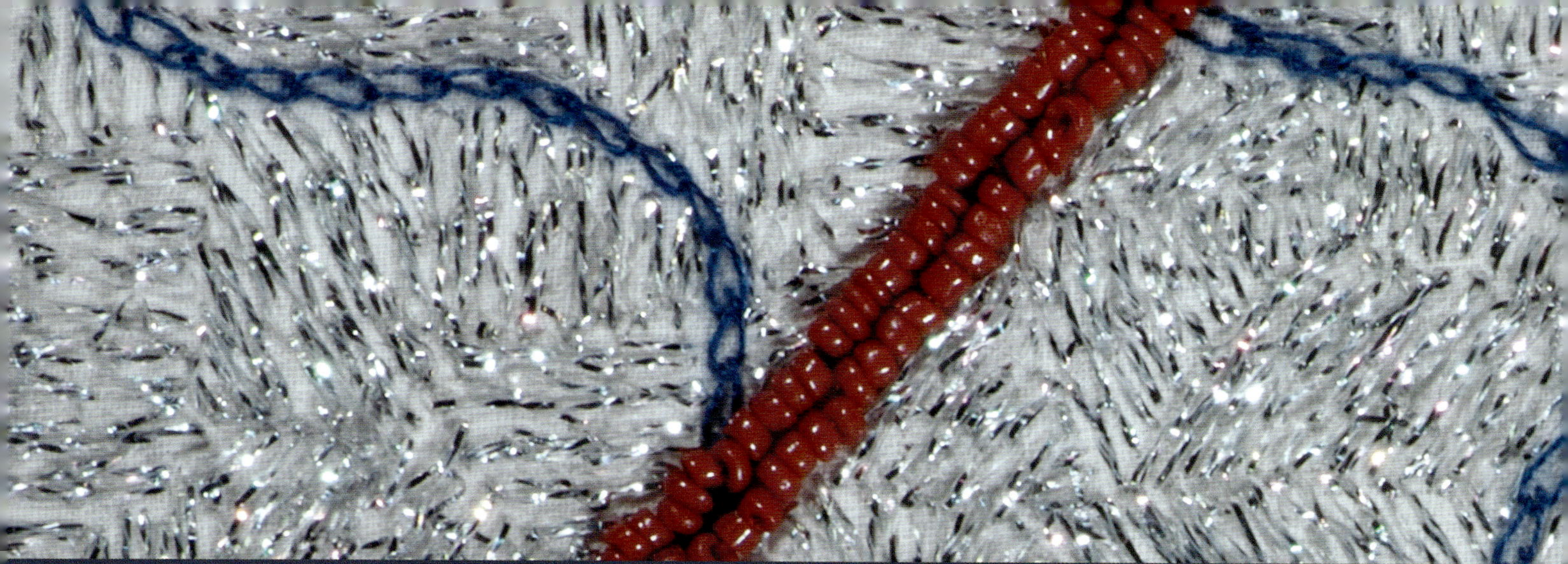

SHOAH SERIES

This series of seven pieces in three colors is a marked departure for Trudie Strobel. Using symbolism and iconography, this interpretive collection of seven works expresses an abstraction of stark feeling. The Jewish star is broken in "Destroyed." The solid, impenetrable, and solo flame in "Flame" appears as a brand, the brand of a devastating history. "Numbered Like Cattle" speaks for it-self, as do the red potatoes of "Starvation." Perhaps the most haunting piece is "Time Running Out," which we leave to your interpretation. All pieces are 9 ″ × 11″ × 7″.

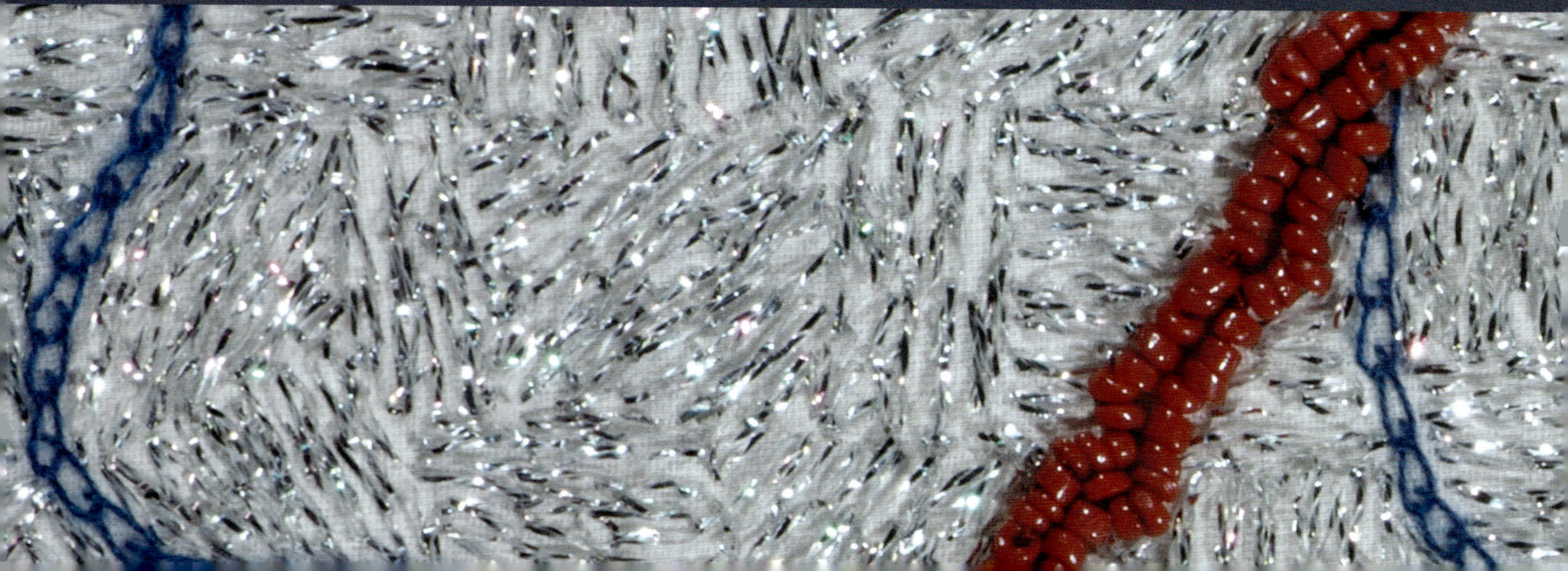

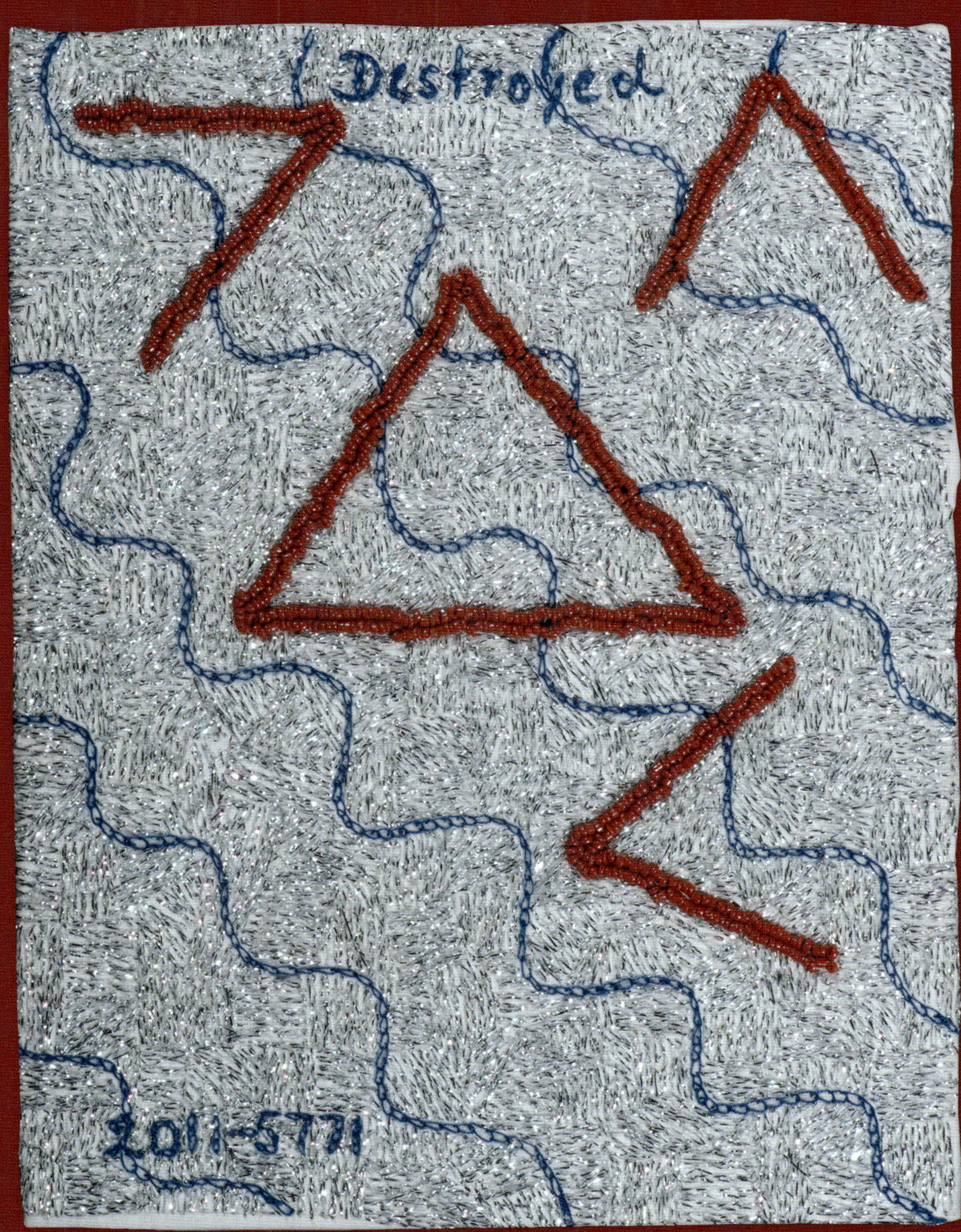

Destroyed

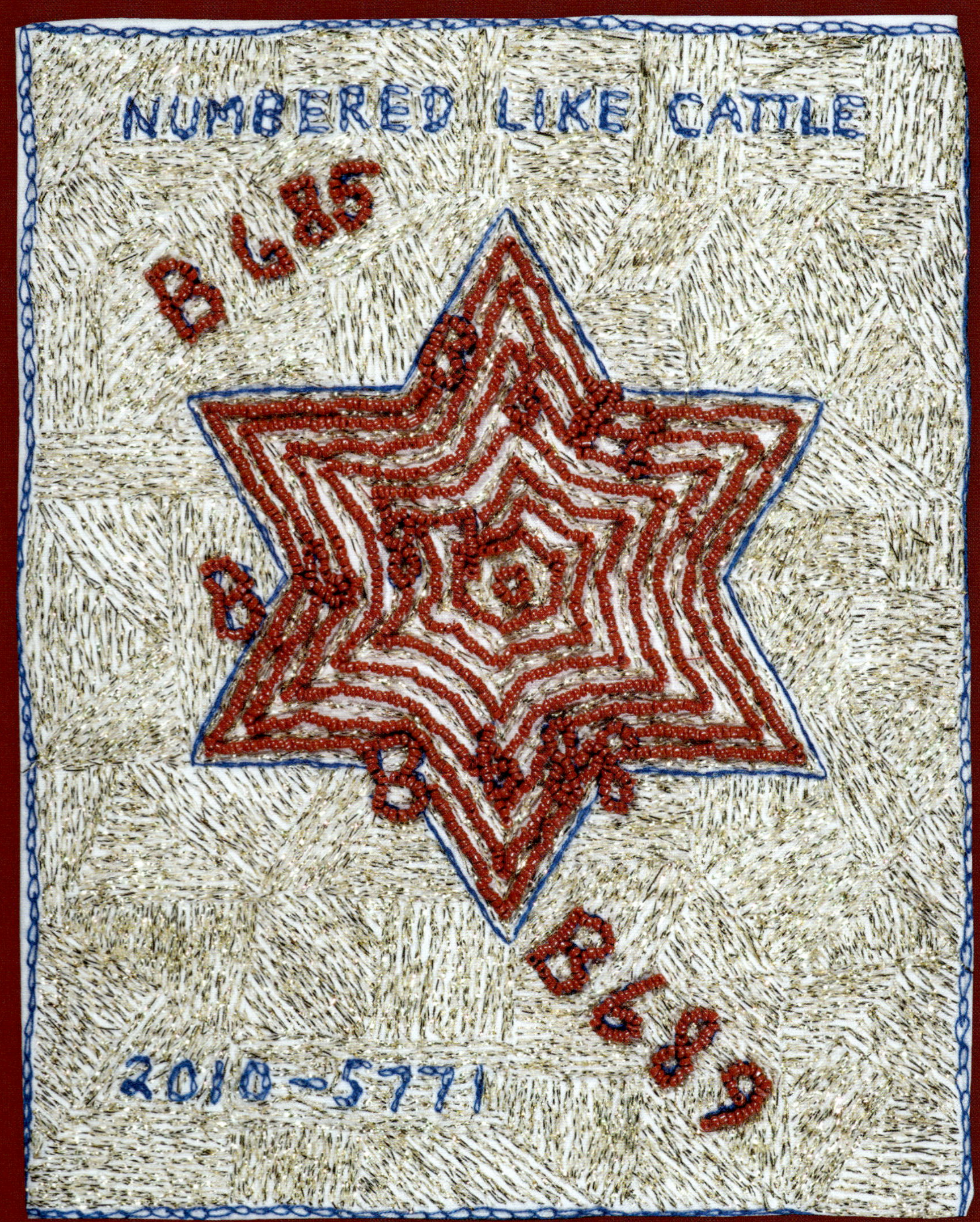

Numbered Like Cattle

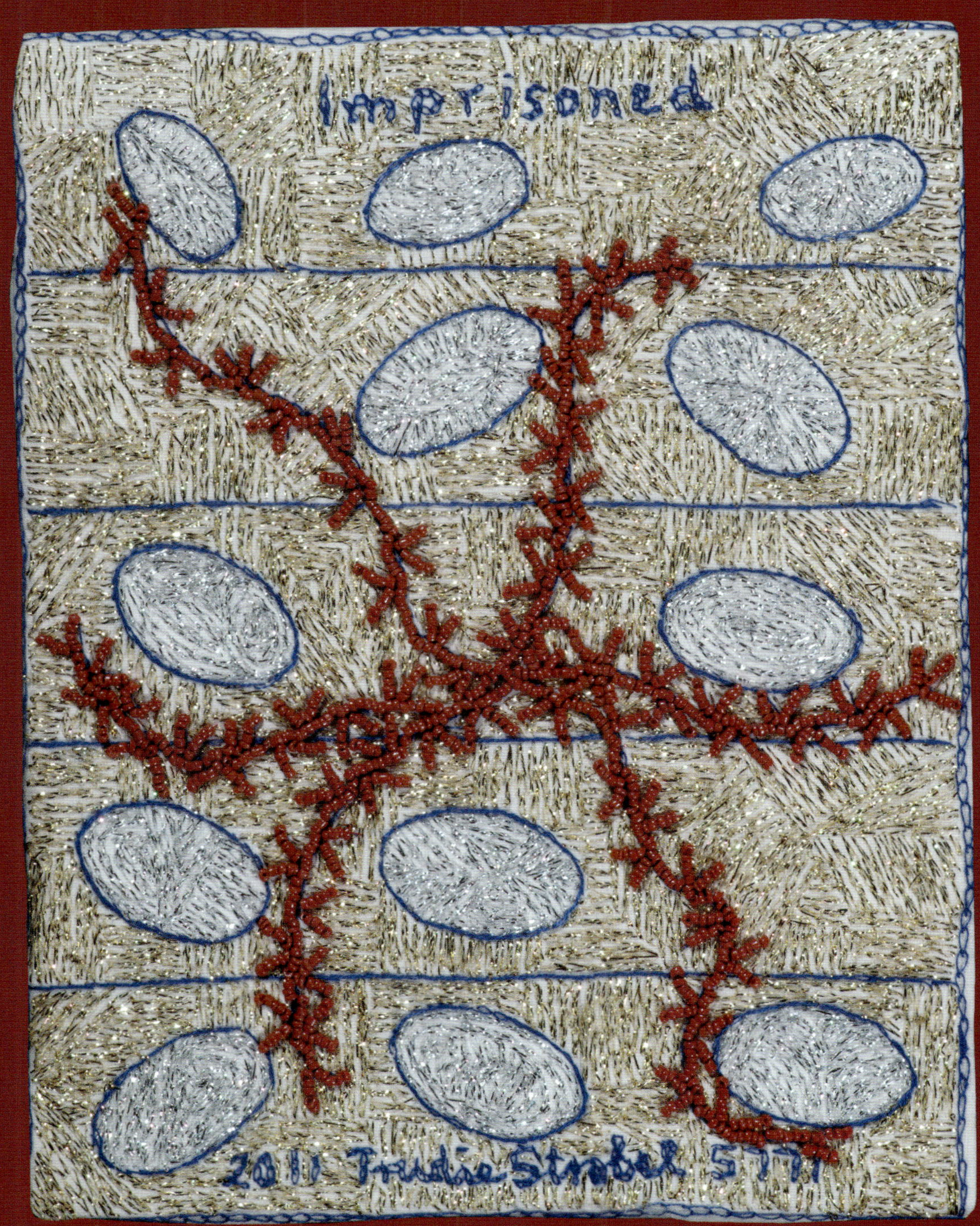

Imprisoned

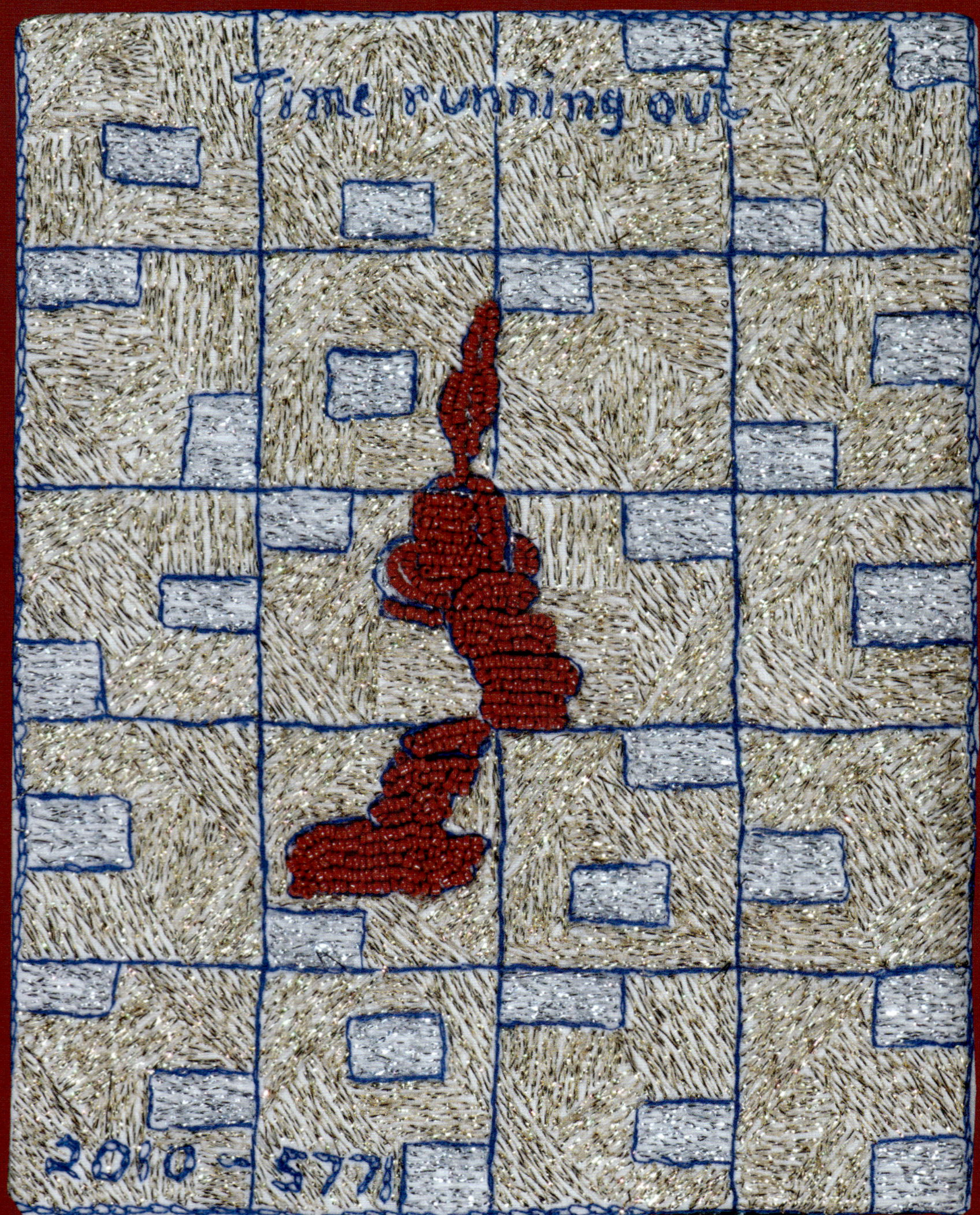

Time Running Out

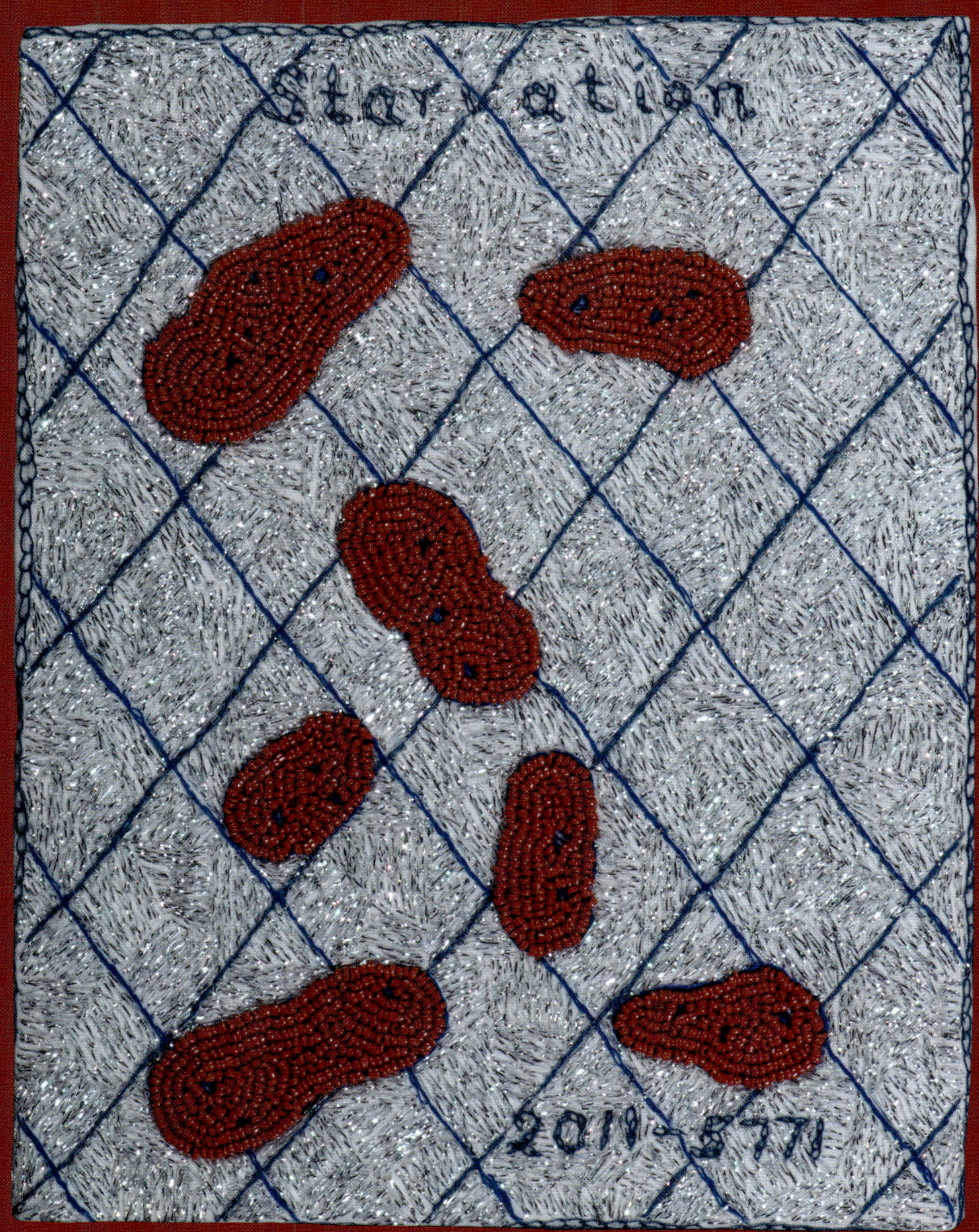

Starvation

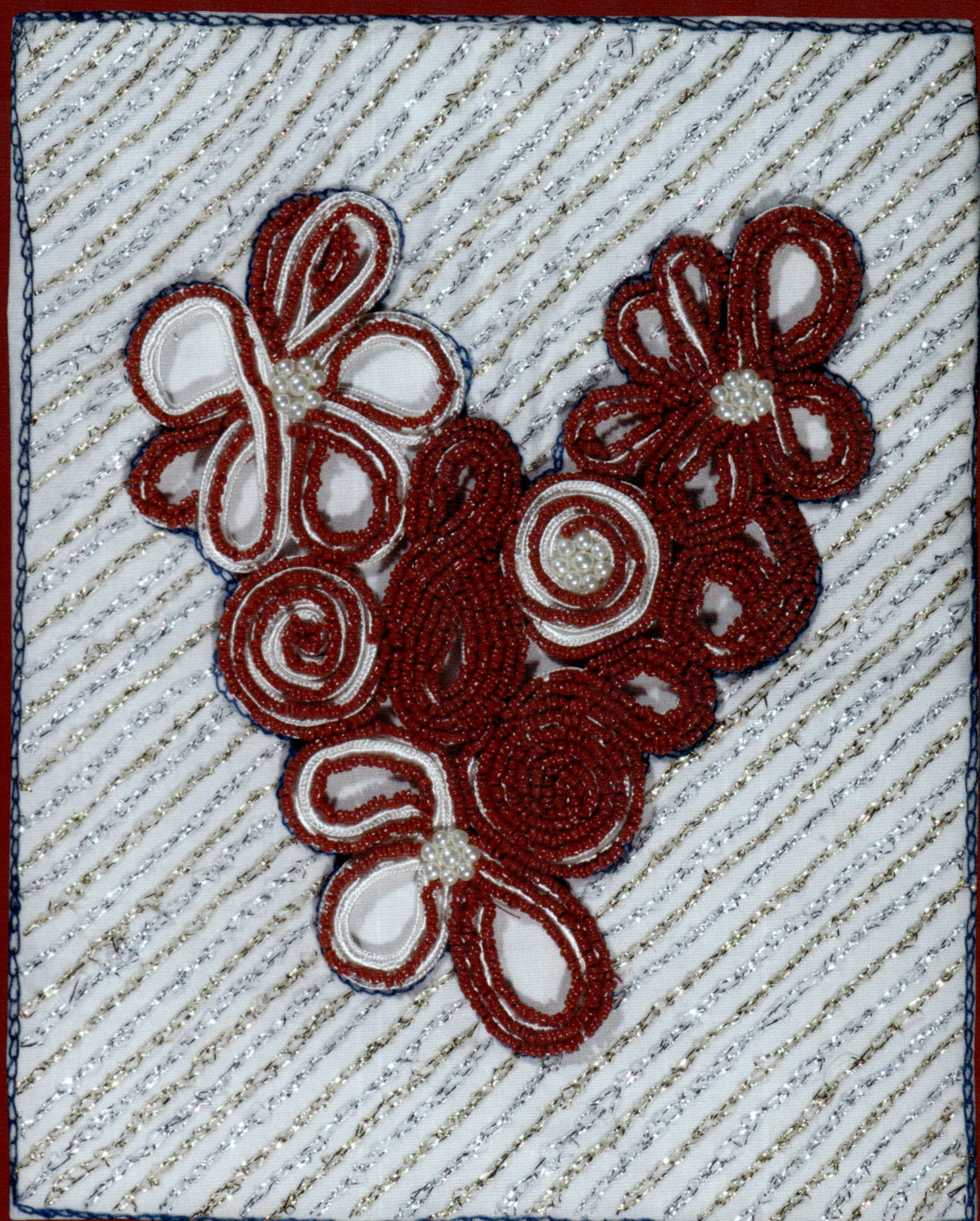

Heart

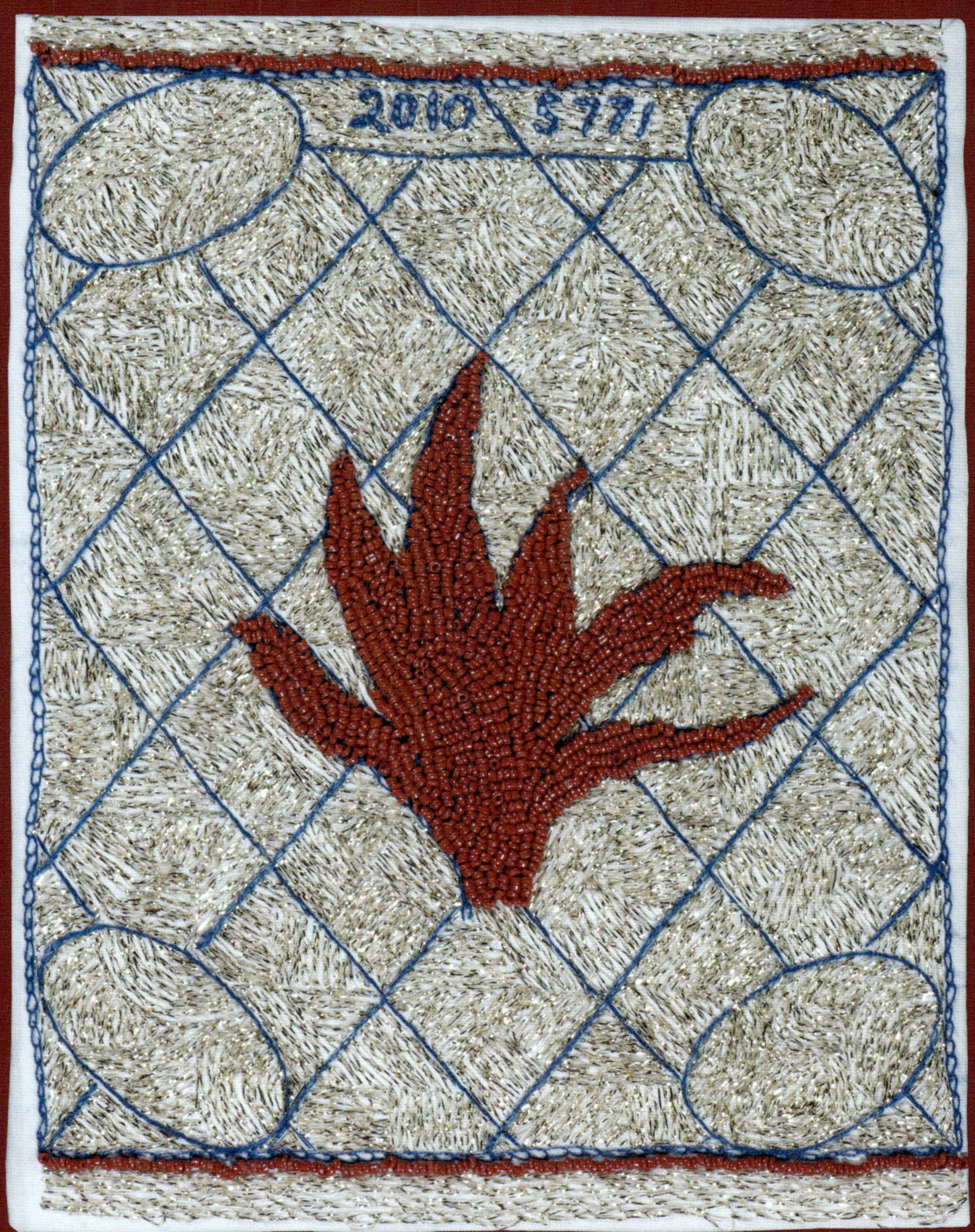

Flame

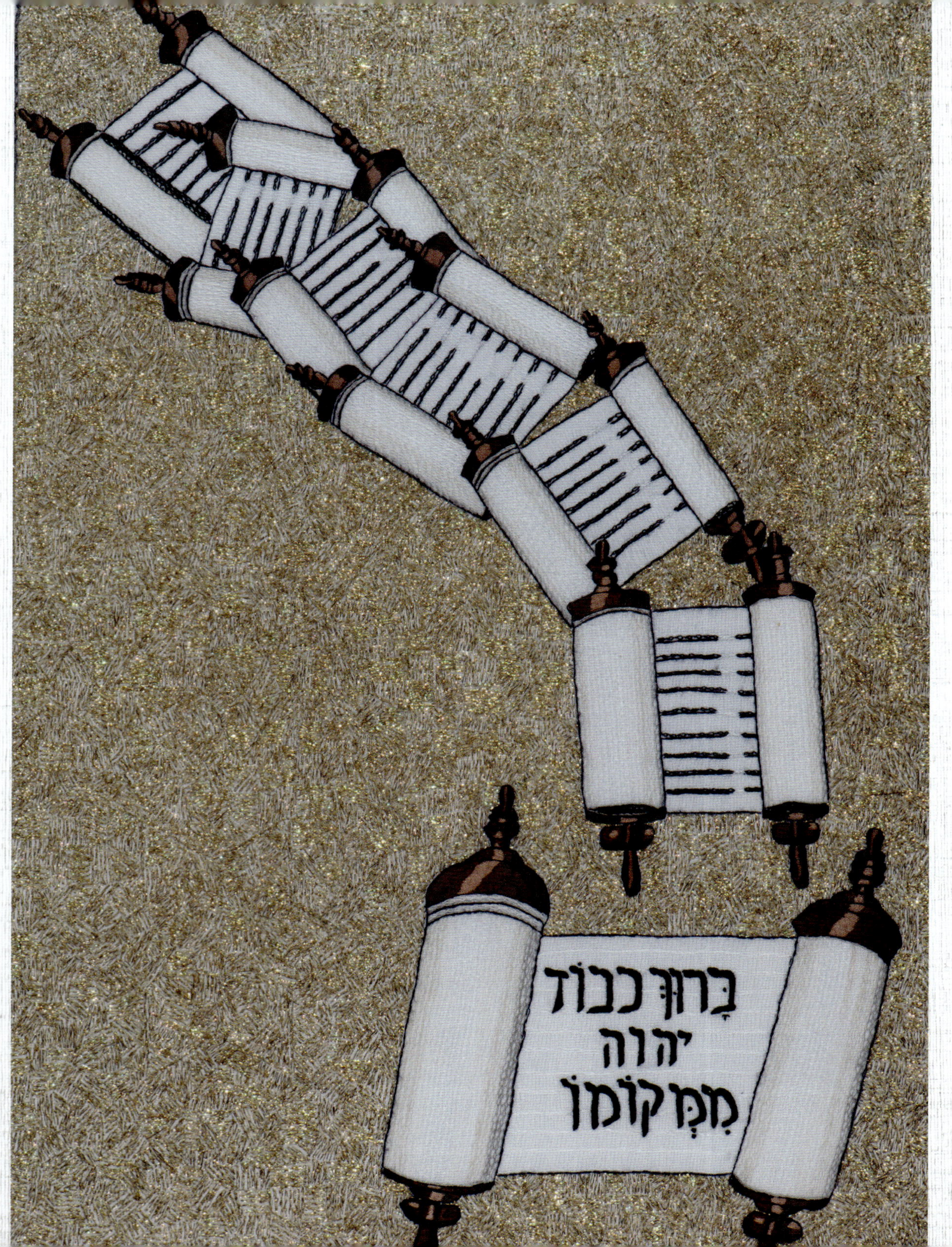
ברוך כבוד
יהוה
ממקומו

CHAPTER FOUR

THE WALK

The world, which is the private property of a few, suffers from amnesia. It is not an innocent amnesia. The owners prefer not to remember that the world was born yearning to be a home for everyone.

—EDUARDO GALEANO

They were not the first to have been seized by the Nazis, and they would not be the last. The caravan grew as they pushed west toward Poland, stopping in towns along the way to seize more Jews and provisions. Masha wondered why Stalin, with his vast and powerful military, would allow the relatively small country of Germany to just march across his borders and take over. Where was Stalin's resistance to these Nazi conquerors? Did the Red Tsar's dislike of Jews trump his national pride? Or had Hitler's forces somehow managed to defeat the Soviets?

The Nazis were always watching, suspicious. Masha felt their eyes on her, constantly looking for any inkling of insubordination. Masha could keep an inscrutable face, but Trudie was a small child who had to be taught to hide in plain sight. Masha was also always aware of the Nazis' ears, listening for any mere utterance of criticism, any grunt of resistance; whispering was dangerous, as it raised suspicion and opened the door to misinterpretation. It was a dueling hypervigilance between captor and captive, with potentially fatal results for the captive. This was another thing Trudie had to learn—how to be quiet, how to be invisible. This was a hard lesson for a child to learn and one that would have repercussions throughout Trudie's life.

Floating Torahs · 2011 · 20″ × 28″ · *Read more about this work in Art Notes, page 188*

Trudie walked some, always carrying her doll, and Masha carried her some, as well as Papa Doll, but at four years old, Trudie was close to thirty-five pounds, and although Masha's shawl could still accommodate Trudie and Papa Doll, it was hard for Masha to carry them for more than a mile at a time. Sometimes the soldiers would let Trudie and the other children ride on the wagons that accompanied them. The motorized Nazi vehicles that had invaded the kolkhoz had moved on to launch the "cleanup" of other towns and villages, to scrub them of their Jews and Slavs, leaving this caravan with mere horse-led wagons to make the 750-mile journey to Łódź, Poland.

All the Jewish prisoners were given a Magen David, yellow star of David, to stitch to the front of their clothing. It made the relentless watching of the "other" easier for the Nazis. Indeed, for centuries Jews had been singled out, ostracized, and forced to wear identifying clothing that marked them as outcasts. For Jewish prisoners of the Nazis, it was the yellow star that often read, *Jude*. Masha helped many of her fellow prisoners stitch the badges to their frocks, their coats, their shawls. Some of the Jewish prisoners were just too shell-shocked to function. And others could not sew. But the punishment for not wearing the star prominently could be severe. Helping others, even with this small, distasteful but urgent task, gave Masha some kind of vague purchase on the elusive sense of humanity that kept slipping under her feet. There was one Nazi soldier with a prominently scarred lip, a venal man with a wicked temper, who seemed to take a particular interest in Masha's sewing expertise. He was clearly taken with the detailed work that had gone into her shawl, as he would ask her about it at odd moments. Once, when he had torn his coat, he ordered her to repair it. His order was harsh and his tone was menacing, but his subsequent attention to her work was incongruously civilized. The attention was terrifying, though, and Masha had to steel herself so she did not physically recoil in his presence.

Uman, once a center of Hasidism[5] and the final resting place of the famous *tzadik* (righteous leader), Rabbi Nachman of Bratslav, had already been disemboweled when Masha, Trudie, and the caravan of prisoners arrived after more than a week of arduous walking. They

5 A movement of Jewish orthodoxy that emphasizes simple, sincere, and intuitive devotion over strict adherence to Talmudic erudition. In Hebrew, the word *Hasid* means "pious" and commonly designates spiritual devotion that transcends the exigencies of Jewish law.

were tired, hungry, filthy, cold, and constantly afraid. In Uman, 10,000 Jews were killed by the Nazis in a span of twelve months. Just a few months before Masha and Trudie passed through on their forced march, in an unthinkable horror, 1,000 Jewish children had been rounded up and massacred. The eviscerated adult community left behind could think of nothing else. Hearing the whispers, Masha's head flooded with thoughts of a thousand young lives, each with his or her own hopes and dreams, each a human treasure in the same way that her Trudie was a treasure—each of these innocent souls obliterated.

Rakivka, the Jewish ghetto in Uman, had already been liquidated. The German troops who ruled the virtually Jew-less town conferred with Masha's captors, and then the herd of prisoners continued on its weary way.

Masha could not help but think that there was something perversely biblical about this forced exodus. But she could not contemplate anything for long, because the walking was so grueling, and she and Trudie were so thirsty and hungry. When they tired and slowed, the grim Nazis would hit them with sticks and shout at them to hurry up. When they stumbled, the vicious dogs would be right there, growling in their faces. When they dropped something, the soldiers would often kick it away, no matter if it was food or jewelry, clothing or coins. And whenever they spoke among themselves, the Nazis were listening. One woman, Zhenya, carried a brass samovar that had been in her family for generations. Zhenya was an older woman, and she was determined. The Nazis snickered about her and her ridiculous cargo, especially the soldier with the scarred lip. Scar Lip would sometimes walk alongside Zhenya, reaching out to turn the samovar's knobs. The older woman held her head high and walked on, not protesting the Nazi soldier's taunting interventions but not accommodating him either as she hugged the large brass vessel that tethered her to a place far away, where she'd known comfort and kindness. Then, two weeks into the endless walk, the older woman stumbled. The samovar fell to the ground and Scar Lip kicked it, like a soccer ball, clear across a field, laughing as it clanked and bounced and finally came to rest against a felled tree. Zhenya stood frozen. The tether had been severed. Scar Lip tried to push Zhenya forward, but she was unmovable. Scar Lip struck her with his baton, once, twice and then brutally hard a third time. Zhenya took the first two blows standing, but the crack of bone caused by the third blow knocked her to the ground. For a moment she lay there, as Scar Lip laughed, but then she began to crawl, dragging her broken body to the discarded samovar. This made Scar Lip mad, and he kicked her harder and harder, fueling himself into a vicious frenzy. Zhenya kept dragging herself, inch by inch, determined to reach that last connection to a life with decency: the samovar. With one last crack of his boot, Scar Lip made sure that didn't happen.

Sometimes in the years that followed, Masha would think about the samovar lying in the field. She'd imagine a peaceful time, when the war would end, when humans would return to their sanity, when someone would come upon the brass samovar lying as it was left, in that field one week's walk northwest of Uman. She'd imagine a little girl stumbling upon it, struck with awe, believing it to be the magical home of a bewitched creature; or she'd imagine an enthralled little boy, certain he had discovered a tiny alien spaceship; she'd imagine a poet discovering the now-tarnished urn and pondering its provenance in verse; or she'd imagine a tank rolling over it, smashing it into oblivion.

Two months later they had walked the 394 miles to Lwów, which was considered Poland at the time. (It is now Lviv, Ukraine.) The Wehrmacht forces had already taken Lwów, too. Before the war, Lwów had been home to more than 75,000 Yiddish-speaking inhabitants. Now, the eviscerated Jewish population was confined to the Lwów ghetto. Thousands had been massacred. Tens of thousands had been sent off to the Janowska death camp. Others would soon be deported to the Belzec extermination camp, where close to half a million Jews were murdered by the SS by the end of World War II.

Trudie and Masha were standing in place, silently waiting for their next orders, when an SS officer smiled at little Trudie holding Papa Doll. Towering over the prisoners in his long black tunic with the swastika on the right collar and the eagle patch, its wings spread, on the left arm, the officer had a chilling smile. "Give that to me," he said. And he strode over to Trudie, who clung to her beloved doll. Masha could feel Trudie tense like a tiny tiger, ready to attack. She could see the eyes of the other Nazis, watching, their hands on their guns. Terrified, Masha uttered Trudie's name, but only her name. She said it quietly but with an iron tone that stopped her young child from reacting when the Nazi yanked Papa Doll from her arms. The Doll Thief laughed and held Papa Doll up to the light, then shoved it under his fat satisfied arm and gamboled off.

Masha could feel the cavern of loss that had just wrenched apart Trudie's soul. "Remember

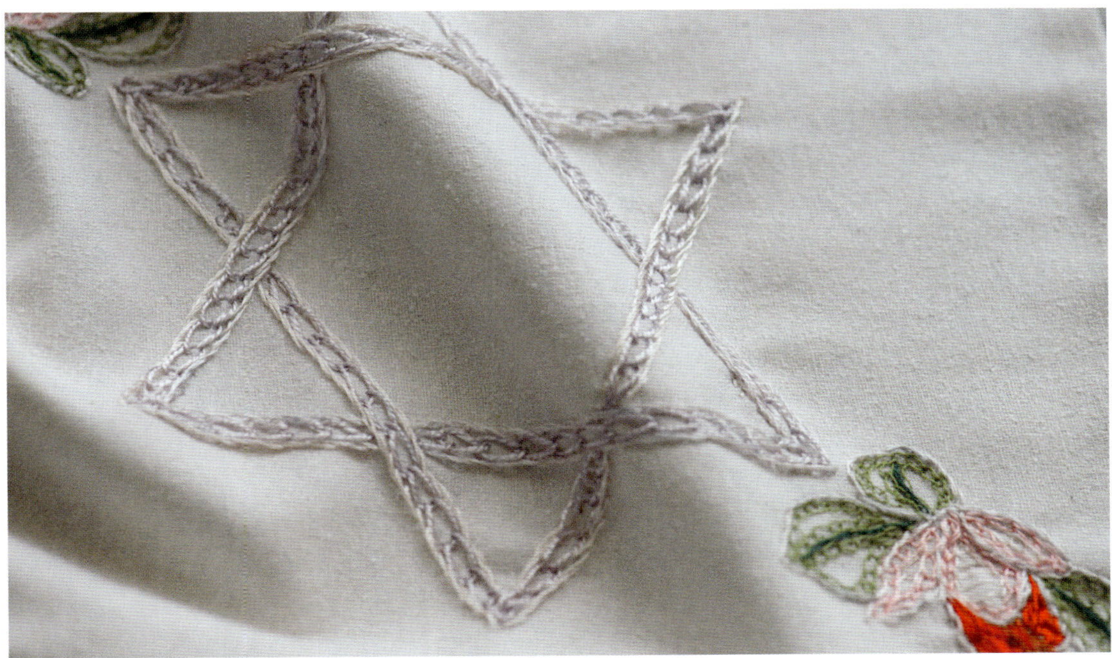

Joseph Ariel's tallit bag—This tallit and tallit bag was commissioned by Liora Elghanayan for her son, Joseph Ariel

Zhenya and her samovar, Trudie," Masha dared to whisper as she hoisted Trudie up into her arms. She hated to say it. She hated that Trudie had witnessed Zhenya's brutal murder. And she hated saying anything that might sound disparaging about Zhenya and her attachment to a brass urn, because she knew she had not died just for an urn. But the words were necessary. And later, when they were huddled together on top of their blankets on the cold ground, Masha told Trudie, "We will both miss Papa Doll. But we have each other."

"Promise?" asked Trudie, still crushed.

"Yes, Trudela, yes of course."

"Always?"

"Always, my love." And Masha determined right then and there that somehow she would make sure this was not a lie.

The Nazis led them north from Lwów to Lublin. It was a bitter walk and took them the better part of a month. Their ranks were fewer and fewer. Many of the prisoners had collapsed along the way from hunger or fever or sheer exhaustion, especially the old and the very young. Some had been injured in a fall or at the hands of the brutal Nazi guards. One woman just walked away. She took her young son by the hand and turned around to go home. The guards barked at her, but she kept going, so they shot her and the boy. When any prisoner became a liability, that prisoner was shot or simply left to die.

What Masha could never understand was why this caravan of prisoners just kept on going. Why were they not left in a ghetto or death camp along the way? Who had mandated that this group of Jews be marched all the way to Łódź? Or was it that no one would take them, that whatever ghetto or camp they happened upon was full or in transition, that their timing was such that they had no choice but to just keep going?

This was certainly the case in German-occupied Lublin, where 34,000 Jews were confined to the Jewish ghetto, the *Wohngebiet der Juden* (Jewish quarter), when Masha and Trudie trudged wearily into town in their pathetic human train. Over the course of the next year, most of the Lublin Jews would be rounded up and killed on-site or deported to Belzec or Majdanek for extermination. But when Masha and Trudie arrived, the town's ghetto was teeming with huddled masses of desperate Jews. Every city had seemed worse than the one before. It was as if they were descending deeper and deeper into a roiling, dark ocean of human iniquity.

"Do you think Papa Doll is all right?" Trudie asked as they sat to rest their aching blistered feet.

"What I think," Masha said, "is that Papa Doll has found a little girl who was all alone, and very frightened, a little girl who needed a companion really badly."

"I'm frightened too, Mama," Trudie admitted softly.

"We are all frightened, Trudela," said Masha. She repeated it half to herself: "We are all so frightened. But..."

"What?"

"But... I have you and you have me. And this little girl, she maybe has no one... *had* no one—until Papa Doll found her."

"Do you believe that?"

Masha could not bring herself to lie to Trudie. "I want to believe it, Trudela."

Russia 1942 · 1991 · 36″×37″

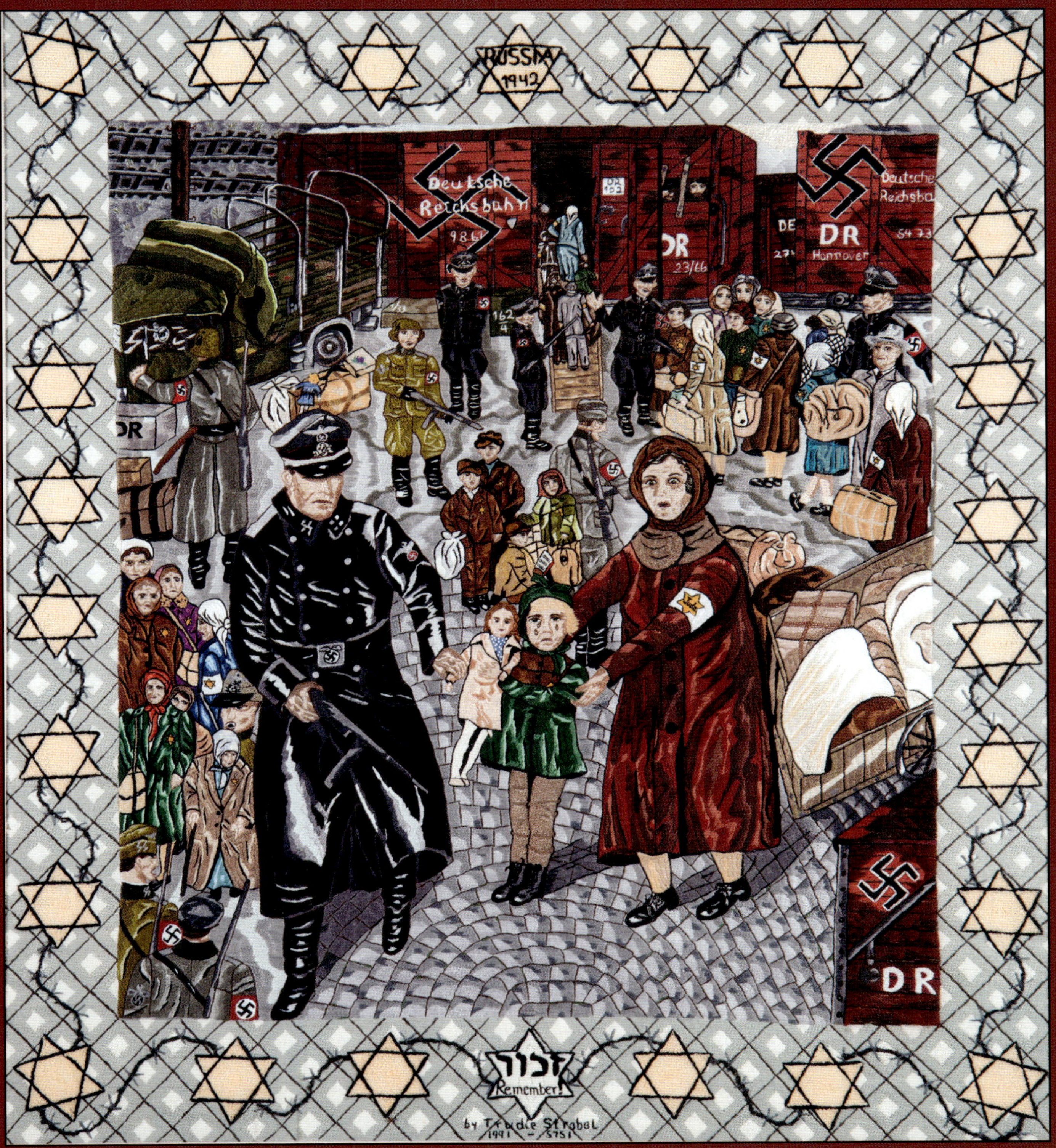
RUSSIA
1942
Deutsche
Reichsbahn
9861
DR
23/66
DE
DR
Hannover
6473
DR
DR
זכור
Remember!
by Trudie Strobel
1991 - 5751

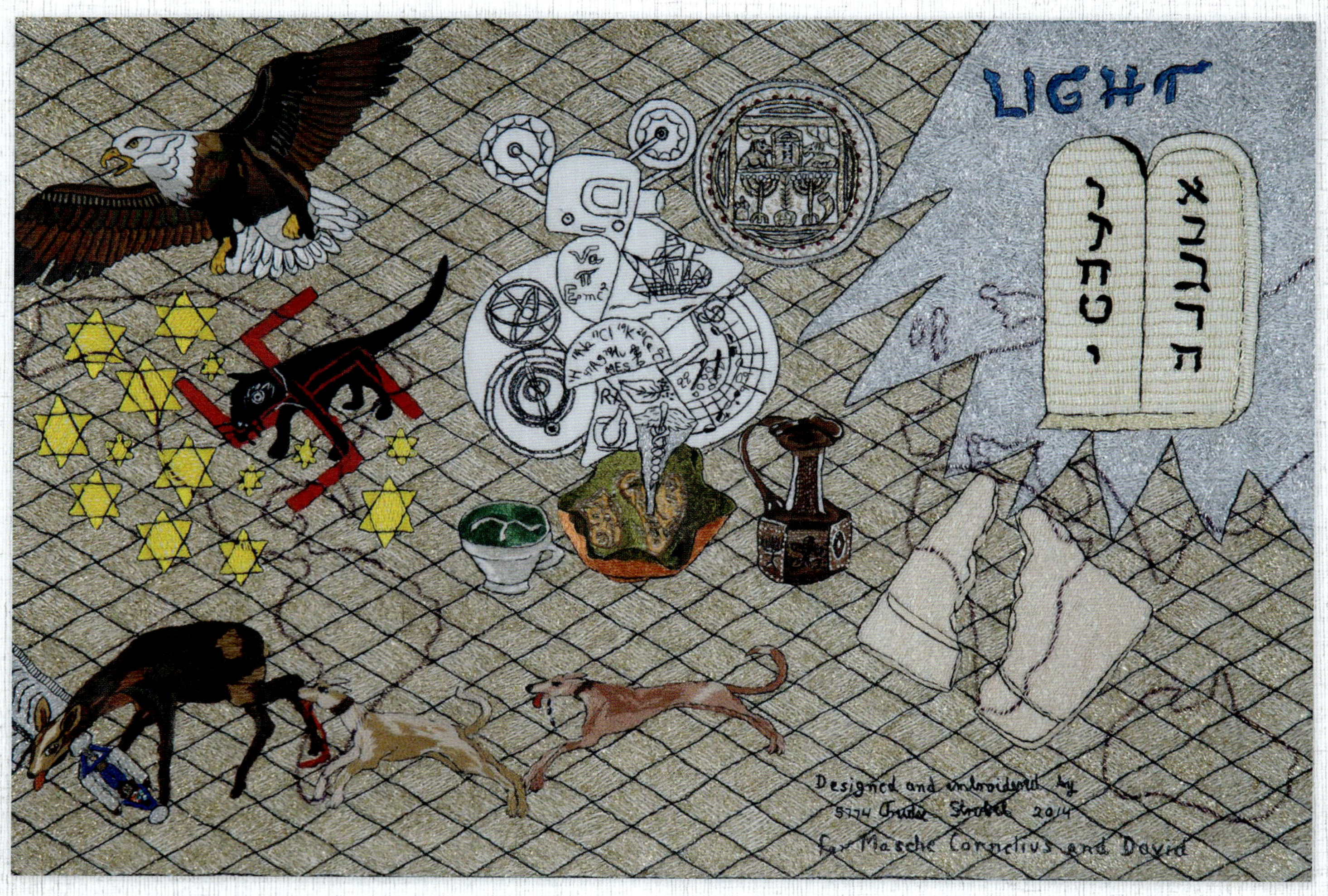

Light #2 · 2014 · 31″×41″ · *Learn more about this work in Art Notes on page 173*

CHAPTER FIVE

ŁÓDŹ

The Great Lie is that this is civilization.

—JOHN TRUDELL

Wohngebiet der Juden – Betreten Verboten read the sign at the entrance to the ghetto: *Housing of Jews – Entrance Forbidden*. The uprooted Jews of the kolkhoz in Neu Chortitza had reached their destination. The Łódź ghetto was encased in barbed wire and guarded by grim German police. Trudie and Masha stood in the interminable line of Jews on the long road laid with embedded round rock that led into the ghetto. There was something incongruously egg-like about those round rocks—embryonic, inchoate, germinal, and thus bearing potential and hope. But this was a miscue. It was not the road to hope; it was the carefully laid avenue to the mass abortion of an entire race.

As Masha and Trudie waited to enter the ghetto, they saw two wagons full of little children being driven away, heavily guarded by soldiers. The children appeared to be dressed for a party. The little boys had on slacks. The little girls had ribbons in their hair. But the children were sobbing and screaming for the mothers they would never see again.

Inside the gates, the ghetto teemed with people, all wearing their yellow Jewish stars, their "badge of shame."[6] (This is the name Trudie Strobel gave to the clothing assigned to the Jewish people by eleven centuries of xenophobic governments to differentiate the Jews

6 Trudie's seminal exhibit in the permanent collection of the Los Angeles Museum of the Holocaust, titled *Eleven Centuries of Degradation*, re-creates these costumes in damning detail.

from the rest of society.) The conditions in the ghetto were miserable and unsanitary. Chronic shortages of food, insufficient clean water, scarce fuel, and inadequate sanitation would cause thousands to die. Some Jews lay starving on the streets. Others waited despairingly in long lines for food, water, books, and the remote possibility of work. The lines did not seem to move, and the crowds never seemed to dissipate. More than 160,000 people were crammed into one and a half square miles of dilapidated wooden structures, with as many as ten people packed into a small room. Most of the houses lacked basic plumbing; "fecal workers" had to haul away waste.

A man in a curiously tidy three-piece suit with a Jewish star on his right breast and an uncanny beige brimmed hat stood on a makeshift platform shouting orders. Chaim Mordechai Rumkowski, often referred to as King Chaim, was the Nazi-appointed *Judenrat* (council representing the Jewish community), chairman of the Łódź ghetto, and the head of the Council of Elders. With his famously white bushy hair, this former director of a Jewish orphanage (a middling career in which he had shown little distinction) now ran the bureaucracy that allocated shelter, rationed food and fuel, and maintained order in the ghetto.

Rumkowski looked hale for a Jew of the Łódź ghetto. So many others shuffled like depleted shadows through the streets, but Rumkowski seemed to be thriving. Trudie remembers his shock of white hair, his apparent command of a very bleak situation. Perhaps Rumkowski naively believed that because the Nazis had elected him to manage the ghettoized Jews, he would be spared, that in cooperating with them, he might not be seen as just another despicable blemish on the racial purity the Germans were fighting to achieve, that he, and maybe others—at least others in his immediate sphere—would be spared, but he would be wrong. The final liquidation of the Łódź ghetto would begin on August 2, 1944. More than 72,000 people, including Rumkowski, would be deported to Auschwitz-Birkenau, where they would be executed. Such would be the fate of ghetto leader Mordechai Chaim Rumkowski. All that time, he had only been organizing paper clips in hell.

But Masha and Trudie arrived in Łódź before the final liquidation. At the direction of King Chaim, they were given a sliver of space on the filthy floor of a filthy room that they shared with a dozen or so others, along with a loaf of bread and some rotten beets. The conditions were miserable; the suffering around them was unfathomable. Today, when Trudie, who experienced so much horror in so many vivid and shocking forms, is asked to speak about Łódź, a mute sadness fills her eyes with tears. Łódź was unspeakable. During its four-year existence, more than 200,000 Jews passed through the ghetto. In that caged community, 43,500 died, mostly of starvation and disease. Hold that cataclysmic loss in your mind and add to it the more than 77,000 Jews and 5,000 Roma (often referred to as "Gypsies") who were taken from the Łódź ghetto to the Chelmno killing center for extermination between December 1941 and July 1944. Chelmno was only thirty-seven miles northwest, a short ride on a cattle car.

When the Jews from Łódź arrived there, they were expecting work, better food, and a shower. Even when they were ordered to remove their clothes and leave them behind for disinfection, the humiliated and disoriented prisoners still clung to hope as they were herded, naked, into trucks to ride to the baths. Chelmno's trucks, however, were engineered so that deadly engine exhaust filled the cargo compartments. German guards sealed the airtight doors. Soon after a driver started the engine, the screams from the suffocating prisoners would commence, only to be extinguished, along with their aspirations, their potentials, and their accomplishments, in merely five to ten minutes. Then the naked bodies were either discarded in mass graves or incinerated in one of two crematoria.

The Nazis came for Masha soon after their arrival. Masha held back her own terror. When she was ordered to follow, she did so, never letting go of Trudie's hand. She had made a promise to never leave Trudie, and she was determined to keep that promise. And the Nazis did not separate them. They left through the door that they had so recently entered, clutching their few remaining belongings, the loaf of bread, and the rotten beets.

But Masha and Trudie were not hauled off to die. Scar Lip had boasted to the Łódź Nazis about the intricate stitching and masterful repair work that Masha had done on his coat. The seemingly endless war had taken a toll on the integrity of the Nazi soldiers' wardrobes. Their admiration for the workmanship that had gone into the overhaul of Scar Lip's coat encouraged him to preen all the more. And thus, word got around. In the wet and cold of the dreary days, an uncompromised uniform was something to covet. A sewing machine was located, and Masha was put to work with Trudie at her side, trying at all times to remain invisible. In that wretched ghetto, Masha found her talents in surreal, perverse demand.

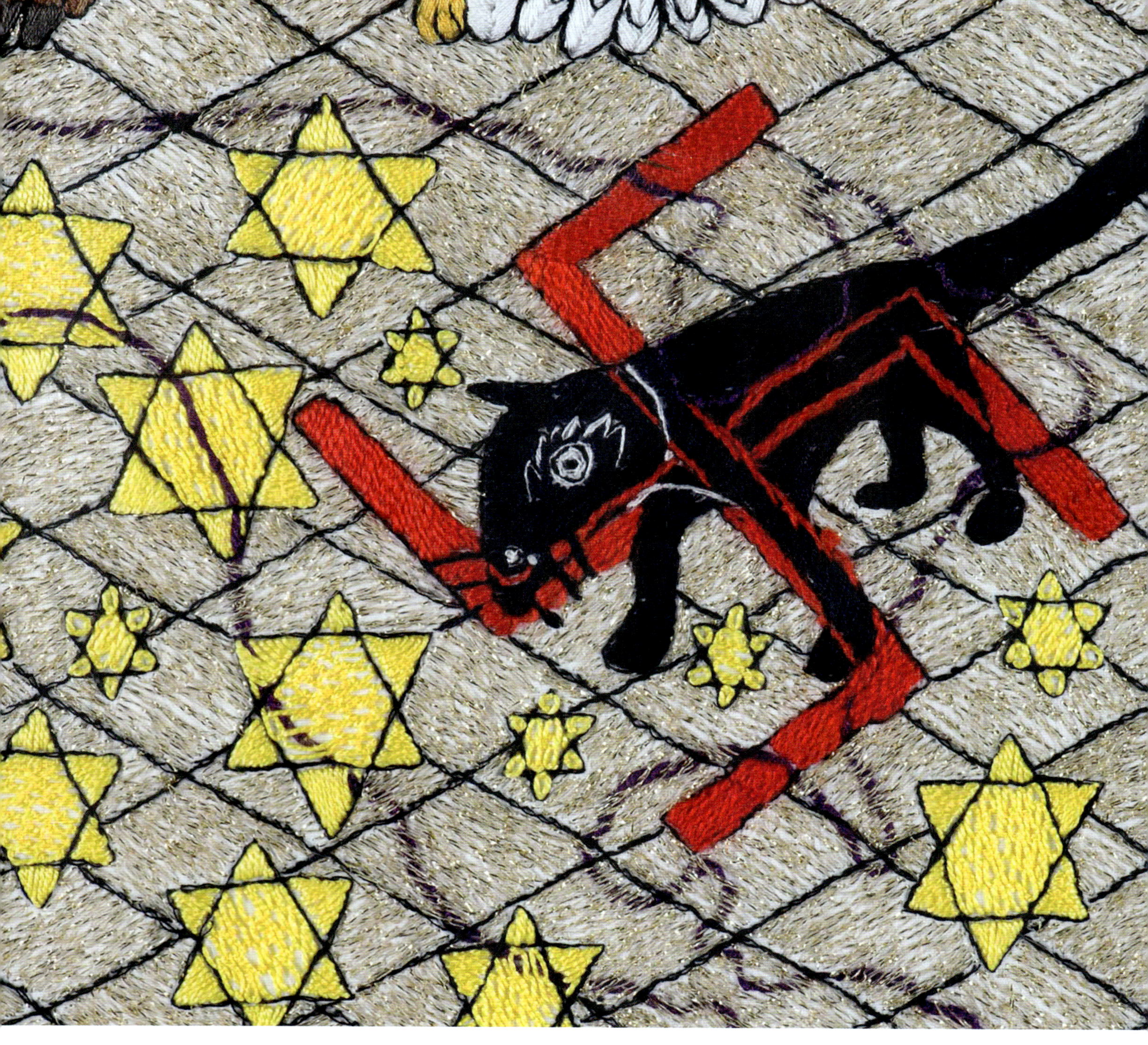

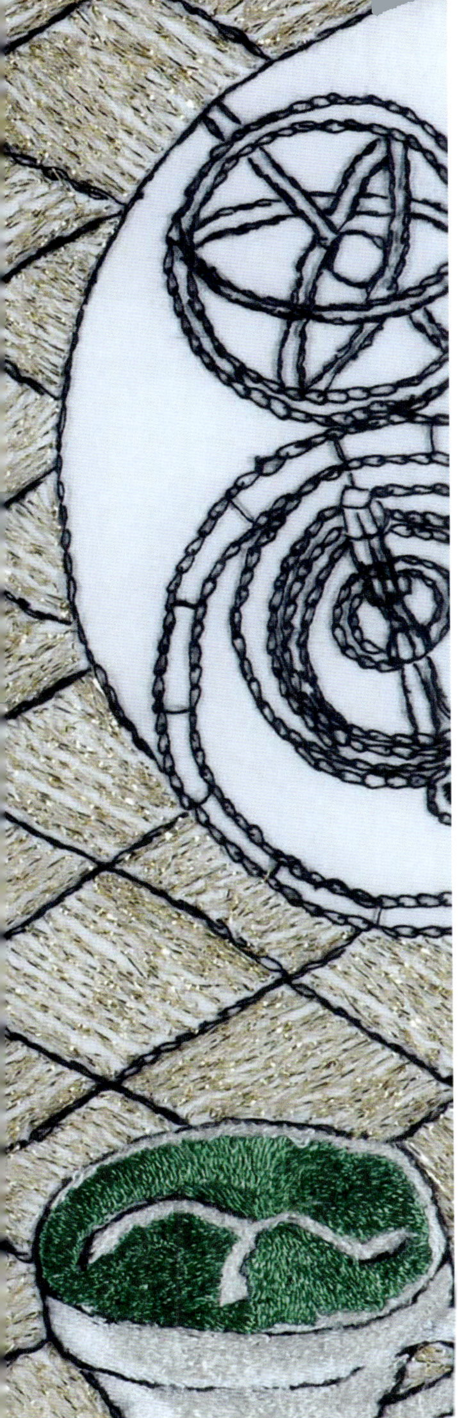

There were others who could sew, of course. And still others who were made to sew. Women and young girls were put to work on primitive assembly lines, stitching the same cuff on the same sleeve of the same shirt with its same pattern, staving off their imminent deaths day after day, week after week, month after month. These sewers, and others whose labors would benefit the Third Reich, were typically sent from the Łódź ghetto to labor camps or sub-camps to work. Indeed, 11,000 laborers were sent to some forty-four sub-camps of Auschwitz. The satellite camps were either *Aussenlager* (external camp), *Nebenlager* (extension or sub-camp), or *Arbeitslager* (labor camp). Some of them were less than ten kilometers away from the main camps, with prisoner populations ranging from a handful to several thousand.

It was the dead of night when the Nazis burst into the filthy room that Masha and Trudie shared with more than a dozen others. Everyone was ordered to grab their belongings and go. "*Shnell*! *Shnell*!" (*Fast! Move it!*) barked the guards as they clubbed a slow-moving arthritic old man with their batons. His wife gasped as he buckled over. But his eyes told her sharply to hush.

"Time to go, Trudela," whispered Masha.

"Where?" asked the exhausted child.

"Anywhere will be better than here," replied Masha, masking her own terror.

"I miss Papa Doll," said Trudie, a tear running down her cheek.

Once outside, they were herded into trucks, packed in tightly, too tightly. There was no room to sit or kneel or even lean. When the truck lurched forward, they were like one solid mass tossed precariously in any given direction. The cruel exodus had resumed.

Detail from ***Light #2*** · 2014

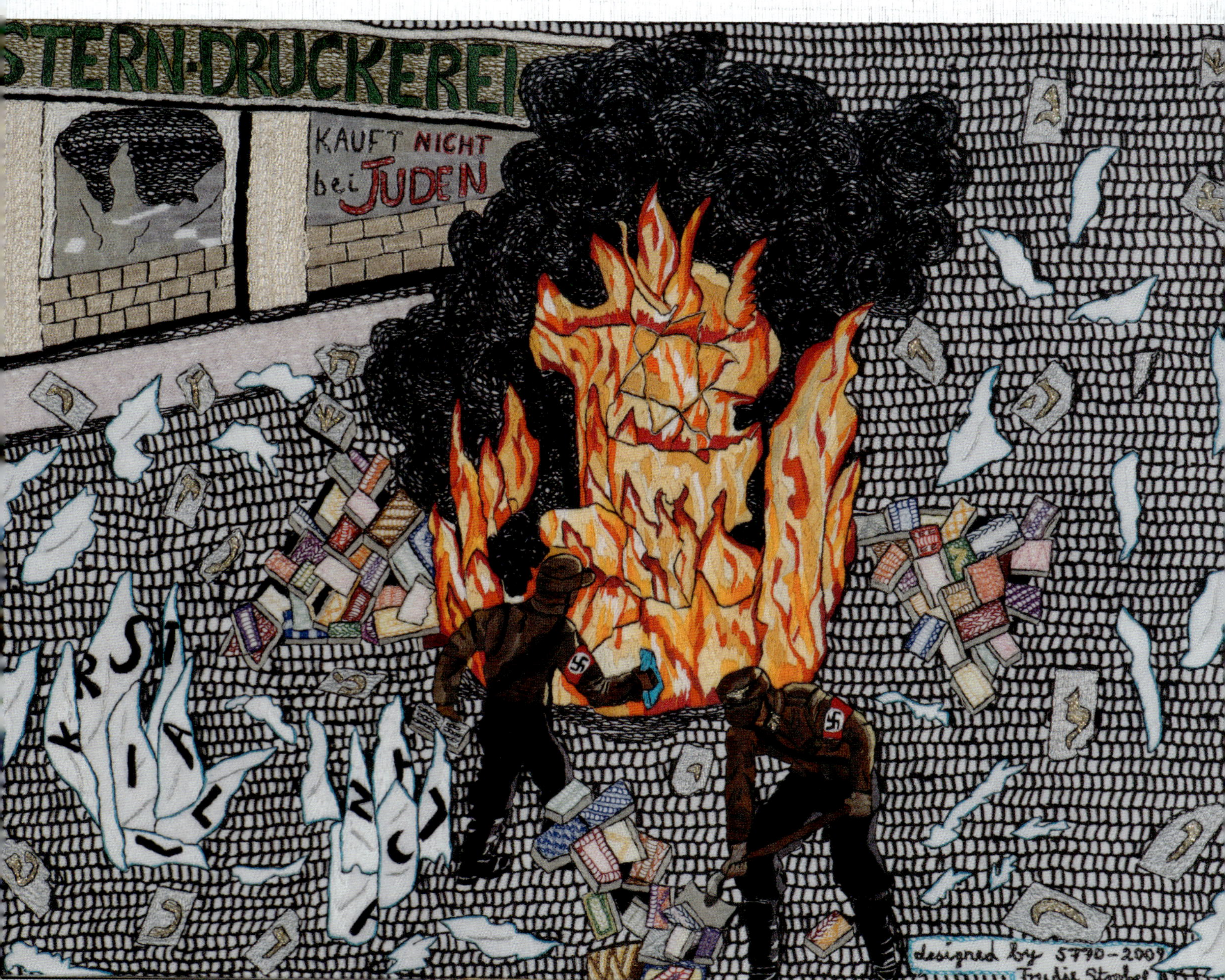

Kristallnacht November 9, 1938 · 2009[7] · 20″ × 29″

CHAPTER SIX

SHNELL!

They tried to bury us. They didn't know we were seeds.

—DINOS CHRISTIANOPOULOS

The trucks drove them to a train. "*Shnell*! *Shnell*!" snarled the Nazi guards as they randomly clubbed prisoners with their batons or the butts of their rifles. The same arthritic man stumbled getting down from the truck, and this time, a squinting Nazi kicked him, laughing as the old man lurched headfirst to the ground. Shrieking, his wife dove to his side. "*Schweigen*!" (Silence!) ordered the guard; the woman's shrieking was intolerable. But she did not quiet; the explosive combustion of horror, outrage, fear, and protest that had ignited in her soul surged forth.

The Nazi shot her in the head. There was a moment of silence, and then her fallen husband began to weep. Quietly. The Nazi shot him too.

Shaken, the prisoners were herded into a cattle car. The guards packed them in tightly. When it seemed like no one else could possibly be squeezed into the car, the Nazis shoved another person in. The doors were shut, and then they waited. Some people prayed under their breath. Others wept quietly. Trudie was the only small child; the few other children were a bit older; all of them were silent. Perhaps they were in shock; maybe they understood that invisibility was critical to survival; or possibly they had mentally capitulated to the hopelessness

7 Trudie Strobel: "Our books were burned and then our synagogues."

of the institutional depravity. There was so little air in the closed car, and it began to get hot. Masha stroked Trudie's hair and felt desperately thankful that they were alive and together.

Suddenly the train lurched forward, slamming bodies against one another, elbows into stomachs, heads against walls. On they went, the clattering of train wheels on tracks a cacophonous metronome of death. Someone started to retch, and the stench of sick made others retch. Trudie buried her face in her mother's skirts and thought about life on the kolkhoz, about Alyona and Eva, and about the geese that could flap their wings and fly away. If only she were a goose. If only she could flap her wings and fly far, far away. Masha began to sing, very softly, the song she sang to Trudie in the womb before they came for Vassiliy, the traditional Yiddish song she had not sung since he'd been taken: "Oyfn Pripitchok."

A fire burns on the hearth
And it is warm in the little house.
And the rabbi is teaching little children
The alphabet.

A few other voices joined in, softly, gently, culling memory and history and tradition from somewhere deep inside, some part of their souls that had thus far escaped being crushed.

Remember, children,
Remember, dear ones,
What you learn here.
Repeat and repeat yet again
Komets alef-o.

Learn, children, don't be afraid
Every beginning is hard.
Lucky is the Jew who studies Torah.
What more do we need?

Air was running out in the cars. But Masha kept singing. Quietly, but in its own courageous way, defiantly.

By the time the train reached its destination and came to a shrieking stop, and the doors slid violently open, many were dead inside the car, which stank of vomit and excrement and death.

Light-headed and reeking, the prisoners were funneled toward the gates of the concentration camp. The guards shouted orders. Their dogs snarled and lunged. One man stopped to read the sign, ARBEIT MACHT FREI, and the frayed tether that had so doggedly connected him to the need to survive suddenly snapped, allowing brilliant and blinding logic to rush in, and he began to laugh. The others around him either froze in fear or moved quickly away. "Arbeit Macht *Frei*?" he said, laughing harder now. "Lies!" he screamed, staring at the gate. There were two quick bullet cracks from a Nazi rifle, and the man would never laugh or scream again. A stifling blanket of collective oppression swaddled the pack of surviving prisoners.

Suddenly, a guard came for Masha, bellowing orders at her. Masha held tight to Trudie as the guard pushed her toward another train. Trudie looked up at her mother, scared. Masha nodded to Trudie reassuringly. It took every remaining ounce of strength for Masha to muster that comforting nod, because inside she was battling yet another volcano of terror on this endless odyssey of horror.

Masha, clutching Trudie, was shoved into another train car. This one was empty. Masha led Trudie to the back corner, where they sank to the ground to finally rest...

When Masha awoke, the train was moving. Inside the car were several others, people she did not recognize, but clearly prisoners too, all with the yellow Magen David, the mark of the Jews. All of the passengers slept. Even the young man whose eyes were wide open did not seem to be awake. Masha adjusted Trudie's weight and fell back asleep.

When the train lurched to a halt, they were at another camp. It was a labor camp, perhaps a satellite of a concentration camp, but smaller than the primary extermination camps.[8] They did not gas prisoners in this camp; they worked them to death. The captives were desperately hungry, and they were threatened and terrorized in an effort to compel them to work harder, but to Trudie, this camp was less evil than the body-strewn streets of Łódź—that is, if there

8 Trudie does not remember the name of this camp or its location. She was only six years old at the time, with no education—and unceasingly terrified. What she remembers clearly is that there were two stacks of beds in the bunk room. Other camps had three stacks of beds. Two was a marked improvement on three. That is the indelible math of memory.

can ever be a barometer by which to measure and compare such exhaustive evil. This camp was an SS farm, and while it was a far cry from the kolkhoz farm of her earliest years, there was at least some living among the dying. Most of the prisoners performed agricultural labor, but Masha Labuhn sewed. And Trudie was her assistant. She would thread the needles. She would separate tatty seams. She would sew the buttons and the buttonholes. As time passed, their bodies grew more and more emaciated until their knees protruded from the skin of their legs like doorknobs and their eyes sunk deep into their distressed dark sockets. Yet mother and daughter would survive to the liberation of the camps in 1945, before Trudie's seventh birthday.

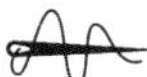

On the day they were freed, Trudie and her mother walked out the front gate of the labor camp. It was still cold, but there in the field was a marguerite. One intrepid flower whose pure white petals radiated out from a fierce yellow eye. "Mama, look!" cried Trudie as she bent to pick that heroic flower for her beloved and indomitable mother. "A marguerite in winter," marveled Masha Labuhn.

The war was over.

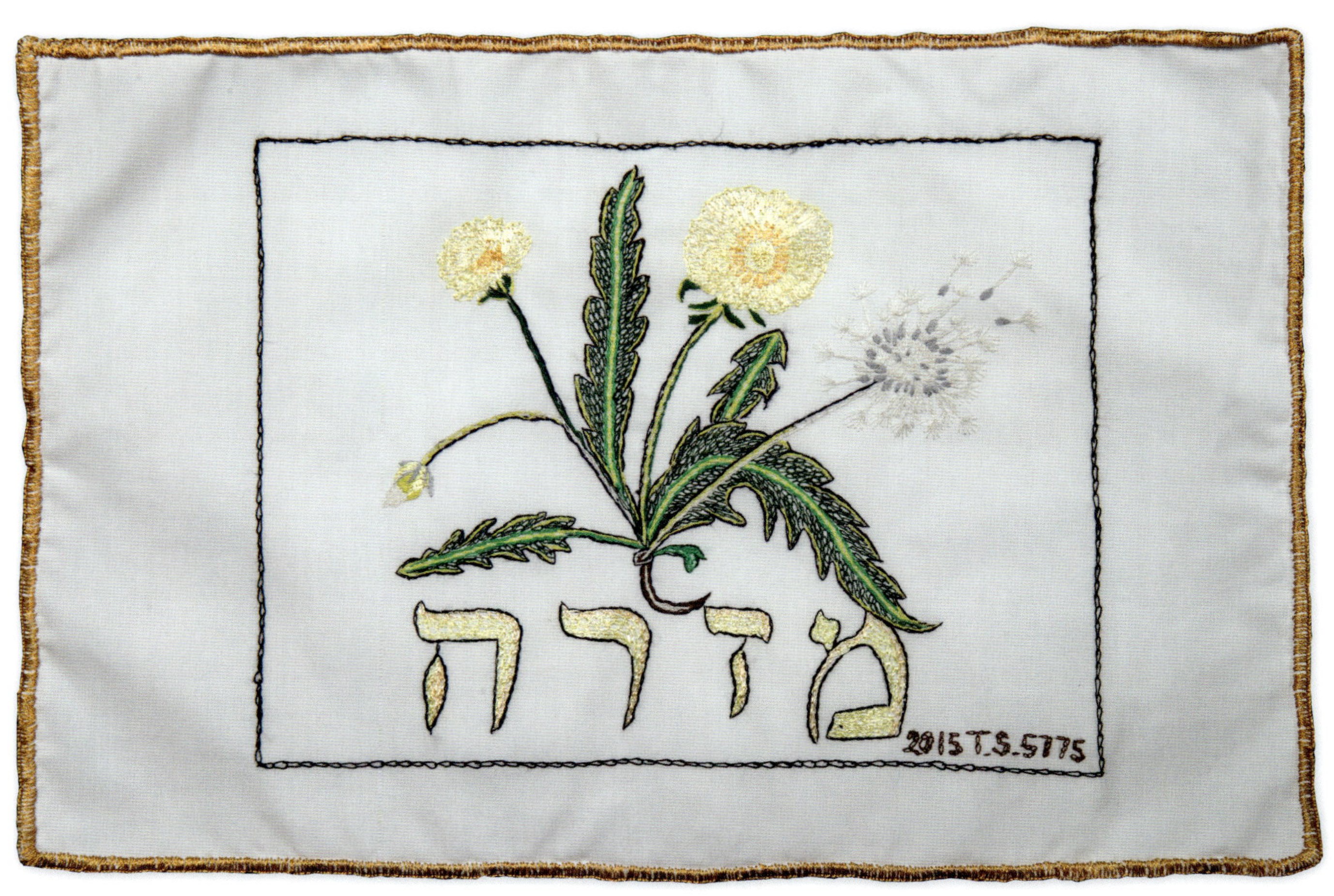

Dandelion · 2015 · 14″ × 16″

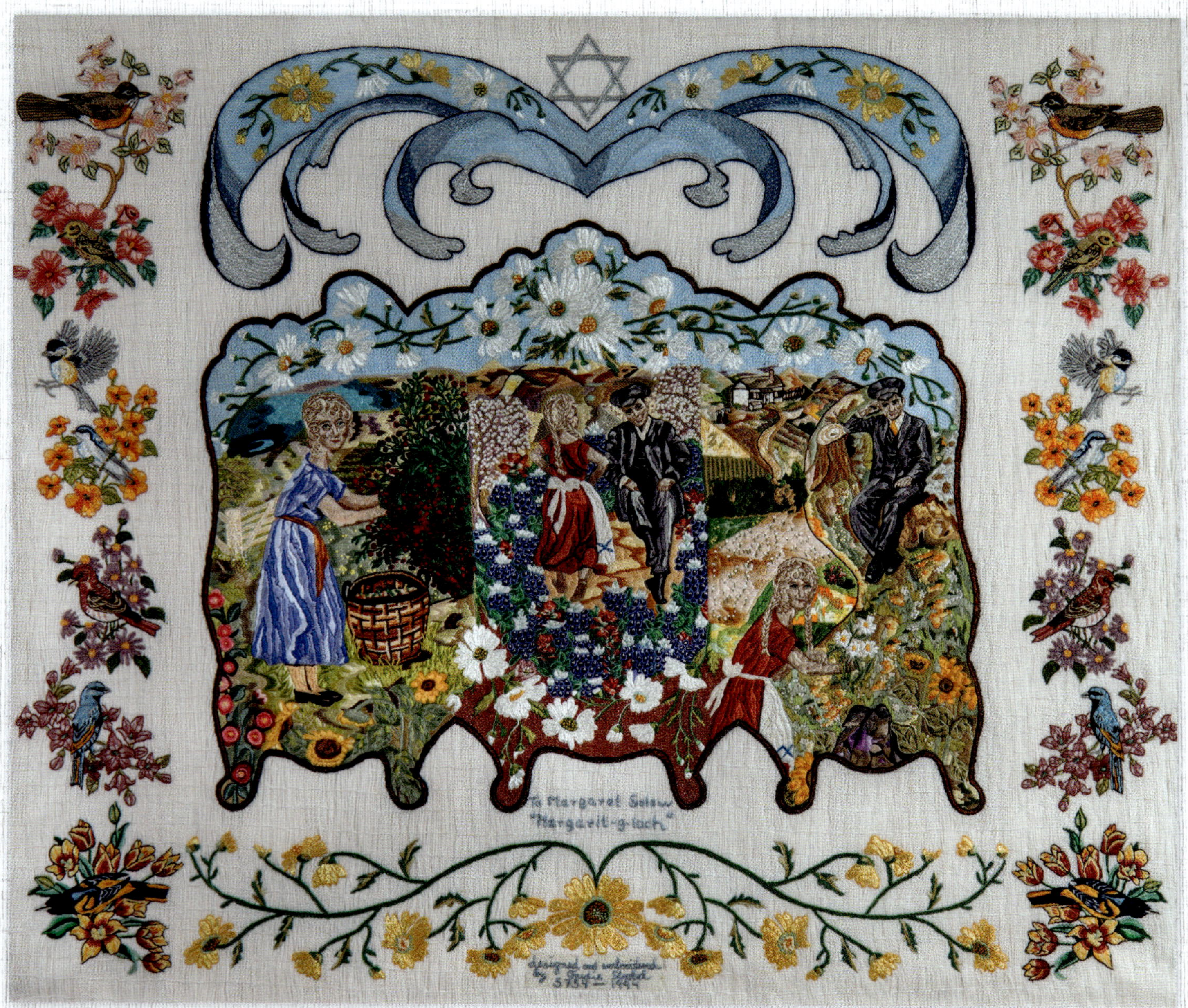

Margarit-g-lach · 1994 · 36″×41″ · *The name translates as "Dear Little Marguerites"*

Trudie has given most of her work away to friends, family, doctors, friends of friends, and museums. What she keeps for herself are her notes, her sketches, and her thoughts about the work itself, which she records with pen. *See Trudie's notes about this work in Art Notes, page 174.*

CHAPTER SEVEN

FREEDOM?

Freedom's just another word for nothin' left to lose.

—KRIS KRISTOFFERSON

They were free from the Nazis. The Third Reich had fallen. Hitler was dead. The concentration camps had been liberated. The scope of the Nazi genocide machine was slowly being recognized by the rest of the world. Around the globe, populations marveled at the photographs of the emaciated victims, the mountains of dead bodies, the massive stockpiles of shoes taken from the slaughtered, the piles of gold teeth that had been systematically collected by the sadistic and greedy, the barbed wire, and the striped "pajamas."

Yet Trudie and Masha were far from free. They had no home; they had no money; they had no family. As far as they knew or would ever be able to find out, everyone they had known or loved was dead or had disappeared. Now they were in a foreign country, first Poland and then Germany, whose blistering anti-Semitism had not been eradicated by the loss at war. Far from it. With nowhere to go and no one to turn to, Masha and Trudie were sent to a displacement camp. It had been a labor camp during the war, so the accommodations, while improved, were nevertheless similar to those from which they had just been "liberated." The camp had been cleaned, and mattresses had been brought in, and they were given soap with which to bathe. To be clean—just to be clean—was such a gift. They were given clean clothes to wear that did not identify them by race, religion, or status. They were given blankets to keep warm. And they were fed. Indeed, there was a cafeteria-style food line. Trudie recalls that they were given "wonderful military-style steel trays with compartments," and the cuisine was American. "Just a *bissel*" (little bit), Masha warned her daughter, who could not remember the last time she had seen an abundance of food. "Just eat little bits so as not to make your stomach sick."

Commissioned by President Truman, Earl G. Harrison, dean of the University of Pennsylvania Law School, surveyed the postwar conditions for the displaced. According to his report to the president, "We appear to be treating the Jews as the Nazis treated them except that we do not exterminate them. They are in concentration camps in large numbers under our military guard instead of the SS troops. One is led to wonder whether the German people, seeing this, are not supposing that we are following or at least condoning Nazi policy." Dean Harrison's report also noted that the displaced Jews "wonder and frequently ask what 'liberation' means." He explained: "This situation is considerably accentuated where, as in so many cases, they are able to look from their crowded and bare quarters and see the German civilian population, particularly in the rural areas, to all appearances living normal lives in their own homes."

Masha was disoriented and stymied in the displacement camp. What would she and Trudie do now? Where would they go? Masha wanted to leave the country that had offered her nothing but horrors. She wanted to leave the continent that had bestowed upon her and her daughter one suffering after another. She wanted to take her precious child far away, across the ocean to America or Israel—to a place where

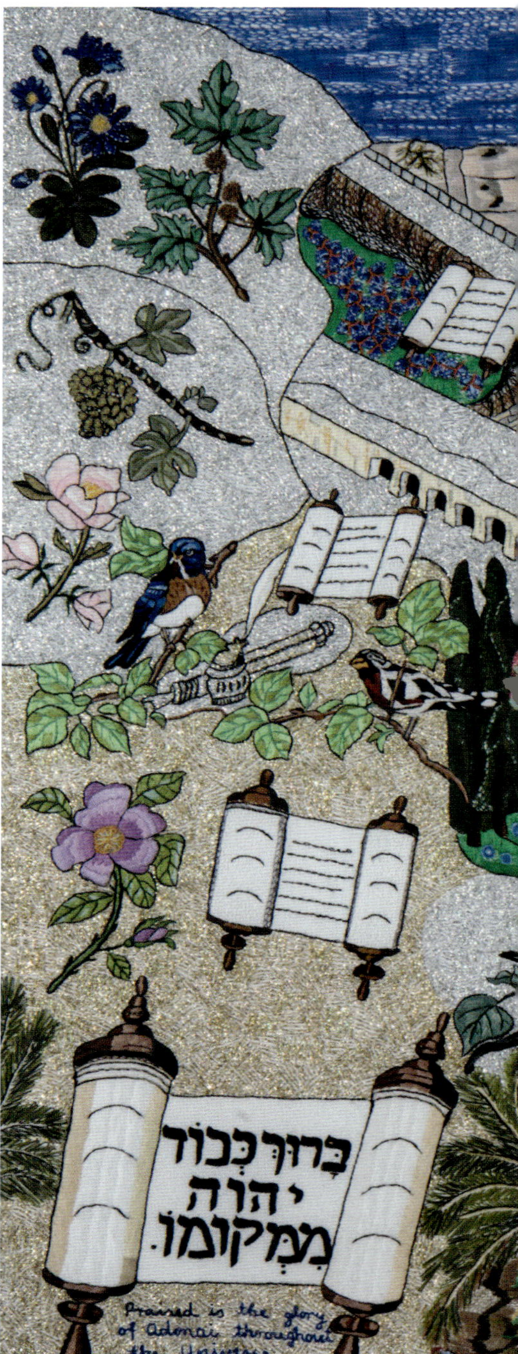

Floating Torahs Over Jerusalem · 2012 · 39″ × 56″
Learn more about this piece in Art Notes, page 188

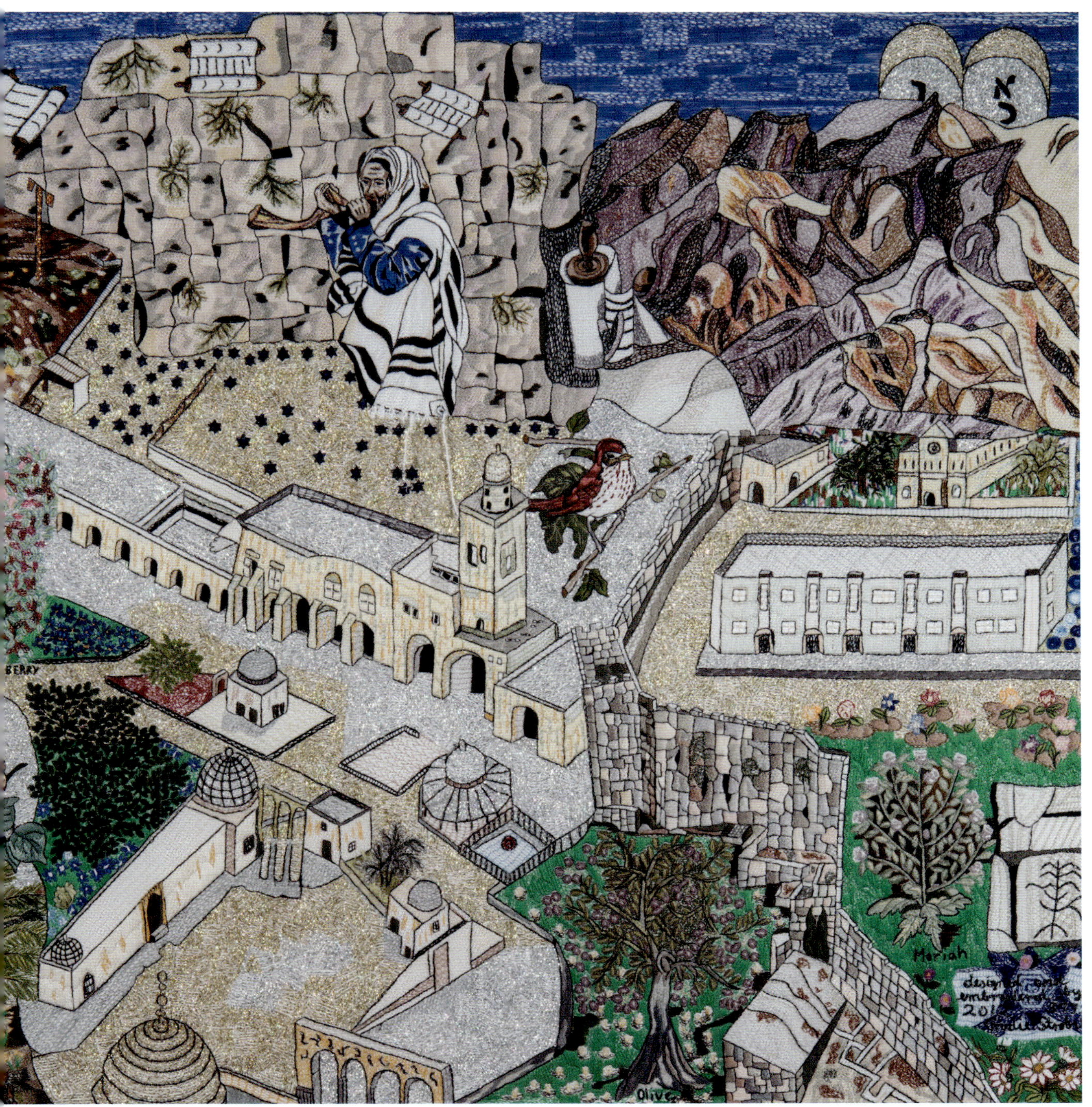
BERRY
Moriah

Trudie could have a chance to find happiness and where they could live without fear. But how? It seemed so improbable, so riddled with hurdles and unknowns, so patently unattainable.

While Masha and Trudie were stuck in a displacement camp dreaming of life far from Eastern Europe, the hypocritical American immigration policies of the time refused to help. There were 250,000 survivors, but in 1945, US immigration quotas allowed only 16,000 to enter the United States. Worse, while US immigration policy turned a blind eye on refugees like Masha and Trudie stuck an ocean away, the Justice Department was busy sneaking Nazi scientists and spies into the country to boost American rocket science and biowarfare programs and to keep a leg up on the Russian spy machine. Paranoia and belligerence reigned as the United States and Russia hurtled into the Cold War. And so, while Masha Labuhn and her brave young daughter languished in a displacement camp in Germany, such programs as Operation Paperclip literally smuggled Nazis across the United States' borders.

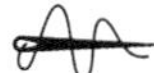

There was always sewing to do, and Masha soon found a way to work in the camp and make a bit of money. One day, women from the Red Cross arrived in crisply fitted uniforms and hats bearing the Red Cross patch. They came with gifts for the children in the camp. Little boxes. Most had pencils, erasers, and a toy. Trudie's "toy" was a small sack of beads: the most beautiful beads she could have ever imagined. Sparkling, tiny glass beads: white, red, green, and silver. Trudie could not believe her great fortune.

"Mama!" Trudie ran to her mother to show her the beads. Masha looked at the smile on the face of her daughter and put down her sewing work. "My dear Trudela," said Masha, "I have not seen you smile since you found that marguerite in the field outside the camp. What do you have?" Trudie showed her the gift from the Red Cross ladies, and now even Masha smiled. "Such magnificent beads! Treasures!"

"Someday I will make something beautiful with them," said Trudie.

"I think today is that day, my child. We will design a picture, and I will teach you how to sew on the beads, one at a time. What shall we make?"

"A goose," said Trudie. "Let's make a goose like the ones in the kolkhoz in Neu Chortitza. With wings so he can always fly away."

“A goose it shall be,” said Masha, and she felt a little smile take root in her soul. “We will need a piece of fabric. Black fabric to show off how magnificently these beads sparkle.” Trudie looked at her mother expectantly. “I have some black fabric right here.” And with that, Masha lifted her black skirt and slashed a wide swatch from it.

“Mama!” Trudie gasped.

“We must save many beads for the neck,” Masha counseled. “The goose’s neck must be stiff and strong so that she can hold up her head.” Just as Trudie would need to hold up her head as she navigated the vicissitudes of life’s fortunes and misfortunes. Bead by tiny bead, stitch by tiny stitch, the goose came to life. Trudie’s goose would be taking flight; a white and silver goose, with a red beak and wide-open eyes, would be heading off in the dark of night to lands unknown, leaving behind flora, fauna, and people, all of whom, anchored by genetics and gravity to an earthen place, were otherwise bound.

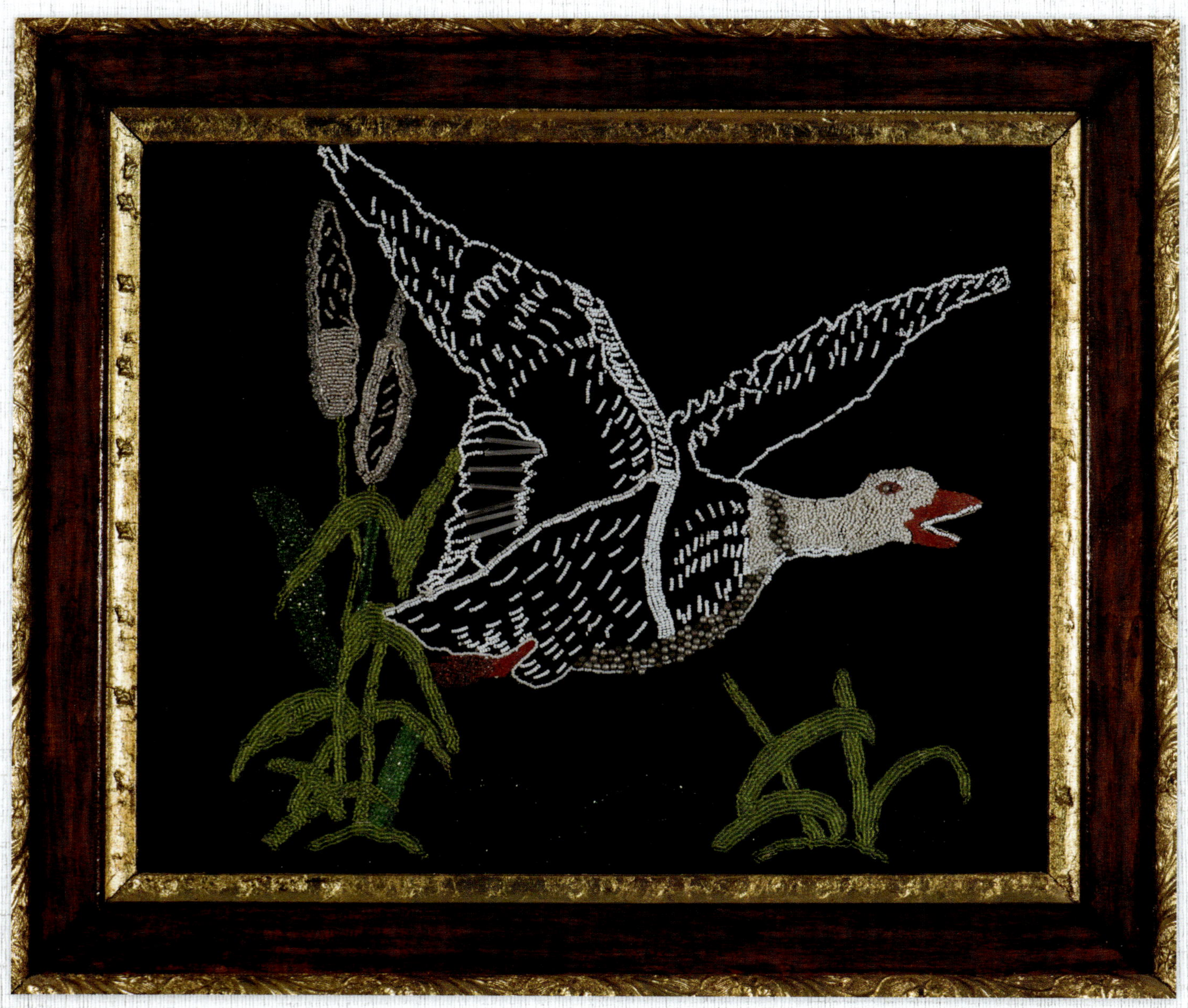

Trudie's Goose · 1946 · 17″ × 21″
This work, which was begun in the displaced-persons camp in 1945, was not finished until Trudie and Masha got to America and were able to purchase more beads.

CHAPTER EIGHT

DISPLACED PERSONS

All the darkness cannot extinguish a single candle, yet one candle can illuminate all the darkness.

—HAIM HAZAZ
From *Broken Grindstones*

Masha and Trudie were soon moved to yet another displaced-persons camp. This one was in Würtzburg, in the Bavarian region of Germany, about seventy-five miles midway between Frankfurt and Nuremberg. Before the war, Würtzburg had been a rabbinic center and home to approximately 2,000 Jews, most of whom had been exterminated in concentration camps. Much of the city had been decimated by the British at the end of the war in a firestorm unleashed by 225 bombers in a span of seventeen minutes. An old theater remained standing, and it was used to house displaced persons. In the theater were two-stack beds, and the refugees (which is, after all, what they were) hung blankets around their beds for privacy. "Imagine the feeling of even a little privacy," Trudie still marvels today, her perennially moist eyes even heavier with the memory. She missed the pristine metal trays with their organized compartments at the previous camp, and while there was food, it was less robust and abundant. This was a time of transition and confusion; Masha and Trudie would soon be "transitioned" again.

Eventually Masha and Trudie were provided with a place to live, eighty-five kilometers northeast in Ermershausen. They were given a room in an empty house with stairs leading up to the front door. A room to themselves. A room with a door on a hinge that closed. A room in which they could finally enjoy privacy. "Can you imagine how rich we were to have space for ourselves?" says Trudie today. Two other families were given rooms in the house, but Trudie and Masha's room of their own was their sanctuary. The town of Ermershausen was still fiercely anti-Semitic. Losing the war had not softened the Nazi heart even if it had disarmed the Nazi offensive. Once upon a time there had been a vibrant Jewish community in Ermershausen. But fierce local anti-Semitism had driven the Jews away even before the Nazis came to power in 1933. By 1933, the Jewish community in the town numbered only fifty-eight people. On November 10, 1938, a night infamously known as Kristallnacht, anti-Semitic townsfolk and the SS laid siege to the local synagogue, destroying the holy vessels and burning the precious Torah scrolls. That night, the Jewish men of Ermershausen were rounded up and sent to their deaths at Dachau. By 1942, the town's entire Jewish population was gone. The luckier Jews had fled. The others had been eliminated. Historians have said that no Jews from Ermershausen returned after the war. It was to this Bavarian municipality that Trudie and Masha were sent to live.

Trudie went to school but had no friends. The local children called her names under their breath or out loud: *dreckiger Jude* (dirty Jew) was the most common. But Trudie kept a stiff neck like her goose with its densely beaded neck. And she kept to herself. She had never been in school before, and so she had to learn to read and write, and she had to do that in a brand-new language, German, the language of her tormentors.

Masha was given vouchers for food, but they were not sufficient and so, to make extra money, she again found work sewing. "I helped my mama sew," says Trudie today. There was no wool to be found in those scarce times, and soon townspeople realized that Masha could disassemble their old coats and reverse the fabric, so that a reconstituted coat looked new. It was painstaking work, and Masha could only earn small sums from the wary, anti-Semitic locals, but every bit of money helped mother and daughter get by. Eventually word spread to nearby communities, farms, and hamlets. Just as a medieval Spanish poet might visit the villa of the landed elite to recite verse and entertain, so Masha and Trudie Labuhn would visit homes and farms outside of Ermershausen to sew and mend. After the long war and with the scarcity of fabric, clothes needed repair and alteration, sheets needed mending, and

Sample of white drawn work · circa 1945–1946

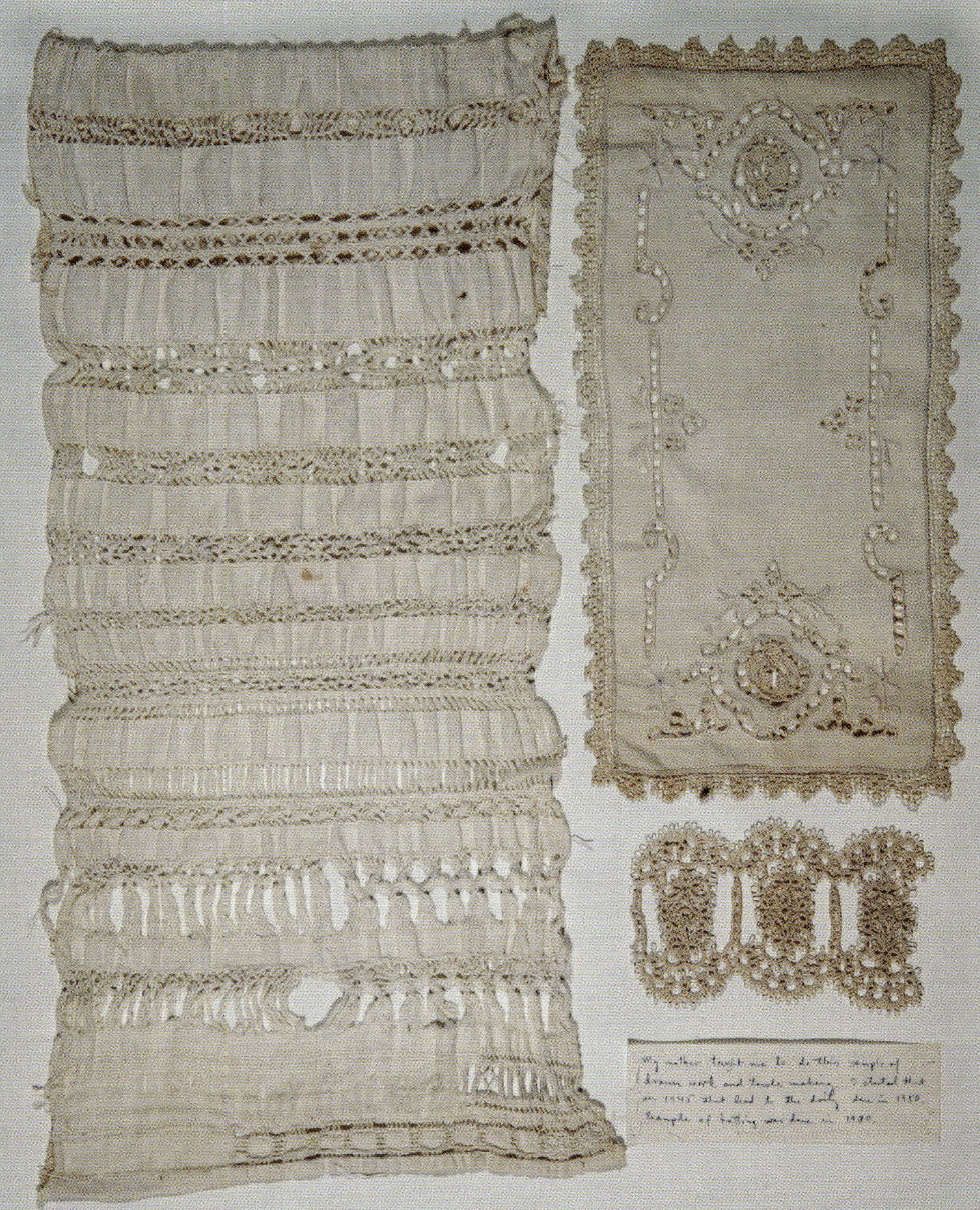
My mother taught me to do this sample of
drawn work and tassle making. I started that
in 1945 that lead to the doily done in 1950.
Example of tatting was done in 1980.

linens needed finishing. And, of course, Masha "turned coats." Traveling for days at a time, they would be put up in a room and they would sew. Trudie learned from her mother. Masha made patterns for clothes, and Trudie stenciled them. Trudie learned sewing, embroidery, beading, white drawn work,[9] knitting, and crocheting.[10] An old woman at a farm where she and her mother briefly took up residence even taught Trudie how to spin wool. Spinning wool was a miraculous endeavor, washing the freshly sheared fleece to remove the oils, carding it to align all the fibers, and then spinning the fibers, winding them, marrying them, and then drafting and spinning the wool. After these sojourns, mother and daughter would return to Ermershausen and hope for another job because their earnings were meager, even from these work-intensive visits.

The house in Ermershausen had a sad history. It had belonged to a Jewish family. The father of the house had served his country in World War I and been terribly wounded. A paraplegic after the war, he found himself confined to a wheelchair in that house with its steep front steps that prevented him from coming and going without community support. Thus, while so many of the town's Jews had left, his family stayed. They had two children, and it just did not seem feasible to flee with an incapacitated father who needed so much care. As the ideologically bellicose fangs of Hitler clamped down on the souls of the German population, and the local population of Ermershausen pledged themselves to the xenophobic national campaign, the remaining Jewish family knew they were in trouble. They sought counsel from a friend, whom they had known their whole lives; they had grown up together in the town; they had gone to school together; even their families before them had been friendly. This was a friend they could trust, even though he had joined the SS and pledged his allegiance to the Third Reich. The friend encouraged them to leave—and to leave soon. He told them what they already knew: They could not stay on in a place as hostile to their kind as Ermershausen. And he told them what they did not know; he told them which bus to take to safety. And so they packed their most precious belongings. The friend helped carry the wheelchair out of the house and

9 Drawn work is a form of detailed counter-thread embroidery. Individual threads are pulled, drawn, or removed from the warp (length) or weft (width) of a fabric's weave. Drawn threads are then grouped, knotted, and patterned.

10 Trudie's education in needlecraft continued throughout her youth and into adulthood. She learned tatting, weaving, lacemaking, and even jewelry making over the years.

down to the street. They said their sad goodbyes, bought their bus tickets, and left the only home they had ever known. The bus took them to a place they had never heard of, a place they could never have imagined existed, a place called Auschwitz. On the advice of their lifelong friend, the paraplegic World War I veteran and his family paid their own way to the crematorium at Auschwitz. They were never seen again.

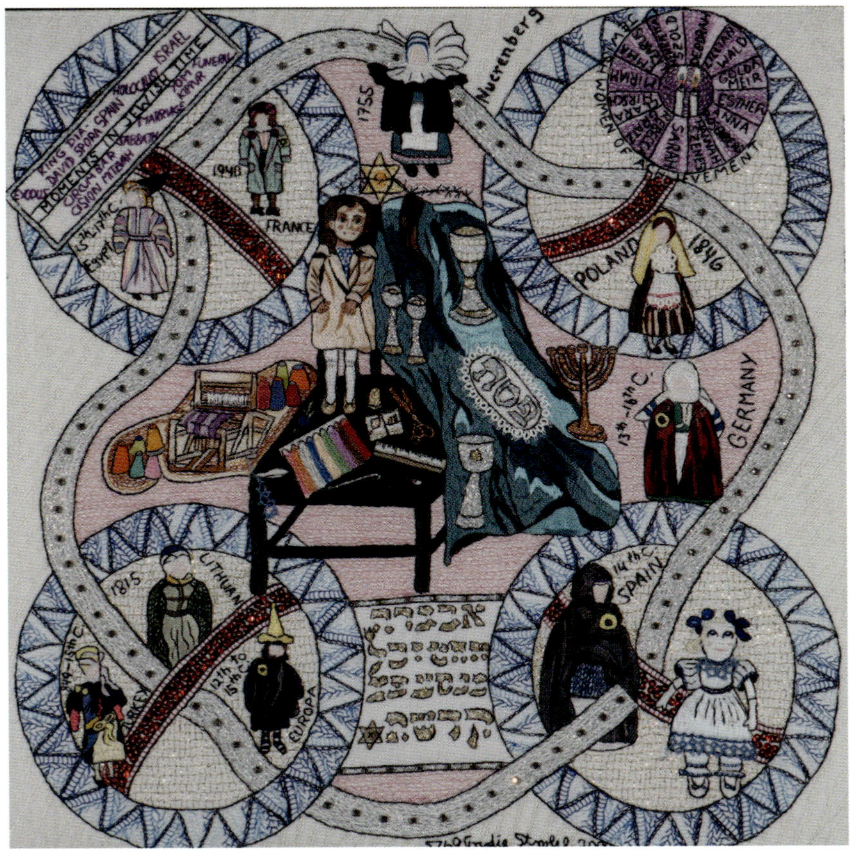

Magical Road to Embroidery · 2000 · 23″ × 24″
In this autobiographical work, all the characters are faceless except for Papa Doll.
Learn more about this piece in Art Notes, page 189.

The two families that first shared the house with Masha and Trudie were able to emigrate long before the paperwork for the mother and daughter was arranged. For five years they were left alone in the small house with its sad history in the town that had been wiped clean of Jews. They were displaced persons in a foreign country beset by "a trail of bureaucratic obstacles and delays, petty red tape, and sometimes brutal disregard on the part of those tasked with helping them."[11] To Masha it all seemed designed for confusion or failure. It started with a Care and Maintenance Form, which asked applicants such inane questions as what were their reasons for leaving. "The mass murder of my people." It asked, "Do you wish to remain in Germany?" That answer was also easy: "*Nein*!" It asked, "Have you any

11 *The Liberation of the Camps: The End of the Holocaust and Its Aftermath*, by Dan Stone, Yale University Press, 2015, p. 204.

relatives, friends, or resources in Germany?" For Trudie and Masha, the answer was another resounding "*nein*!" They had nothing left but each other. Until 1947, the forms were reviewed by the United Nations Relief and Rehabilitation Administration. After 1947, the review board of the International Refugee Organization stepped in. New forms had to be filled out. And the waiting continued.

Finally, in 1951, they set sail from the port city of Bremerhaven, Germany, aboard the *USS General W.G. Haan*, a former troop ship. (*Hahn* means "rooster" in German, so Trudie and other refugees remember the name of the ship as Rooster.) Masha and Trudie Labuhn of Neu Chortitza were going to America. Trudie was thirteen years old. It was the start of a new life. Masha would never return to the continent of her birth; it would take Trudie nearly seven decades to return. Once the *General Haan* left the Weser River, crossed the North Sea, and entered the North Atlantic Ocean, the sailing got rough. The petulant seas knocked the huge ship around, and while there was ample food for the passengers, the smell of it made most of them sick. Nevertheless, the passengers, all World War II refugees, were buoyed by hope. They were leaving behind centuries of Jewish life on a continent that had betrayed them.

When the captain called out, "Statue of Liberty," Masha wept.

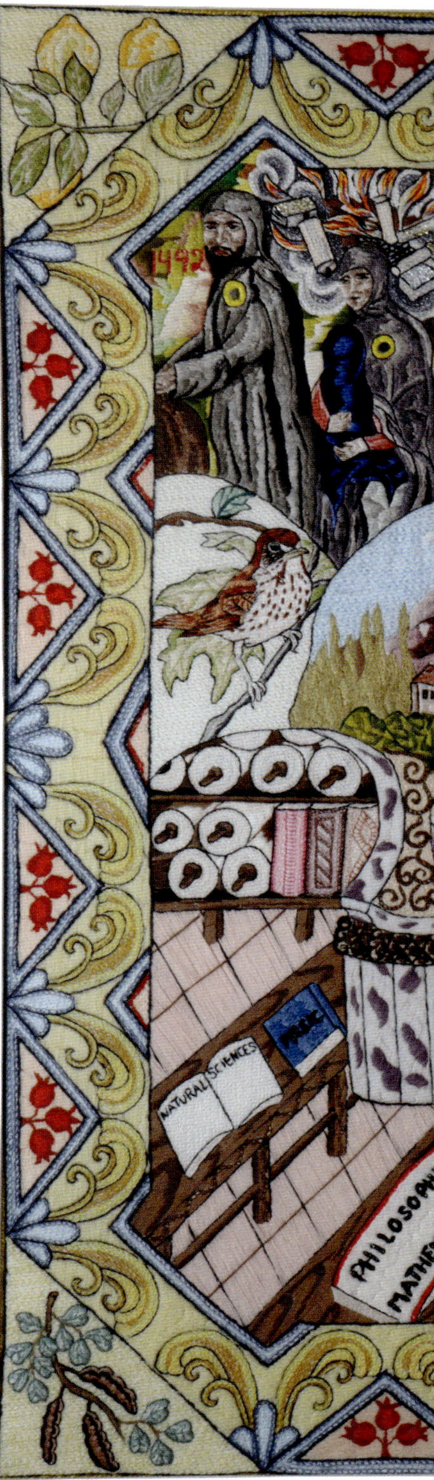

Golden Age of Spain · 1995 · 36″ × 48″
Read more about this work in Art Notes, page 185

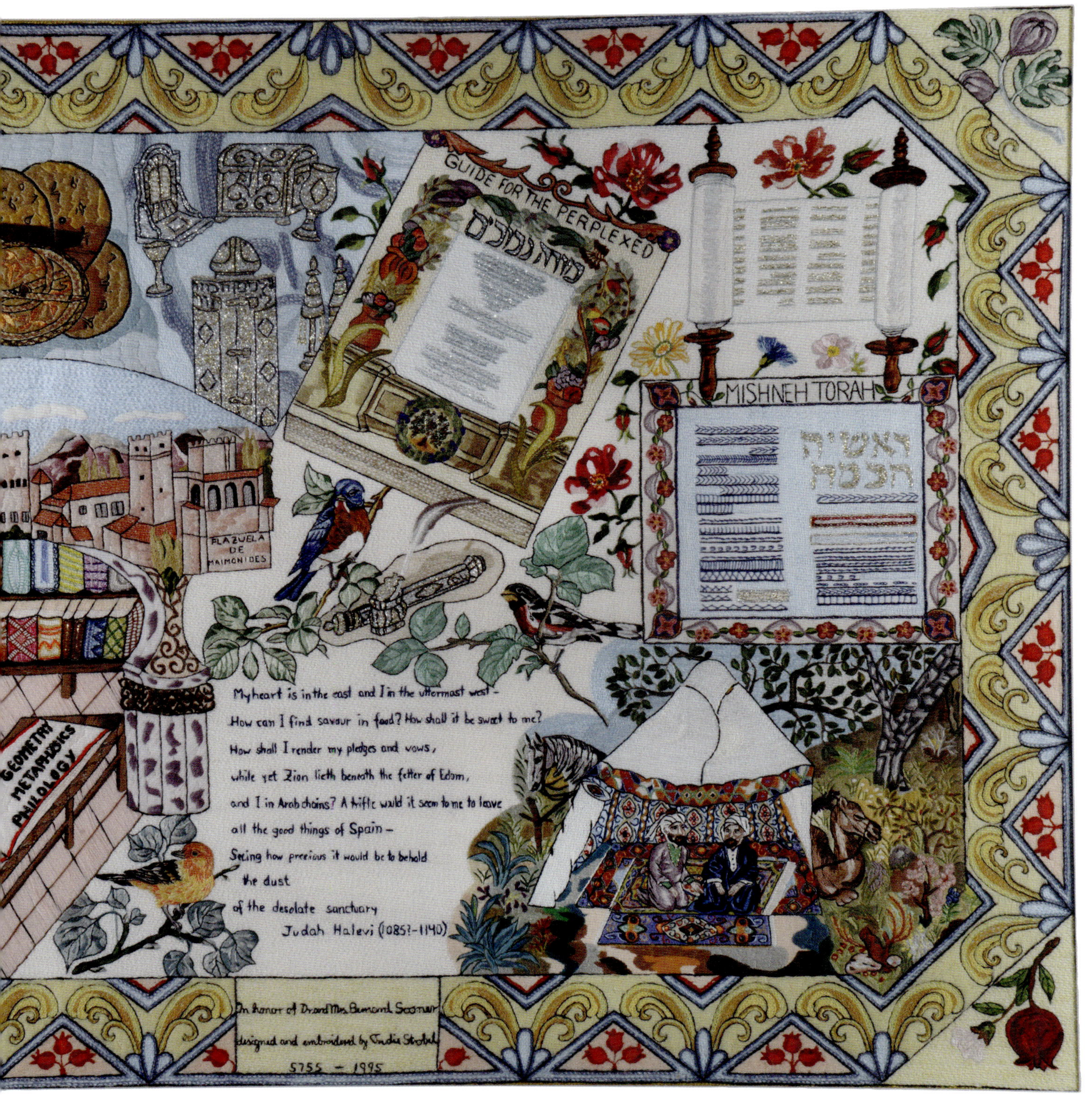

GUIDE FOR THE PERPLEXED
מורה נבוכים
MISHNEH TORAH
ראשית חכמה
PLAZUELA DE MAIMONIDES
GEOMETRY
METAPHYSICS
PHILOLOGY
My heart is in the east and I in the uttermost west –
How can I find savour in food? How shall it be sweet to me?
How shall I render my pledges and vows,
while yet Zion lieth beneath the fetter of Edom,
and I in Arab chains? A trifle would it seem to me to leave
all the good things of Spain –
Seeing how precious it would be to behold
the dust
of the desolate sanctuary
Judah Halevi (1085?–1140)
5755 – 1995

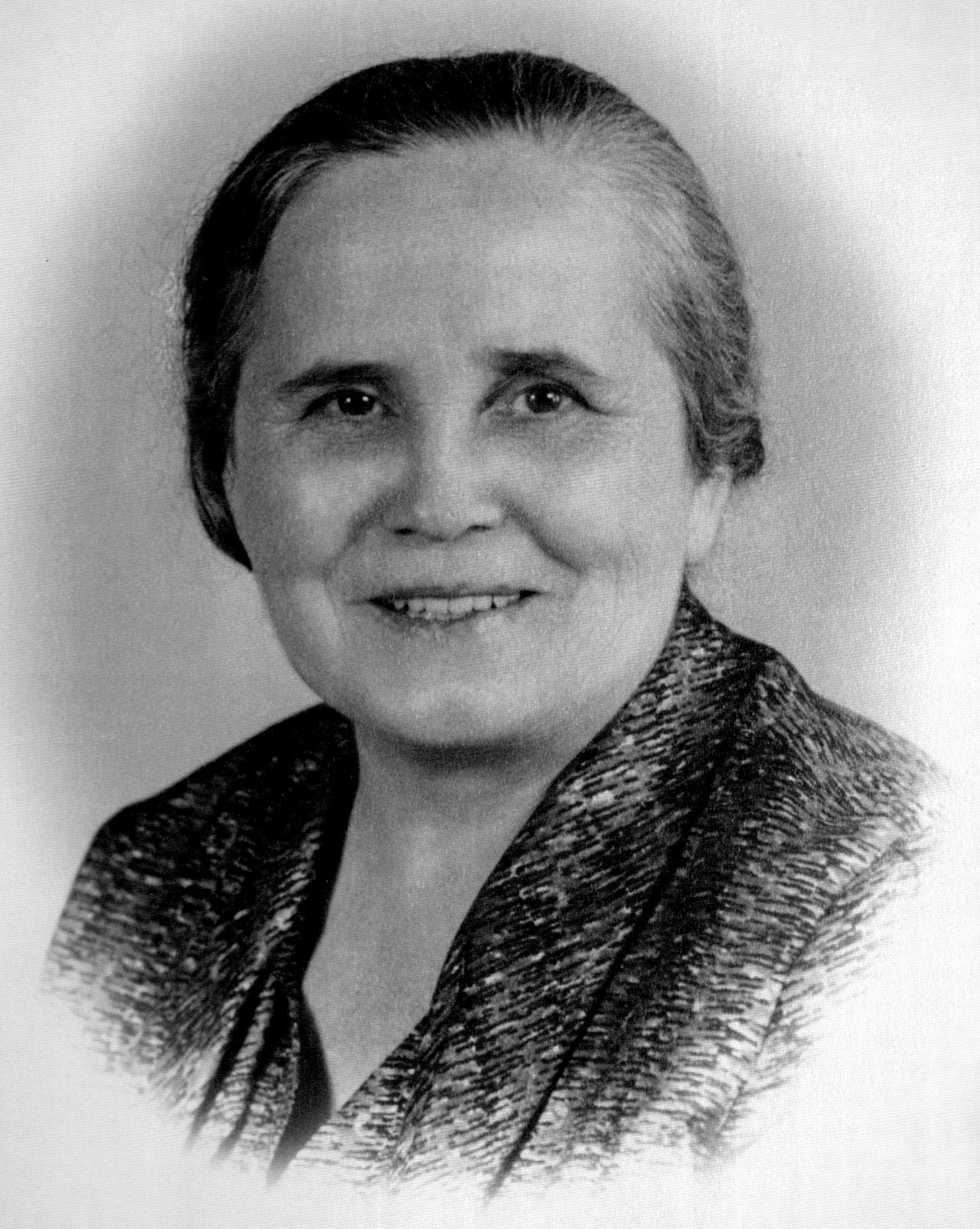

CHAPTER NINE

AMERICA

Nobody teaches life anything.

—GABRIEL GARCÍA MÁRQUEZ
Love in the Time of Cholera

Trudie Labuhn met her future husband, Hans Strobel, in Chicago, where she and Masha had settled after arriving in America. A friend of Masha's, Tanta Teresa, suggested the match. Trudie had some concerns about this "nice German Jewish boy" whom Tanta Teresa had "found." Trudie pictured a young man showing up in lederhosen, and she tried to resist the arrangement. But Tanta Teresa was insistent, and the next Sunday she brought Hans Strobel to the home. Today Trudie says, "I come into the living room and I see this beautiful man across from me. I still remember he had a tan suit on, and he was so gorgeous to me. And he had the same feeling for me because we could not stop looking at each other." At this point Trudie slips into a pointed whisper: "He ate me up with his eyes."

A German Jew, Hans had survived the war in hiding. But Trudie and Hans rarely talked about the past.

Two weeks passed before Trudie and Hans saw each other again. This time they met in private. Four weeks later, in 1956, when Trudie was eighteen years old, they were married. Trudie had only been in America for five years. Trudie and Hans Strobel would be married for more than fifty-five years.

Left: Masha Labuhn, Trudie's mother; photo taken in America

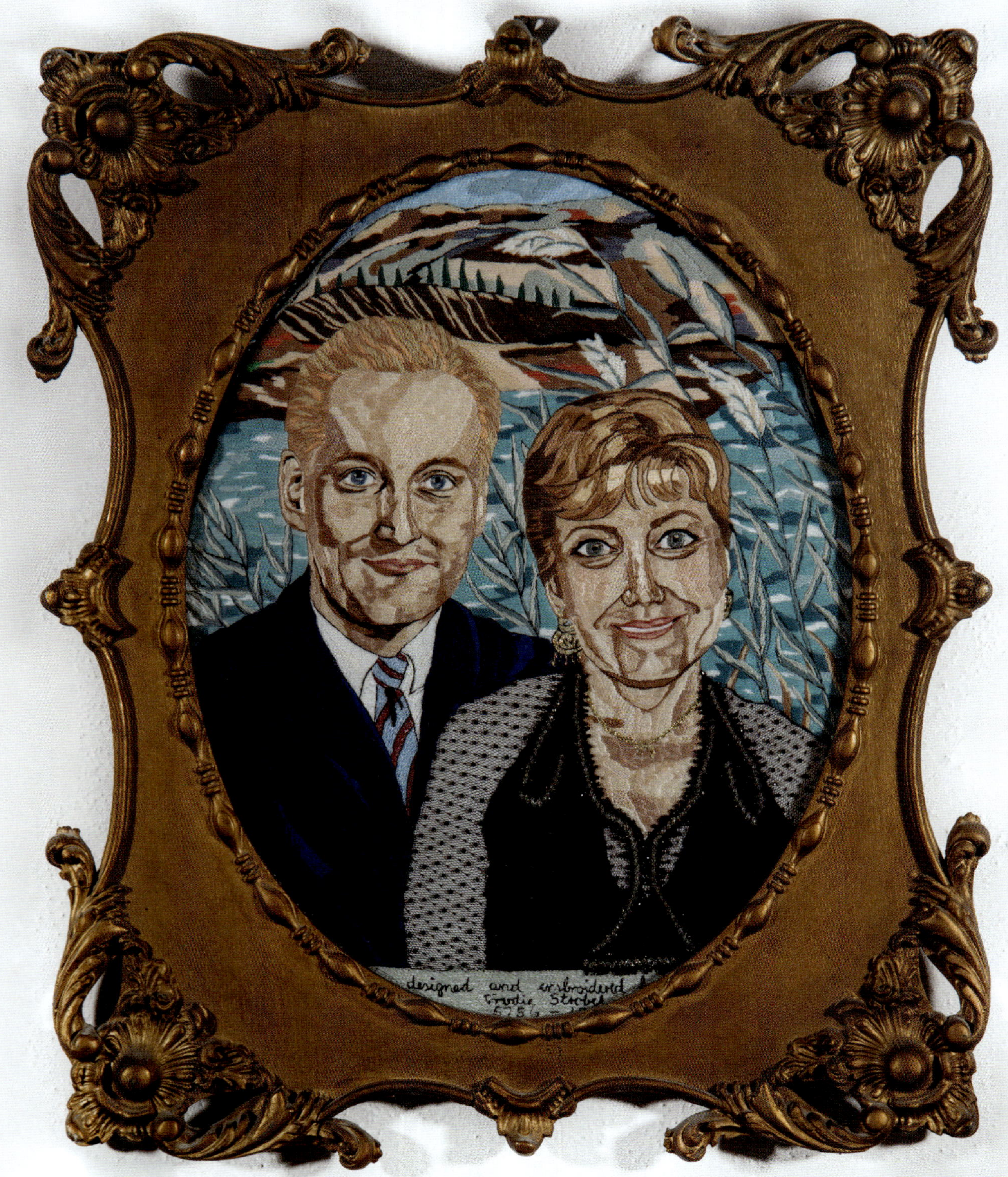

Portrait of Trudie and Hans Strobel · 1996 · 16″ × 20″

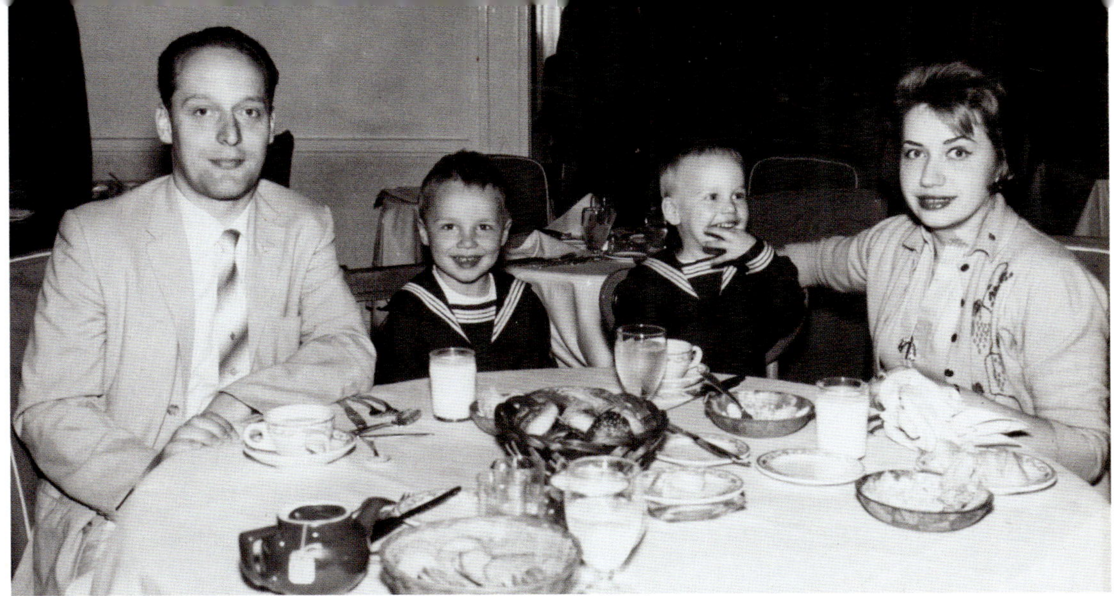

Hans and Trudie Strobel with their sons, Paul and John, 1963

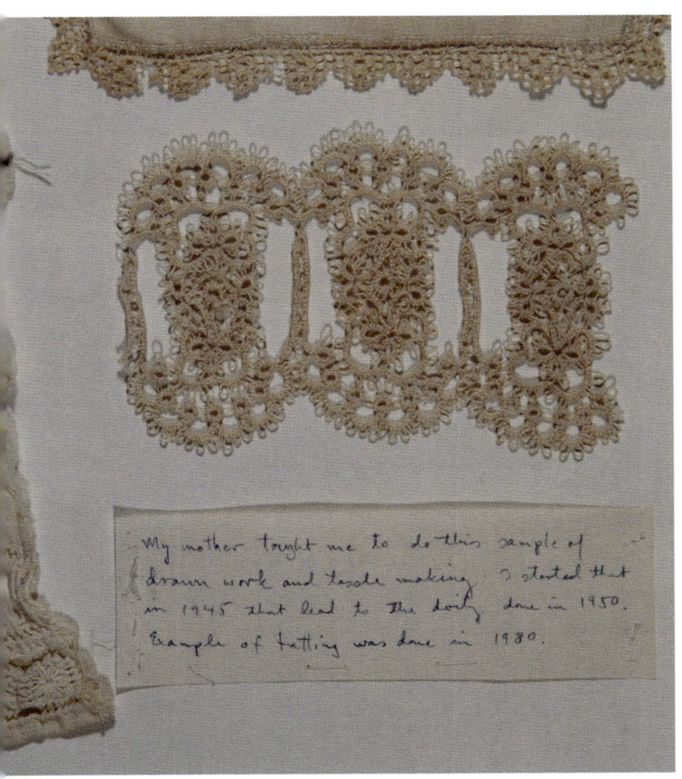

Tatting · circa 1980

John Strobel was born in 1957 and Paul Strobel two years later. Their spines were not twisted like those of the boys who had been born to Masha. They were two American miracles. They would be raised in the upscale Los Angeles suburb town of San Marino, in a kind and tolerant world where food was plentiful, where religion was a choice, and where, for the most part, dreams were encouraged. They would never know the hardships that their grandmother, their mother, or their father had known. Indeed, it was not until their sons were teenagers that Trudie and Hans even revealed that they were Holocaust survivors. Trudie had put that horrible past in a drawer and shut it. Masha also kept that drawer shut until her death.

Trudie missed her mother desperately in the

months and years after her death, but she had children to care for, a house to maintain, a yard to keep up with, meals to cook, mending to do, and needlework. Trudie never abandoned her education in needlework. And needlework never abandoned Trudie Strobel.

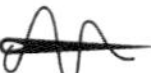

Masha would have been so happy for Trudie, whose boys soon grew into men, and who eventually became a grandmother to two healthy girls, Corinne and Nicole. The traumas of the past were locked away in a history she was determined to keep buried.

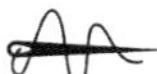

Trudie's sons were well into their twenties, long out of the house and making lives of their own, when her world went dark. She didn't know where she was. She stopped talking. She stopped eating. She lay in bed curled up in a fetal position, enveloped in darkness. This went on for months.

Trudie had gone back to school after her sons left home. Having only completed high school when she met and married Hans, she decided to go to Pasadena City College and get a degree in nursing. She was an A student and had only half of a semester left to complete her studies when she stopped functioning. She was not yet fifty years old.

She dreamed she was in a thrift shop, looking for dolls. There were so many dolls, beautiful dolls, and they were just a dollar each. Trudie selected the most precious ones and put them in her basket. But when she went to reach for another, the dolls in her basket were gone. She would awaken from the dream drenched in sweat and tears.

Hans found a doctor, a psychiatrist named Dr. Solow. Hans drove Trudie to see him. The Strobels lived in San Marino and Dr. Solow was in Beverly Hills, so the drive was a long one, but his office was not far from the Los Angeles Museum of the Holocaust, where Trudie and Hans had volunteered for years. Trudie sat in Dr. Solow's office in silence. The doctor would ask questions, but she could not bring herself to respond. He would encourage her to shake her head or to nod. But she couldn't even manage that. It was hard enough to get up out of bed, get dressed, and leave the house, and now this man wanted her to talk, too.

"Trudie, do you want to go to the hospital?" asked the doctor after a few silent sessions.

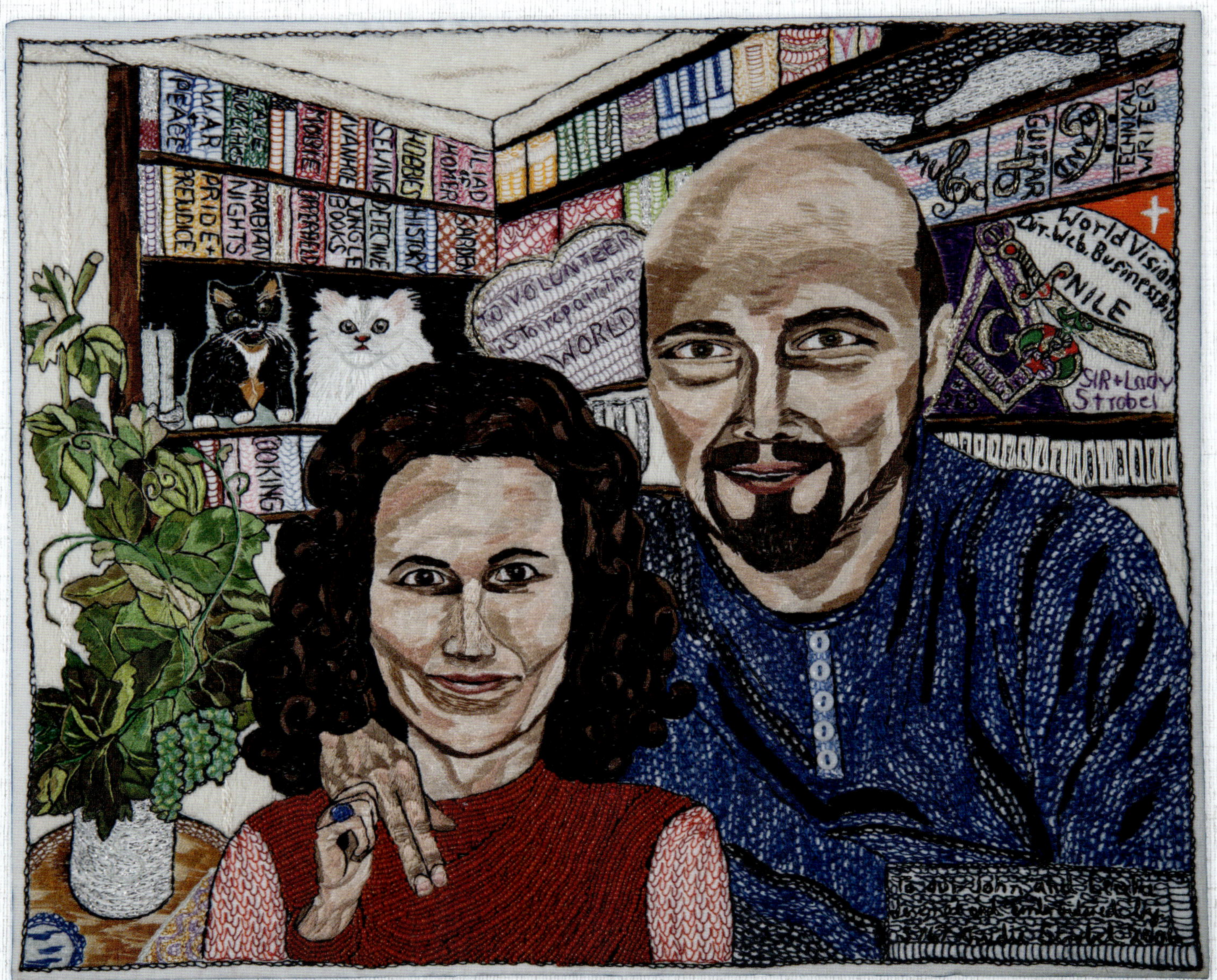

Portrait of John and Leala (Trudie's son and his wife) · 2006 · 20″ × 15.5″

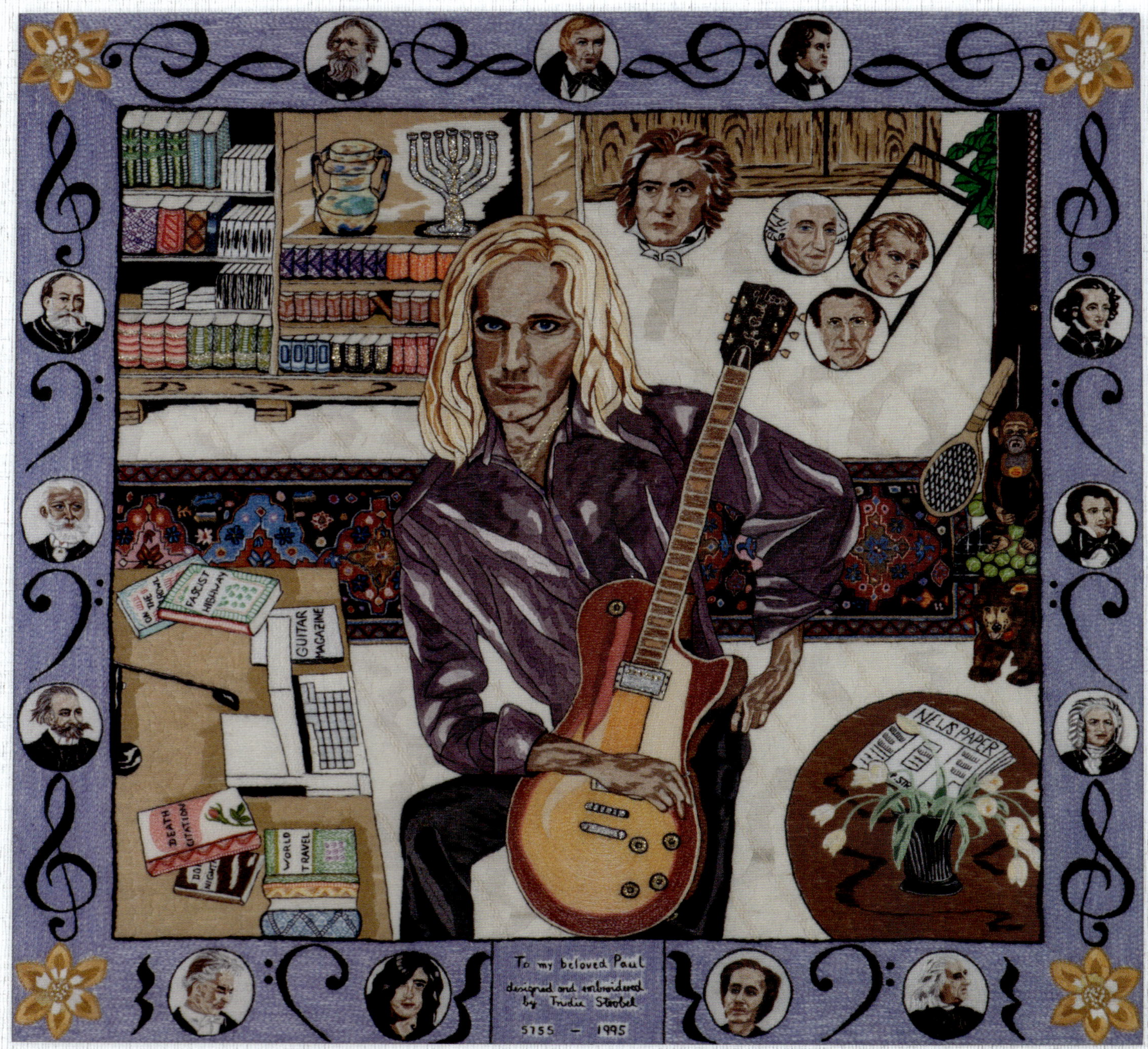

Study of Paul Strobel (Trudie's son) · 1995 · 35″×38″ • Opposite: Details

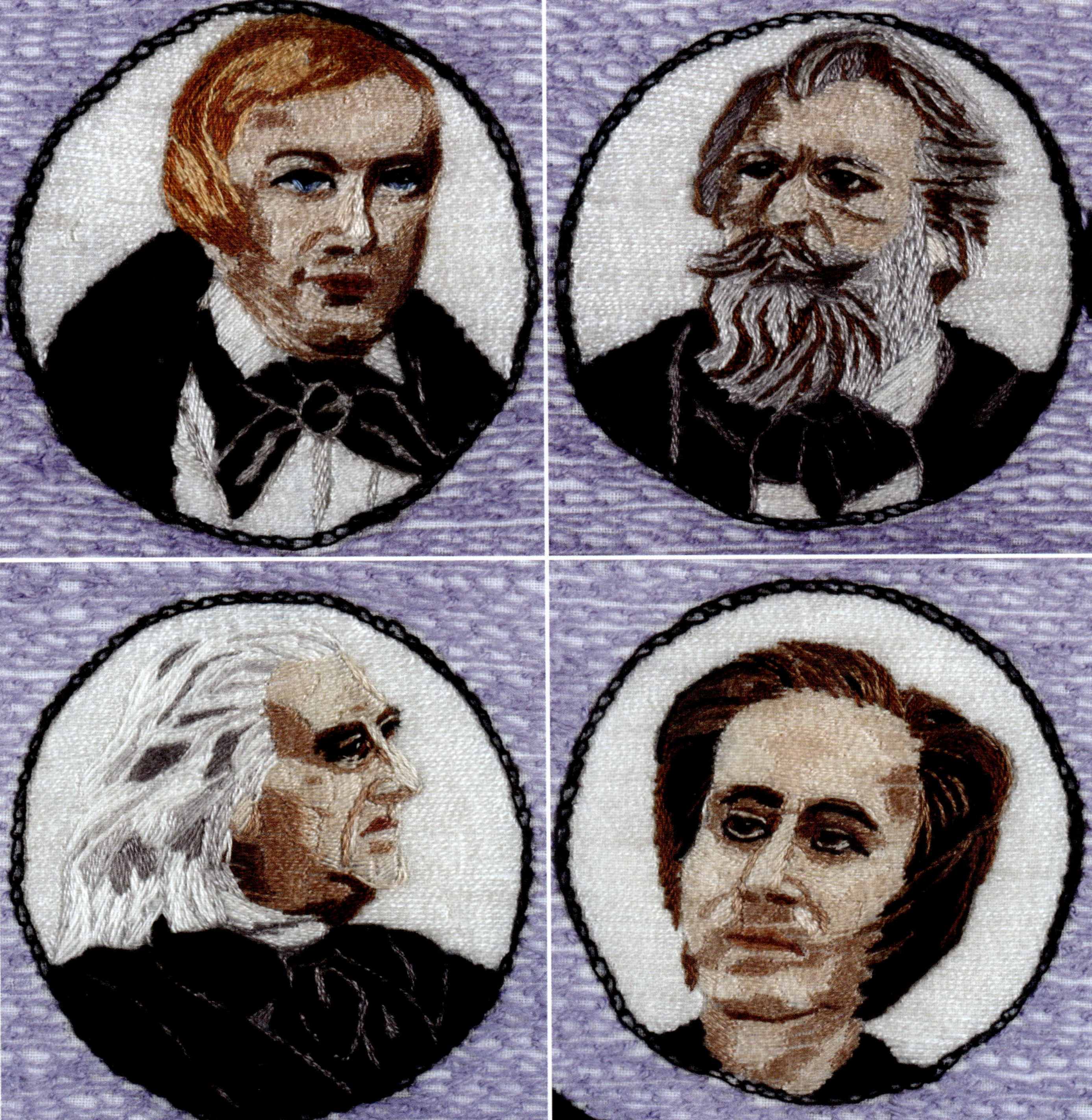

"If you won't talk—"

"No," said Trudie, scarcely audible. Finally, an utterance.

"Then we are going to have to find a way to talk. Okay?"

"Yes," Trudie answered, her lips barely moving, the sound almost imperceptible. This was engagement. This was a beginning.

Eventually Dr. Solow managed to exhume the theft of Trudie's Papa Doll from her fiercely guarded catacombs of memory. He had a suggestion: "Perhaps you would like to dress a doll just as your Papa Doll was dressed." It was something to think about. It was an action she might be able to take. It could be a way to ever so gingerly reach back to those raw memories that recoiled from exposure.

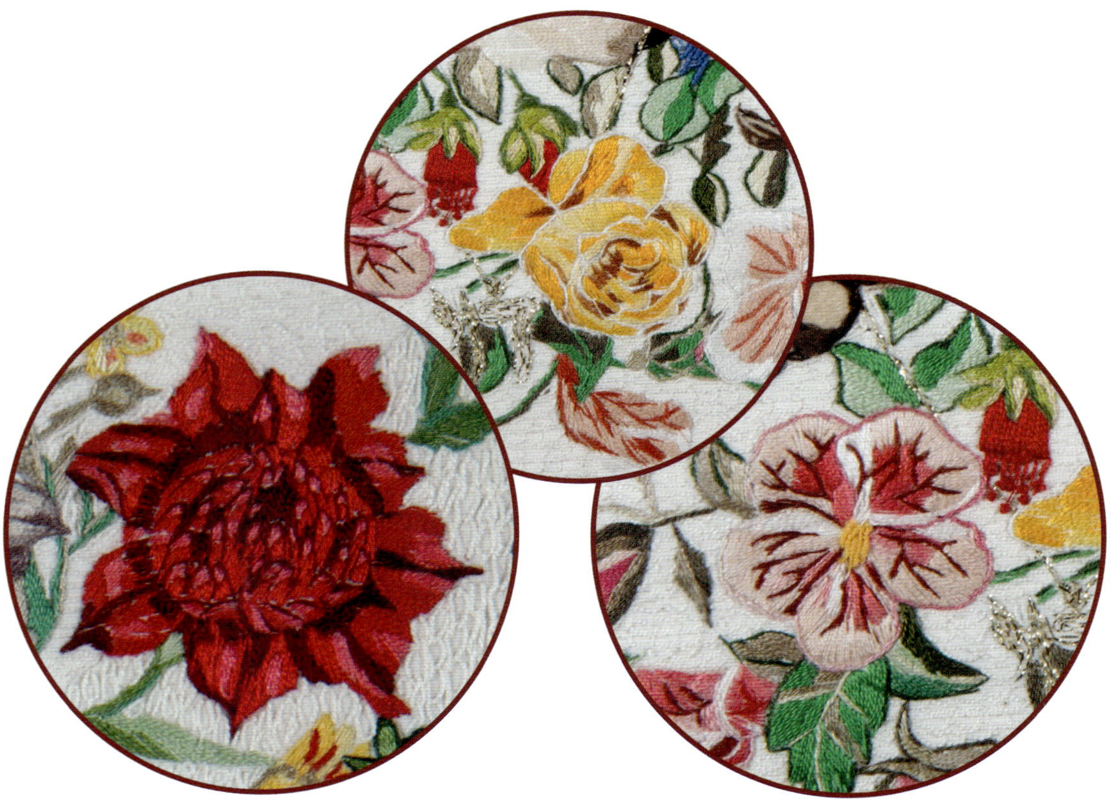

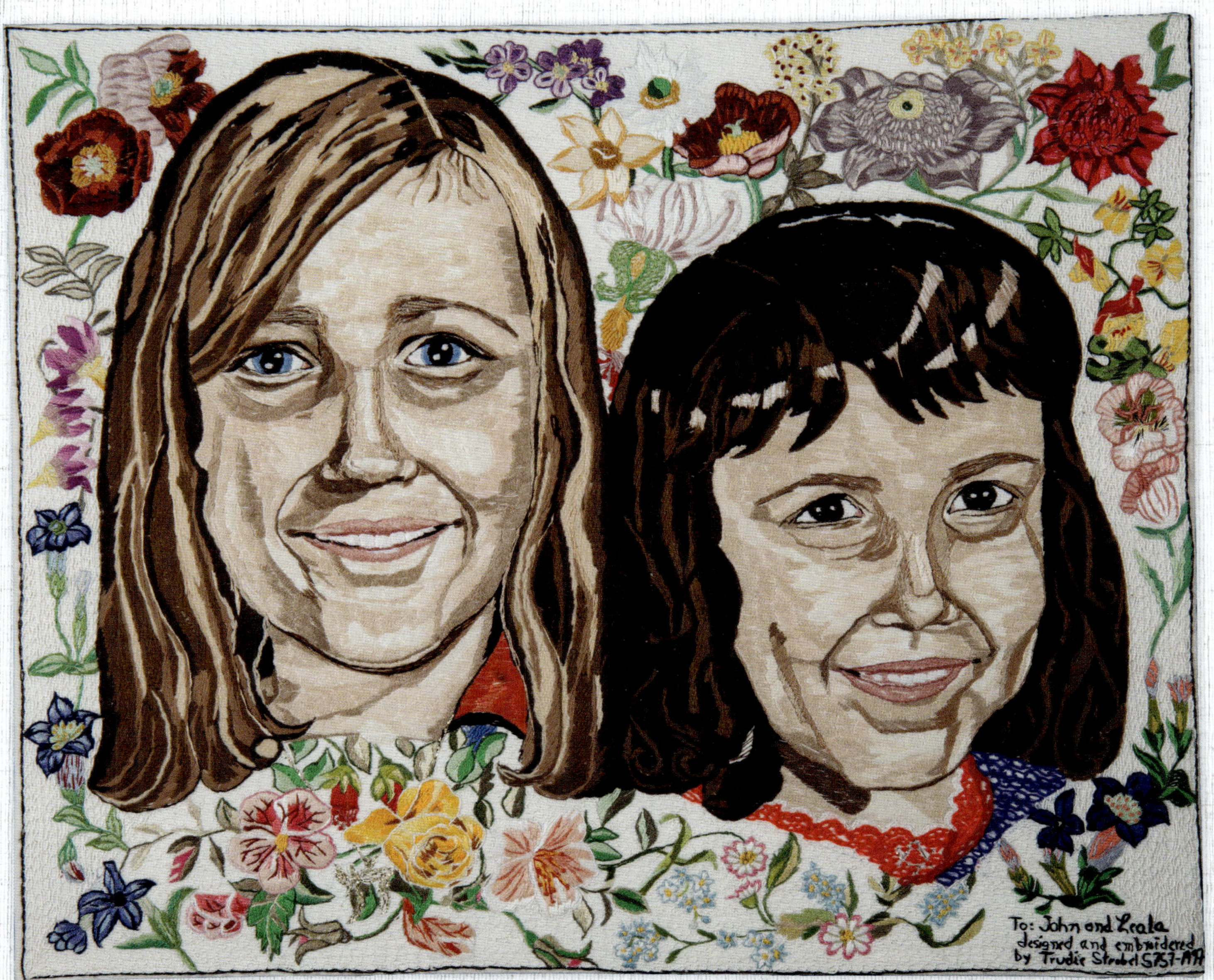

Corinne and Nicole Strobel (Trudie's granddaughters) · 1997 · 22″ × 18″ • Opposite: Details

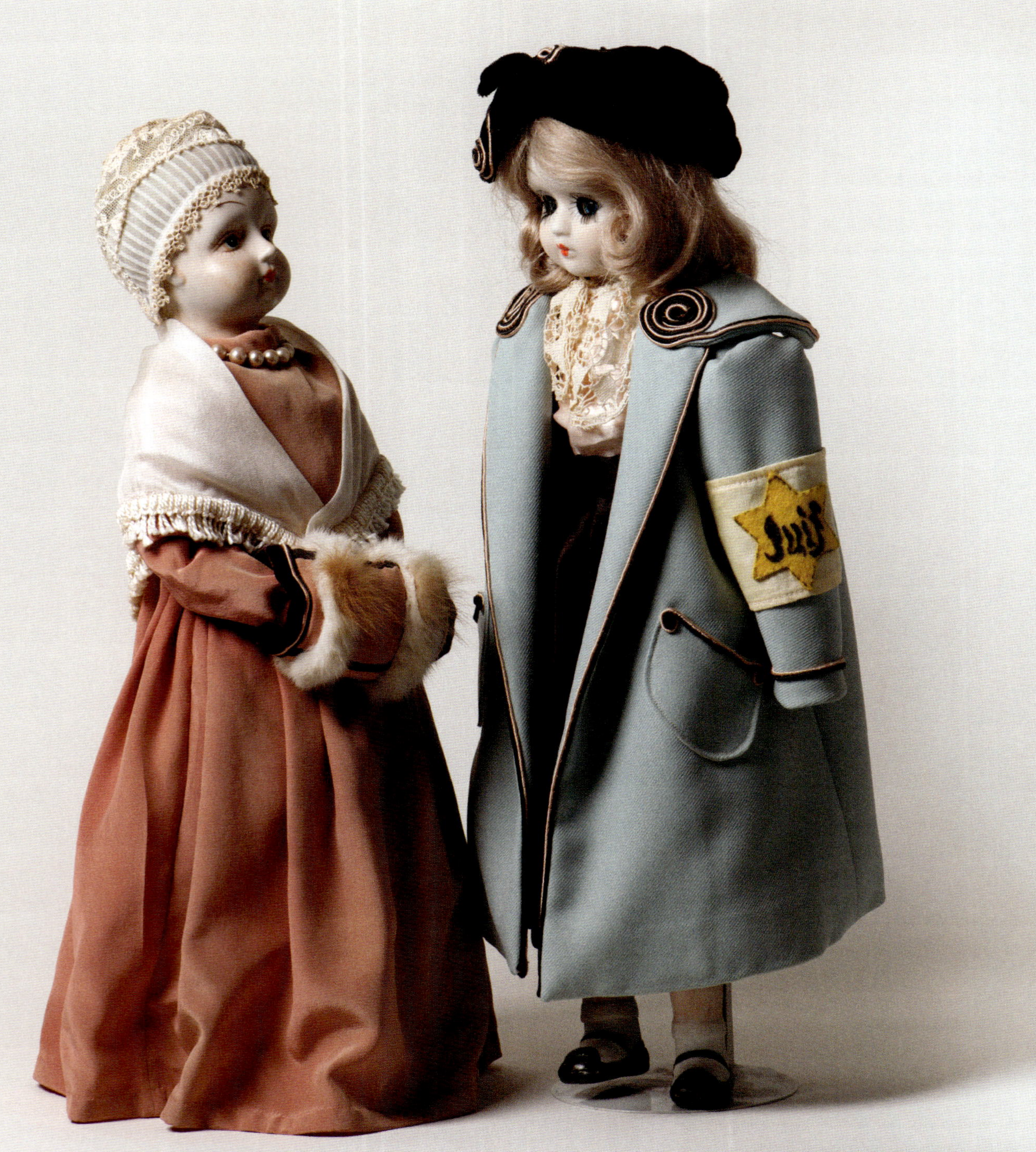
Juif

CHAPTER TEN

BADGES OF SHAME

To Our Children's Children's Children
—THE MOODY BLUES

Trudie took Dr. Solow's suggestion. She would dress a doll. She wanted to get it just right, so she started with patterns, drawings, samples of material. Dr. Solow wrote her a prescription. It was not for medicine or rest. The "prescription" directed her to the library on the twelfth floor of the Jewish Federation of Greater Los Angeles to do some research.[12] If she was going to do this project, she was determined to do it accurately. She found *A History of Jewish Costume* by Alfred Rubens, which became her bible. In its vast collection of images and detailed descriptions, the book traced Jewish clothing from biblical times through the nineteenth century.

Trudie's research expanded the scope of her project. Instead of replicating her irreplaceable Papa Doll, which would live on in her heart, she decided she would dress eleven dolls in the costumes Jews were forced to wear to identify them as targets for discrimination over the course of eleven centuries. She named the project *Badges of Shame: Eleven Centuries of Degradation*. The twentieth-century badge of shame, which Trudie and Masha had worn throughout the Shoah, was the yellow Magen David sewn on the breast or worn on an armband. Masha

Europe, eighteenth to nineteenth centuries, and France, 1940

12 This library has long since been closed and its volumes transferred to the libraries at the American Jewish University.

had helped many fellow prisoners stitch a yellow Star of David to their clothing, heralding their Jewishness to the Nazis. That badge Trudie knew well. Indeed, that is a badge the world knew well. Trudie elected to begin with a different World War II badge, the yellow armband worn by the French Jews under the Nazi occupation. This figure wears it over an elegant sea-green jacket.

Trudie soon discovered that the first recorded evidence of restricted dress was in the Eastern world under Islam and Caliph Omar I in the ninth century. Jewish women in Turkey in 849 CE were required to wear two round yellow patches on their outside garment. If they wore a turban, it had to be yellow. Two of the buttons on their garment had to be a different color from the other buttons. By the fourteenth century, Jewish women were also required to wear a corded girdle and shoes of different colors. All of these eccentric details mandated by the Turks are featured in the wardrobe of Trudie's ninth-century Jewish woman from Turkey.

In 1215, the Fourth General Council of the Lateran was convened by Pope Innocent III. Seventy-one patriarchs and metropolitan bishops, 412 bishops, and 900 abbots and priors attended. Among the seventy canons presented to the council, number sixty-eight required Jews and Muslims to wear distinctive clothing to distinguish them from Christians, so that no

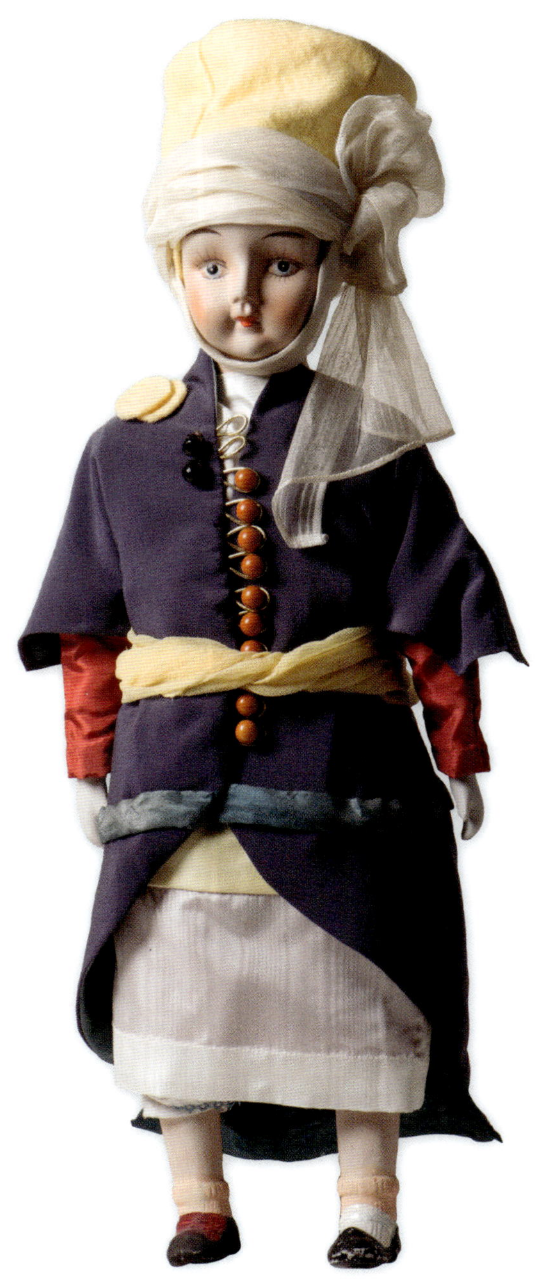

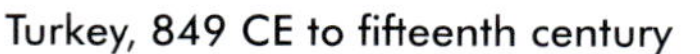

Turkey, 849 CE to fifteenth century

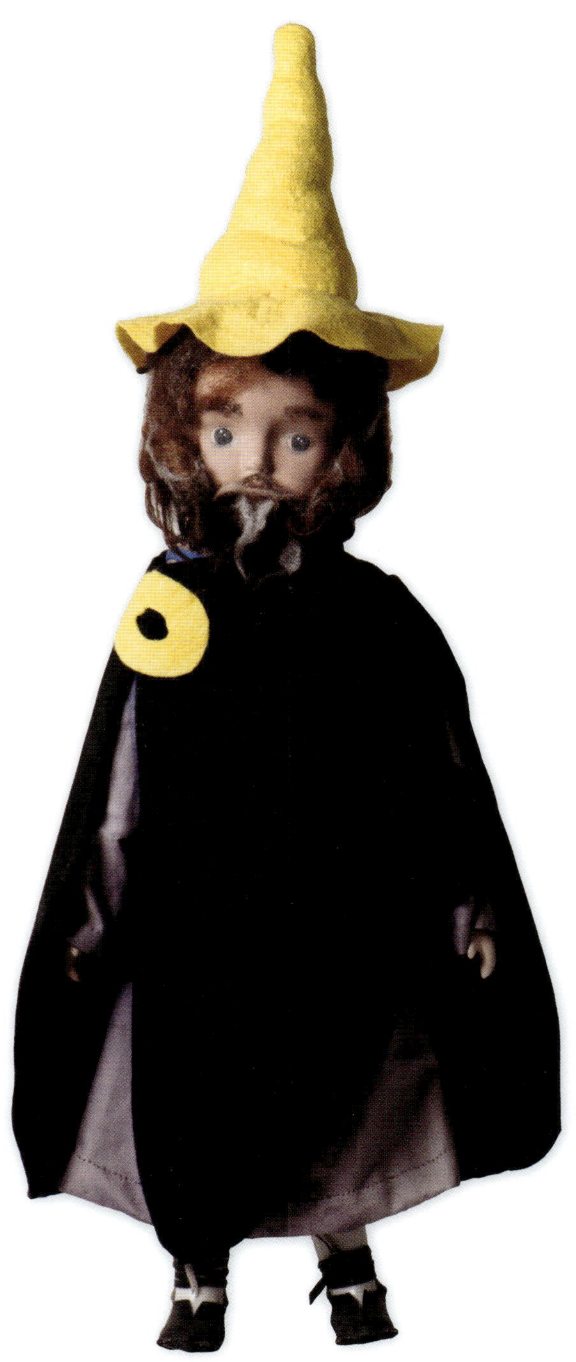

Christian would be ignorant of their otherness, and so that no Christian might make the egregious mistake of marrying them. Furthermore, secular authority relied on the badge as a means of exaction, an extorted tariff, levied with severity. For generations, this mandate remained the authority on all disputed points of canon (church) law. Jews had to abide by this canon intermittently for four centuries in every Christian country; regarded as a mark of degradation, it was always bitterly resented.

The original badge was in the shape of a ring, hence the name "rouelle," which means "wheel" in French. By 1227, it was worn by all Jews. In many kingdoms, a pointed yellow hat was a garish complement to the rouelle worn on the breast. In Trudie's thirteenth-century costume, a male doll wears this humiliating yellow hat in the shape of an inverted cone. Trudie refers to it as a witch's or dunce's hat.

In 1257, a Papal Bull (or edict) added a veil (headdress) with two blue stripes to the restrictive dress of Jewish women. This new requirement for women only is curiously reminiscent of a traditional tallit. The coverings of women's head and shoulders took

Europe, 1227

different forms for the next four centuries.

Trudie's fourteenth-century German female wears a maroon cape-like, floor-length coat with a long, white apron under it. Throughout the 1500s, Jewish men, women, and children had to wear a yellow rondelle in the shape of a ring.

In 1396, in the Kingdom of Aragon, Juan I changed the cape to a long outer gown, called a *gramalla*, which extended over the feet to the floor, covering even the toes. He again ordered that the yellow badges be in the shape of a ring. Trudie's fourteenth-century Spanish gramalla is a sweeping gray tunic, lifted so that one can view the floor-length apron beneath.

By the end of the seventeenth century, Egyptian restrictive dress required that Jewish women wear long black stovepipe hats with a white kerchief accented with gold and

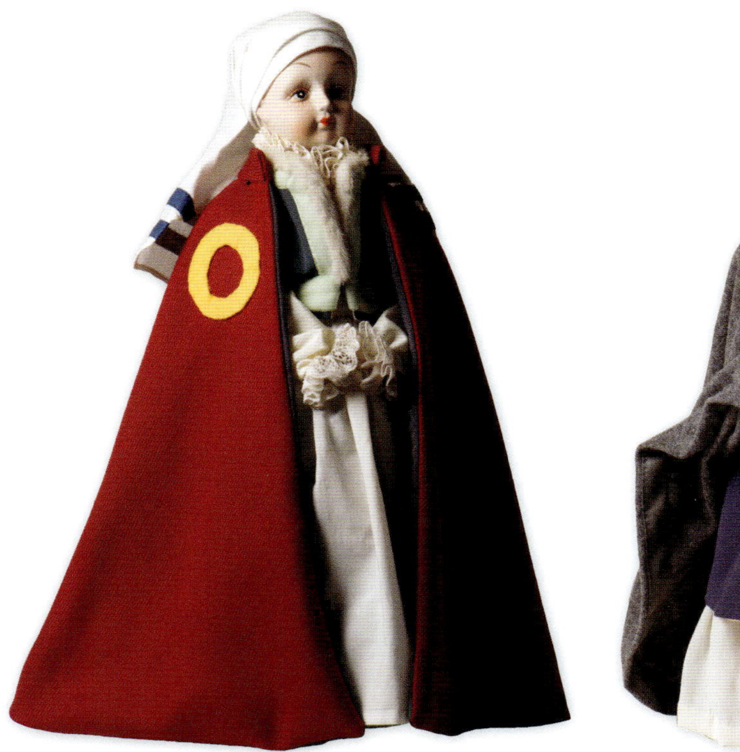

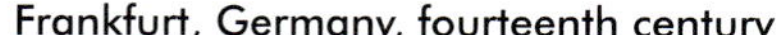

Frankfurt, Germany, fourteenth century

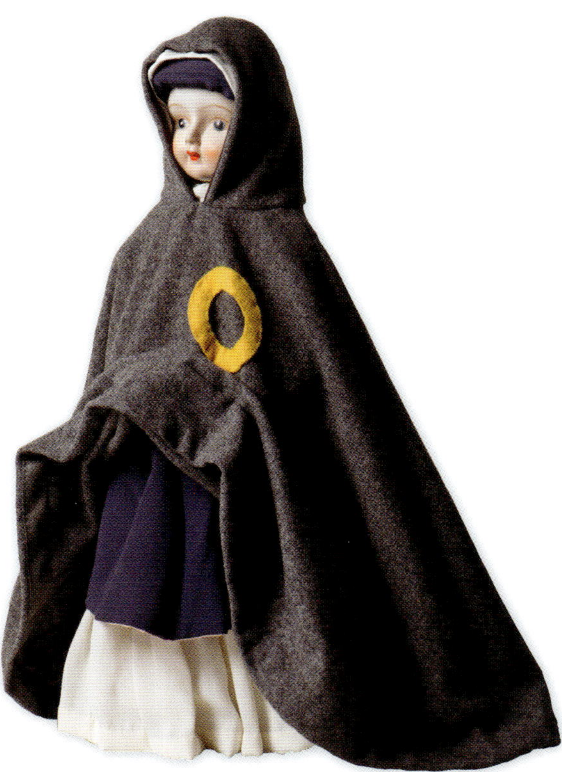

Spain, fourteenth century

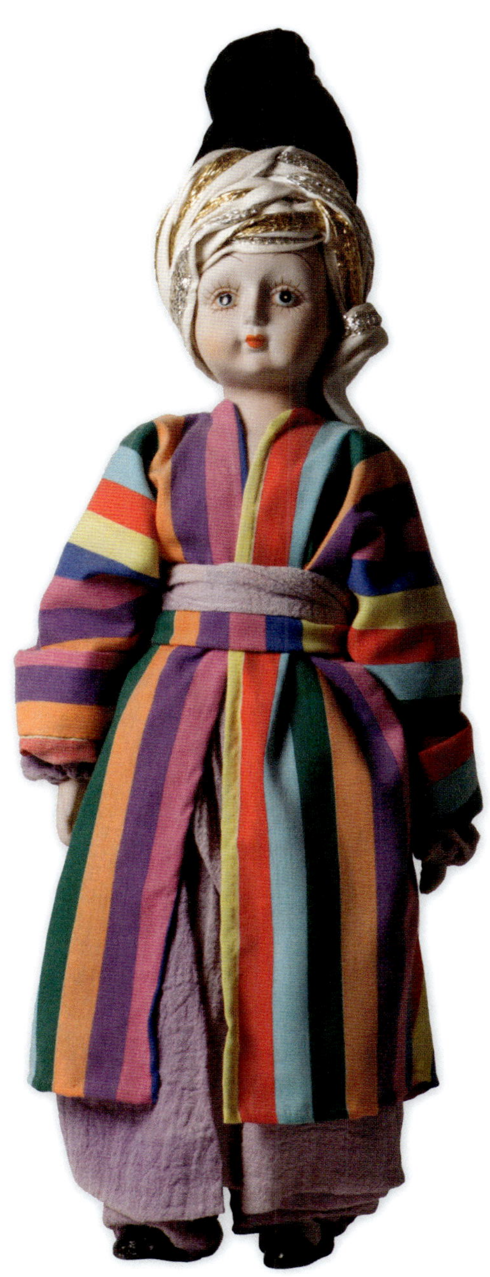

silver accessories. Trudie's Egyptian figure is outfitted in a striped outer garment and proudly wears the gold and silver head wrap that Trudie meticulously reproduced.

In Germany, the aforementioned veil of the fourteenth century evolved into a cap with two stiffly starched pointed wings of white linen, which closely covered the hair but still had the two blue stripes. Trudie's replication of this *viereckiger schlier*, or square veil, is accompanied by a ruff, or pleated collar, that was typical at the time. With this new restrictive dress, the yellow badge requirement was jettisoned. However, this extraordinarily conspicuous and cumbersome nun-like headdress had to be worn by Jewish women in Germany through the eighteenth century.

As the 1700s trundled into the 1800s, European Ashkenazim in some principalities evolved their own distinctive style of dress to conform to the restrictions imposed upon them. Women wore decorated lace caps and forehead bands, or *stirnbindel*, a chest covering, or *brusttuch*, and bib-like trimming on their dresses. Note the delicate tatting on the cap of the doll's costume. Think of the hours Trudie spent combing through thrift shops and antique stores, fabric shops and craft shops, searching for the perfect materials from which to fashion each of the doll costumes. This particular doll wears pearls and fur cuffs with intricate seam detail.

Egypt, seventeenth century

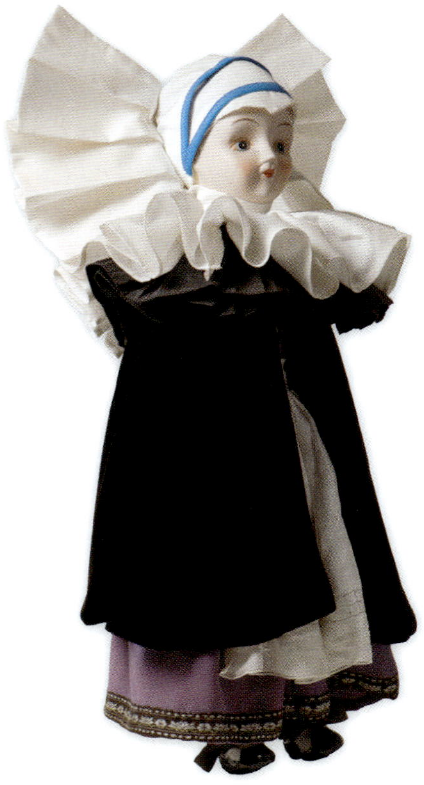

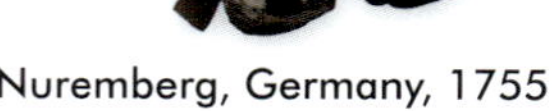
Nuremberg, Germany, 1755

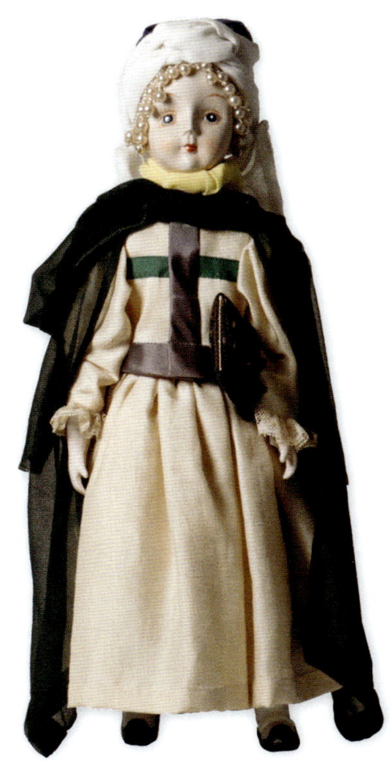

Lithuania, 1815

In Lithuania, statutes were enacted in 1566 that forbade Jewish women from wearing costly clothes or gold and silver ornaments. Instead, they were directed to wear kerchiefs of yellow linen, along with the now familiar veil with two blue stripes. These rules of dress continued for several hundred years. The doll representative of this era wears pearls but not a shred of gold or silver. Trudie crafted her modest, though quite pretty, vestments out of ordinary fabrics. This doll is dressed like a Jewish Lithuanian woman in 1815.

The Russian government wholly embraced the diktat that Jews must wear special clothing to marginalize them. A Russian Jewish woman circa 1843 would have worn a tall, yellow bonnet tied with a scarf, which heralded her Jewishness. The painstaking detail with which Trudie crafted even the folds of the yellow bonnet, along with the intricate lacework of the collar and tunic, and the masterfully embroidered flowers on the smock, highlight the juxtaposition of xenophobic costume mandates with the dignity of the Jews who wore them.

After the French occupation of Poland in 1812, Polish Jews became fanatically attached to their Polish costume, even though its political intention was to single them out for ostracism. This included, for women, the restrictive yellow kerchief, the stirnbindel, now worn in red, and the brusttuch, which is magnificently replicated on Trudie's Polish doll. In 1850, a Russian Imperial order formalized the edict mandating this distinctive attire. The order also prohibited peoth for men, a constraint that must have caused intense anxiety, fear, and, most likely, significant rebellion among the Jewish population. *Peoth*, or *peyos*, are the long sidelocks hanging in front of the ears that are worn by religious Jewish men. The Torah says, "You shall not round off the peyos of your head."[13]

Trudie made a twelfth doll in this series later. It was not until we went to the Los Angeles Museum of the Holocaust (LAMOTH) to photograph the dolls in their collection that they brought this doll out of a box held in the back room. It has never been displayed. It was made at the request of Cheryl Zoller of the Gonda Foundation and fashioned after her aunt in 1940 Warsaw. This twelfth doll takes us back to World War II. A Jew, with the Star of David stitched to her chest, she carries the few belongings she has managed to hold on to as she is forced from her home and flung into exodus.

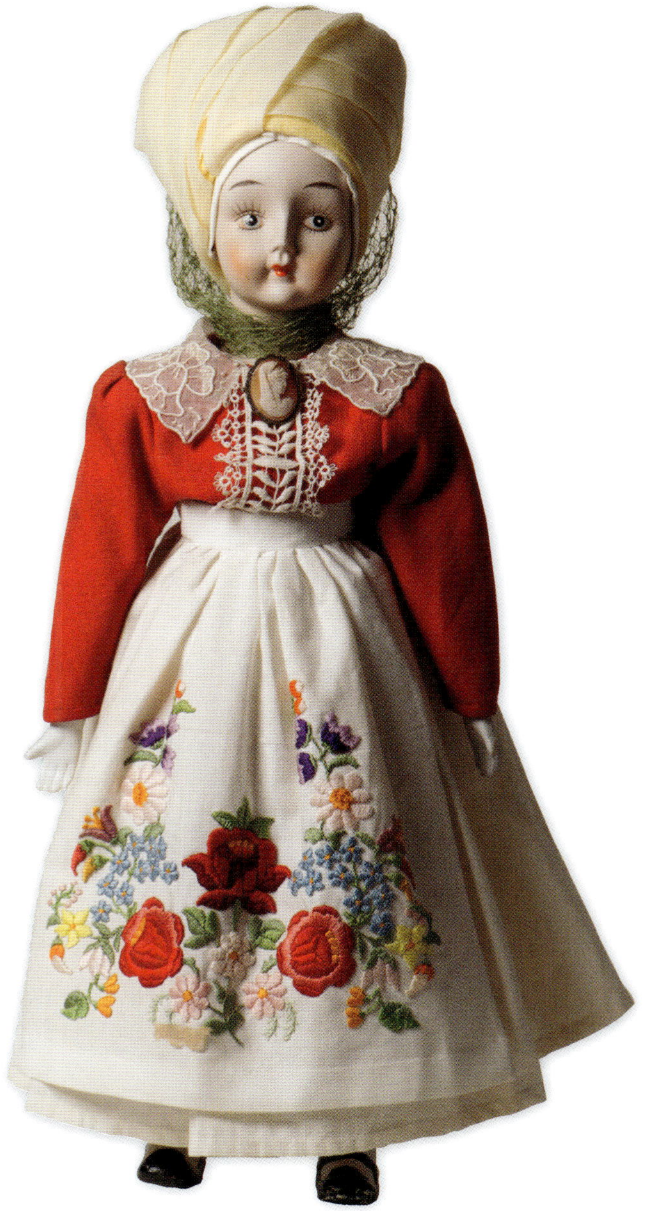

Russia, 1843

13 Leviticus 19:27

Trudie was forty-eight years old when she started work on *Eleven Centuries of Degradation*. Utilizing all of the many disciplines of needlework that she had learned throughout her life, she strove for historical veracity in each doll she costumed according to centuries of sumptuary laws[14] and xenophobic fiats that mandated Jewish attire. Committed to authenticity, Trudie handmade the lace, which took long hours. She even labored with exactitude over the undergarments and the length of the aprons. She cut many of the fabrics from her own blouses and coats. When Trudie talks about this collection, she says, "This is me. This is Trudie Strobel." She did copious research.[15] She studied the text of European Jewish sumptuary laws of the fifteenth century to the eighteenth century, along with the massive historiographical works of the first-century Jewish historian Flavius Josephus, including *Antiquities of the Jews* and *The Jewish War*.

In 1986, Trudie gifted the dolls to the Martyrs Memorial and Museum of the Holocaust, now known as the Los Angeles Museum of the Holocaust. *Eleven Centuries of Degradation* is the most popular exhibit in LAMOTH's permanent collection.

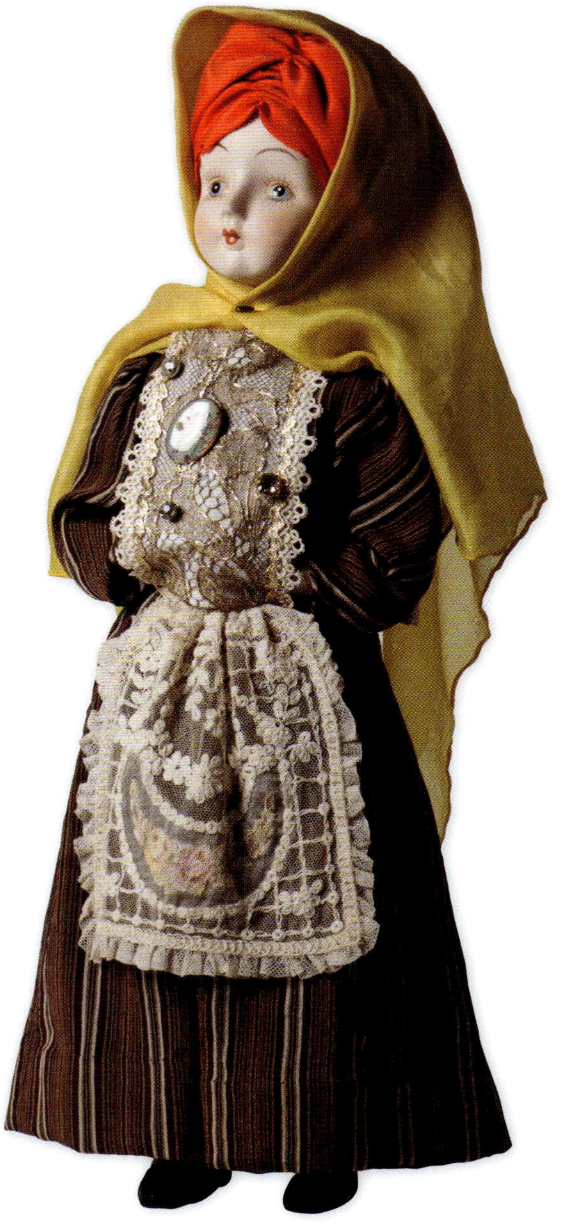

Poland, 1846 • Opposite: Warsaw, 1944

14 Sumptuary laws, which regulate consumption, are designed to restrain luxury or extravagance in such matters as apparel, food, and furnishings.

15 Some of her principal sources were: Abba Eban's *Heritage: Civilization and the Jews*; *Costumes and Styles* by Henny Harald Hansen; Th erese and Mendel Metzger's *Jewish Life in the Middle Ages*; and what became her costume bible, *A History of Jewish Costume* by Alfred Rubens, whom she befriended and consulted. She also consulted *Th e Encyclopedia of Islam*, *Encyclopedia Judaica*, *The Psychology of Clothes* by J.C. Flugel, G. Kisch's *Historia Judaica* (specifically the chapter called "The Yellow Badge in History"), *Ivanhoe* by Sir Walter Scott, and *Th e Merchant of Venice* by Shakespeare.

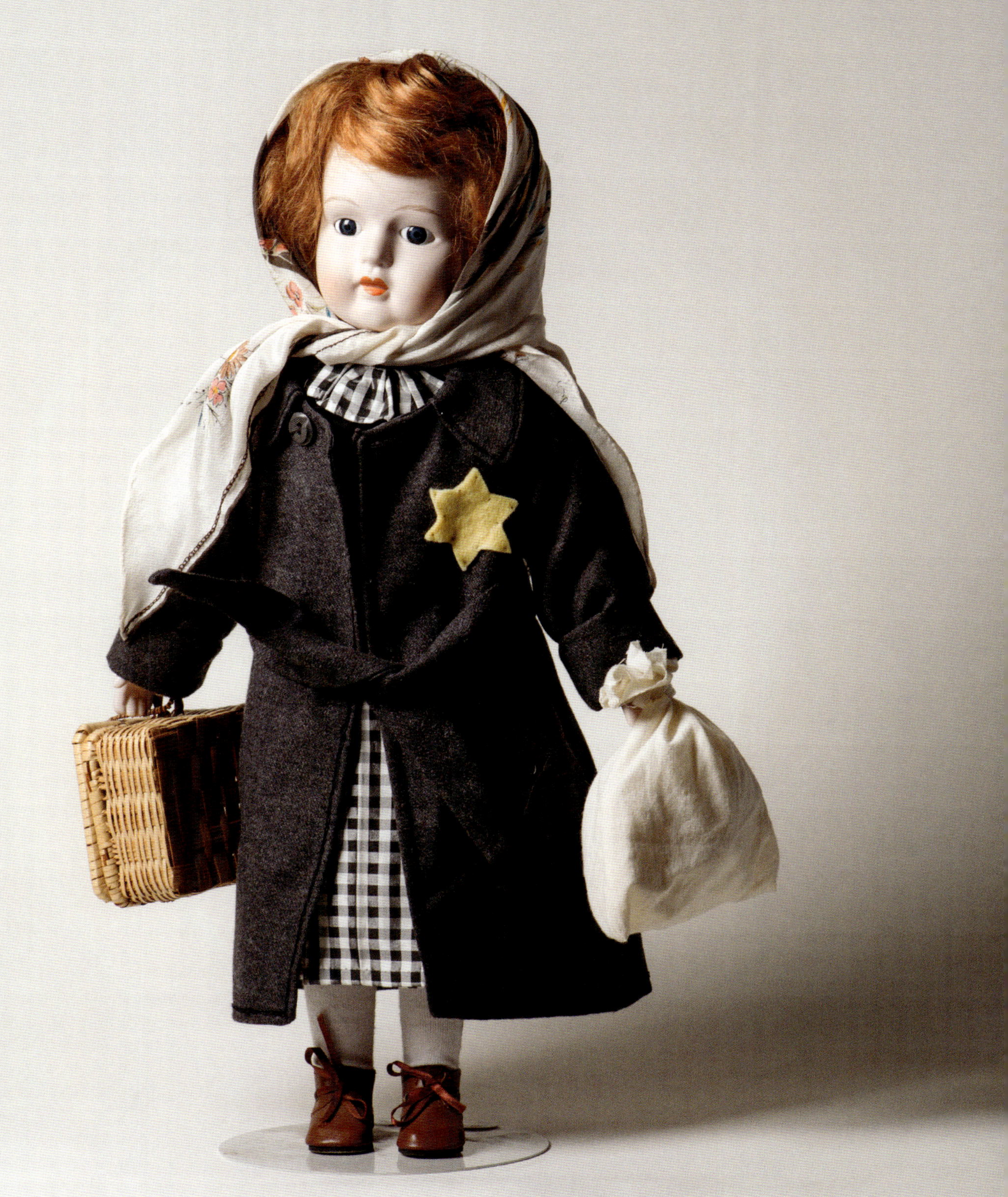

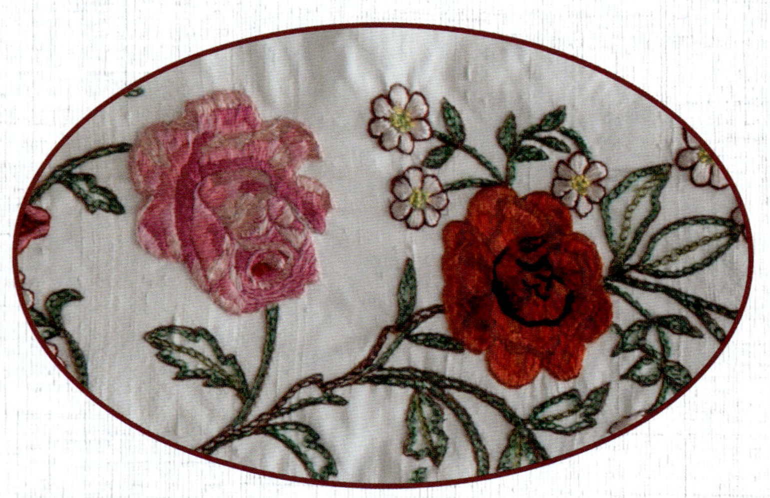

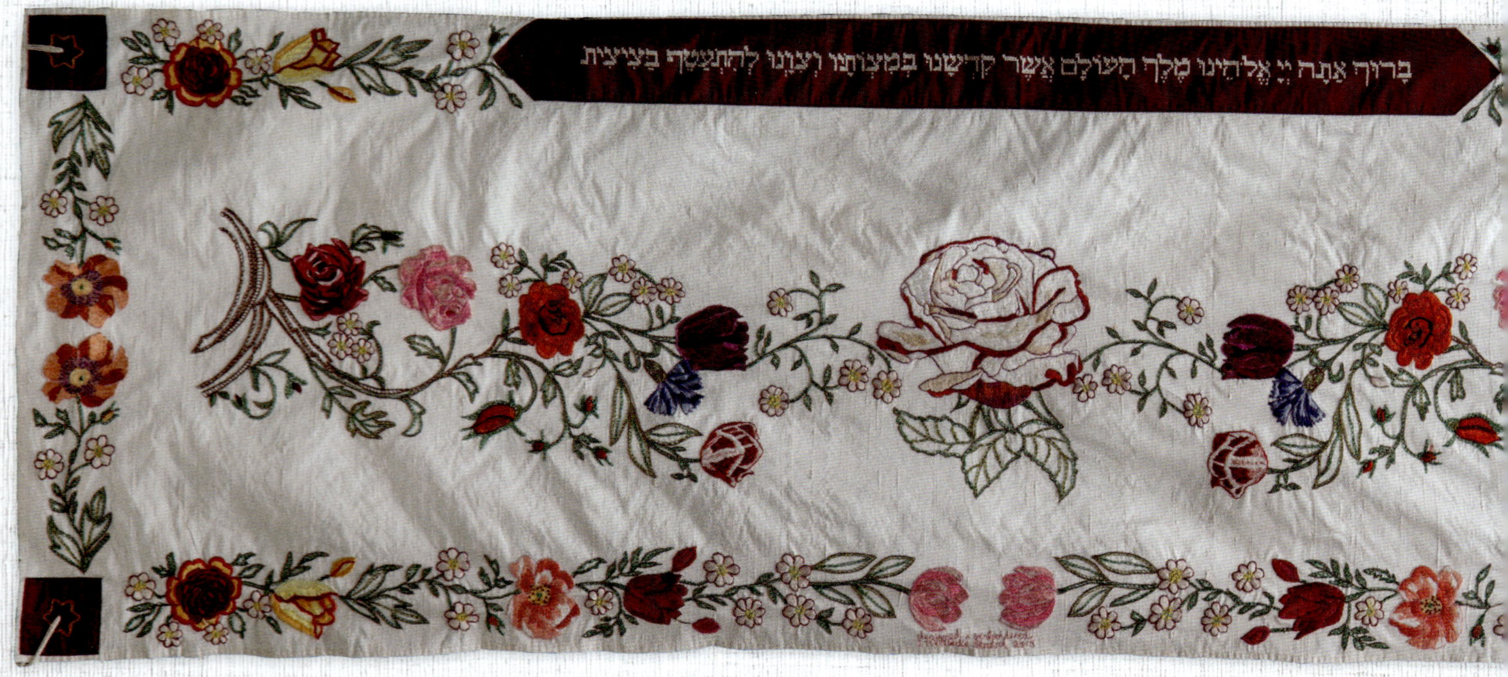

ברוך אתה יי אלהינו מלך העולם אשר קדשנו במצותיו וצונו להתעטף בציצית

Faye's Tallit · 2013 · 24″ × 72″

CHAPTER ELEVEN

TAPESTORIAN

Her art is humble and noble.
Her name is Trudie Strobel.

— From "Paint Her as She Is"
LEO EGAN (née Zgierski)

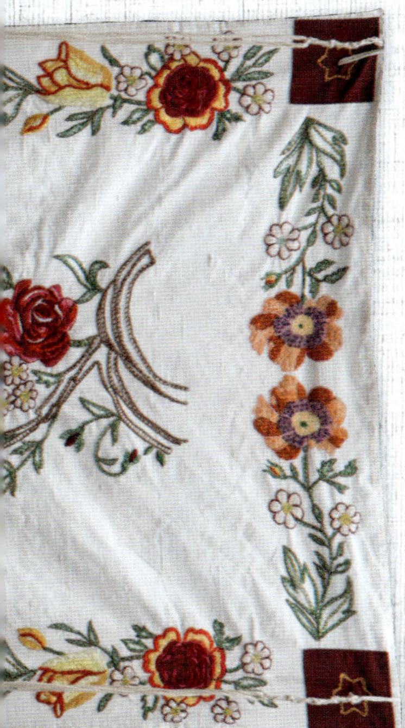

Trudie still did not speak often or audibly (even to her family), and she was still battling haunting nightmares and overwhelming depression, but her work got her out of bed and initiated a healing process.

One day in 1988, she came home from an appointment with Dr. Solow and saw a picture of a rose. It made her smile. So she copied it. Her drawing was very precise and realistic, and, in that moment, she realized she could draw.

Not only could she draw a flower, but she soon learned that she could draw people, faces, towns, animals—anything her mind saw she could draw. It was an amazing gift. She had never been trained in anatomy or perspective. She had never studied color or shading, and yet, if she saw it, she could illustrate it. The logical next step for Trudie Strobel, whose childhood had been salvaged by stitching, was to paint in thread. It was an unusual string of logic, but it was inevitable to her.

Trudie says that it took a lot of thinking to develop a story that she wanted to illustrate. Most of her work, and certainly all of her larger pieces, are narratives. The first large piece that she illustrated in thread is a series of twelve panels, each depicting a moment in Jewish history.

MOMENTS IN JEWISH TIME: TWELVE PANELS

PANEL ONE

"Exodus from Egypt" is set around 1290 BCE. The Israelites flee Egypt and enslavement to the Egyptian Pharaoh, and during their exodus, Moses receives the laws from God on Mount Sinai.

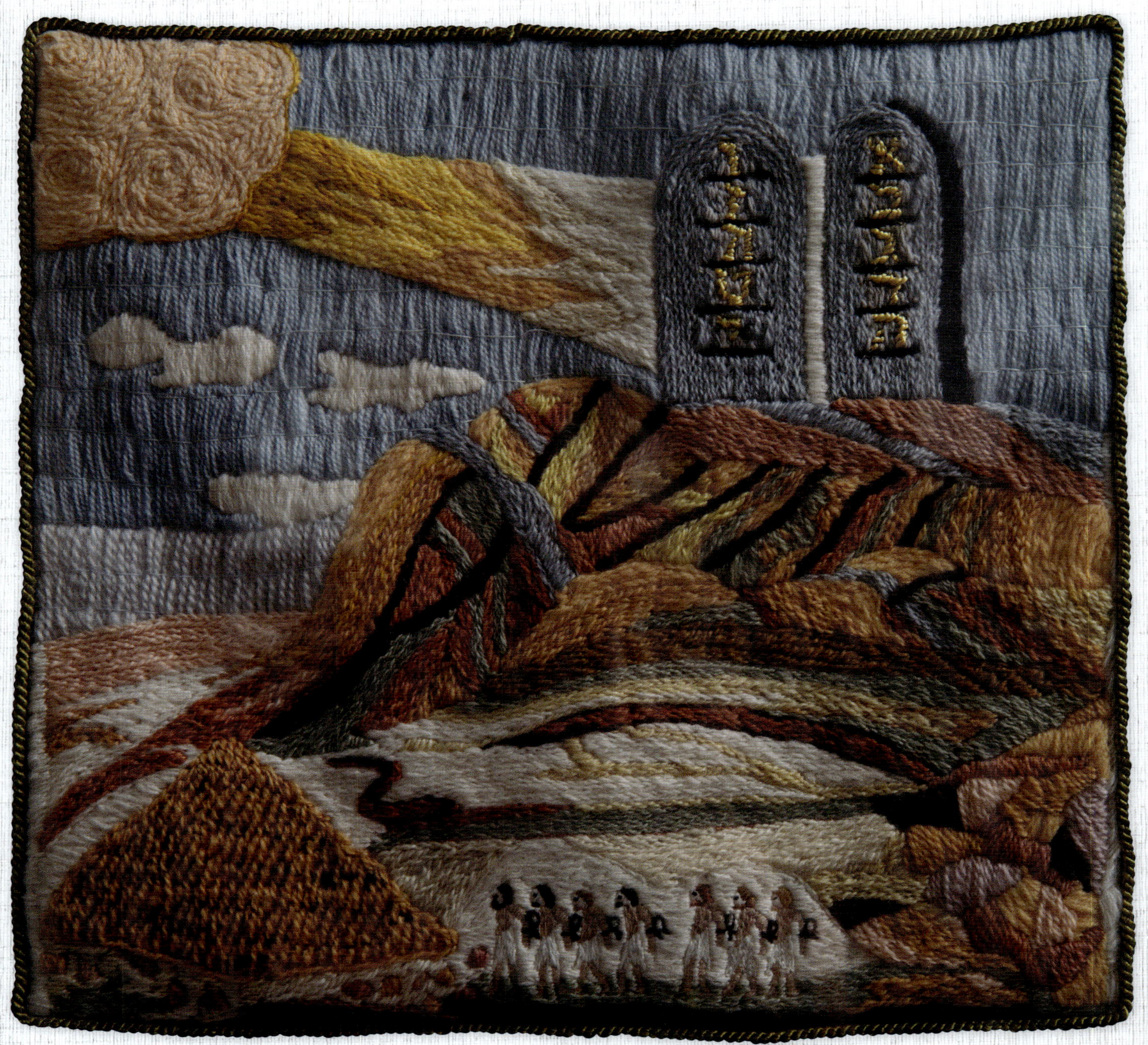

PANEL ONE: ***Exodus from Egypt***

PANEL TWO

"King David" is set around 1000 BCE. David, the second King of Israel, is the most beloved and heroic figure in ancient Jewish history. He was a poet and a warrior who also played the harp. The lions holding the crown over his head symbolize the land of Judah, of which he was King. It was the spiritual and intellectual center of the Jewish people for more than a thousand years.

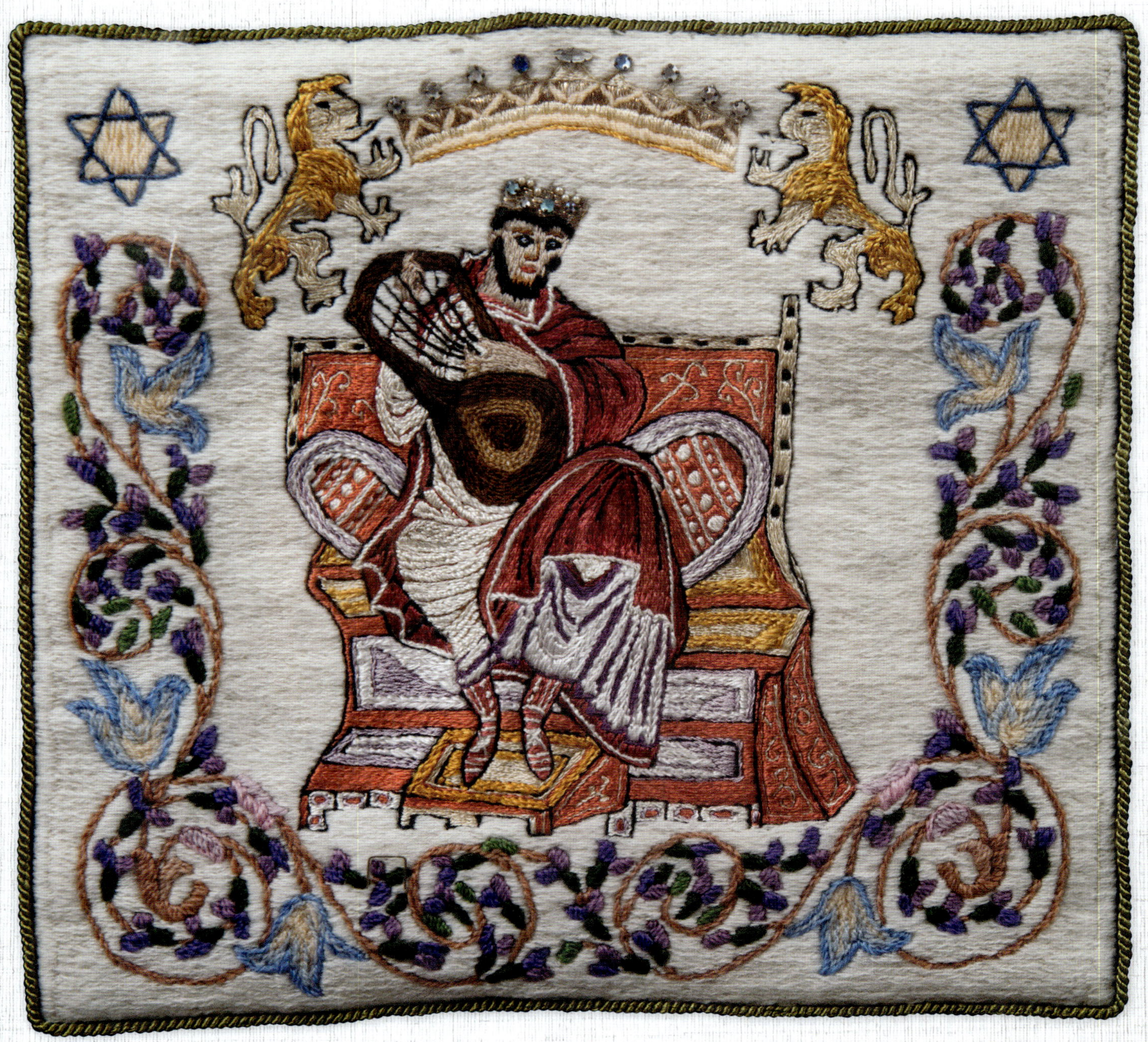

PANEL TWO: ***King David***

PANEL THREE

This panel, "Diaspora," is set between 586 BCE and 70 CE. Diaspora, from the Greek word meaning "scattering" or "dispersion," commonly refers to the dispersion of the Jewish people outside of Israel. Jews have lived outside of Palestine even before the period of kings. After the downfall of the kingdom of Judah, which was conquered by the Babylonians, Jewish settlements developed in Babylonia, Egypt, and elsewhere. One of the original Talmuds was compiled in Babylonia. The first temple, built by King Solomon, stood for more than 600 years until it was destroyed by the Babylonians in 586 BCE. During the reign of Alexander the Great and subsequent Greek rule in the Middle East, new Jewish communities were established in Alexandria, Egypt, and Syria. Alexandria, which became the leading Jewish community in the diaspora, is represented in blue thread. Jewish scholars in Alexandria translated the Hebrew Bible into Greek, the Septuagint.

The second temple was destroyed in 70 CE by the Roman General Titus, who erected an arch in Rome in 81 CE and struck coins to commemorate his victory over Judea. The burning menorah[16] at the bottom of the panel symbolizes the destruction of the temples, both on the month of Av. The arch stands on the place where Jewish captives, bearing the burning menorah from the temple, were dragged into the forum. All of these historical points are depicted in this one panel.

---

16 The menorah was an integral part of the temple and was safeguarded within its sanctuaries.

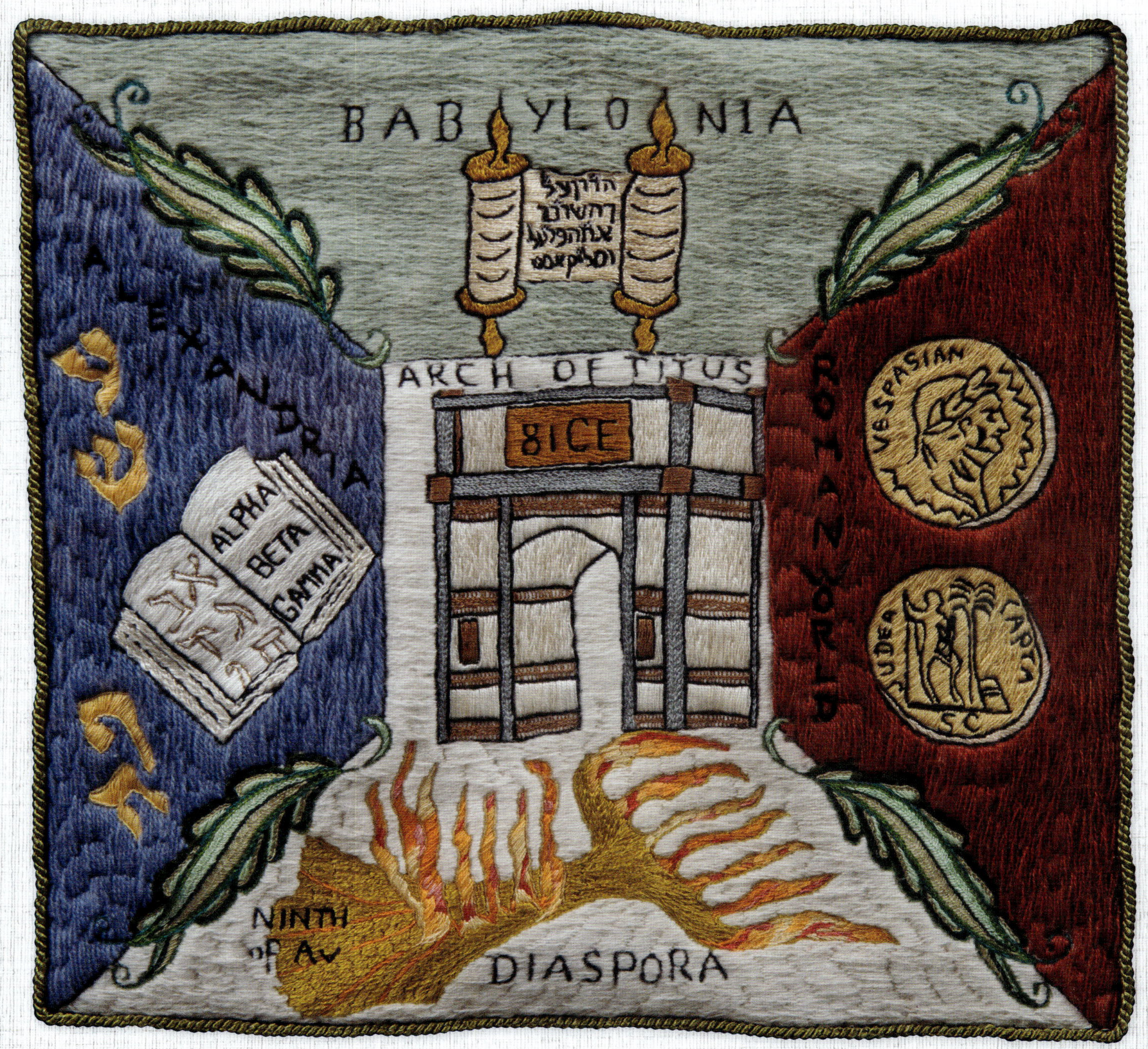

PANEL THREE: ***Diaspora***

PANEL FOUR

Set between 1100 and 1500 CE, "The Golden and Dark Ages of Spain" depicts a page of the Mishnah Torah, which was one of the most important works of Maimonides.

Moses Maimonides, also known as Ramban, lived in Spain in the twelfth century. Undoubtedly the foremost intellectual of medieval Judaism, Maimonides was a scholar of Hebrew literature, the religious leader of the diaspora Jews, and a prominent physician.

As a counterpoint to the beautiful page of the Torah, the right side of this panel depicts March 31, 1492, the date the edict expelling Jews from Spain was signed by King Ferdinand. It was an era of burning of books, torture, and inquisition that led to the Jewish exodus from Spain.

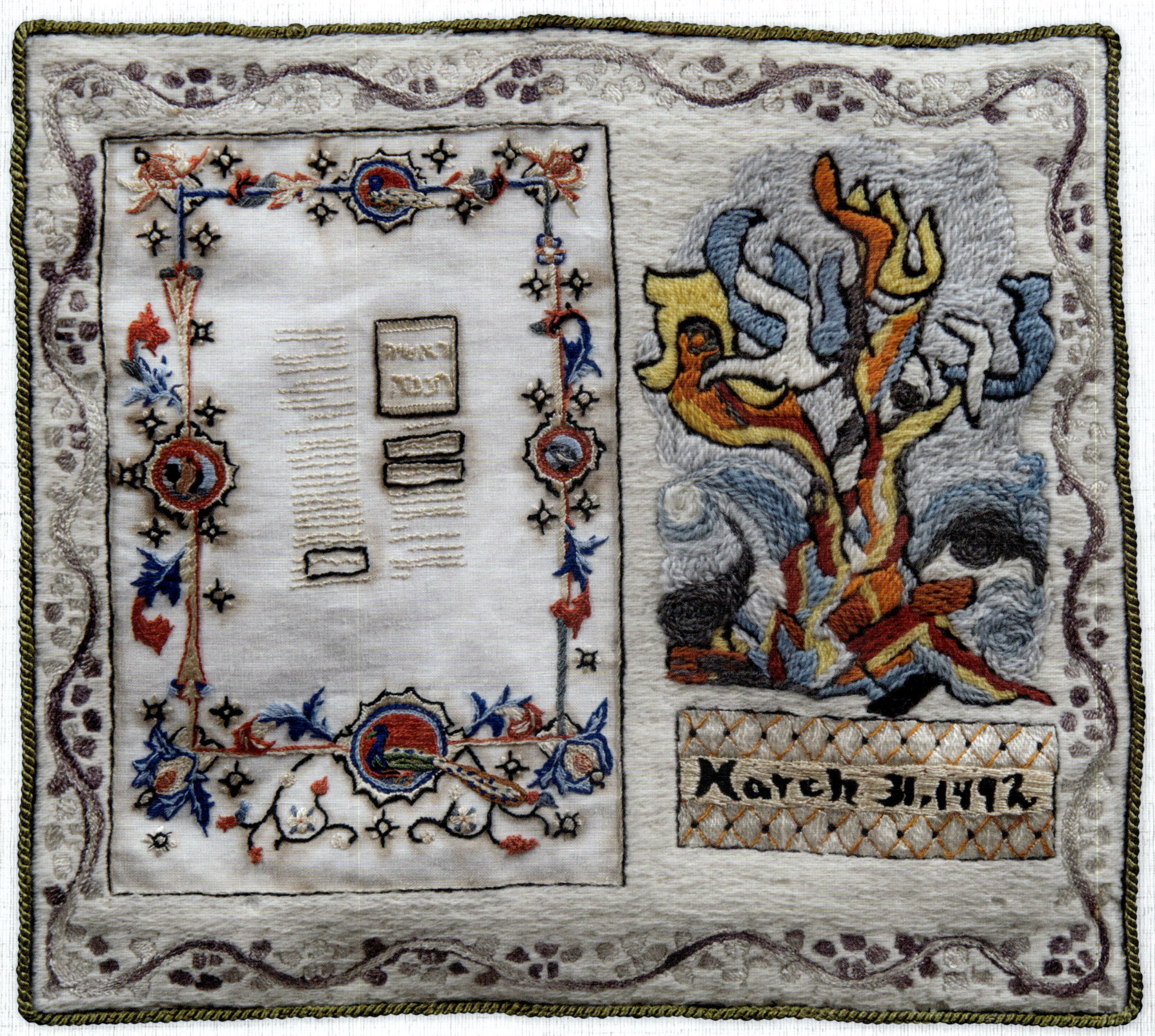

PANEL FOUR: ***The Golden and Dark Ages of Spain***

PANEL FIVE

Unlike Trudie's later Holocaust work, "Holocaust—The Horrifying Years" is executed with a stark, modernist use of reds and black dominated in unsettling prominence by the yellow Star of David. This panel, with its interpretive, almost Pop Art feel, is Trudie's first attempt to address, in tapestry, what she calls "The Horrifying Years." Note the railroad tracks and barbed wire. During the Hitler regime, 6 million Jews—men, women, and children—were killed in gas chambers and by firing squads. The disciplined stitching of this panel is also a departure from the other panels in this series. In this panel, each stitch is identical; no one stitch stands out. The effect of the uniformity of technique is eerie, echoing the mass victims of genocide who were numbered, catalogued, and deprived of all the particulars that identify an individual.

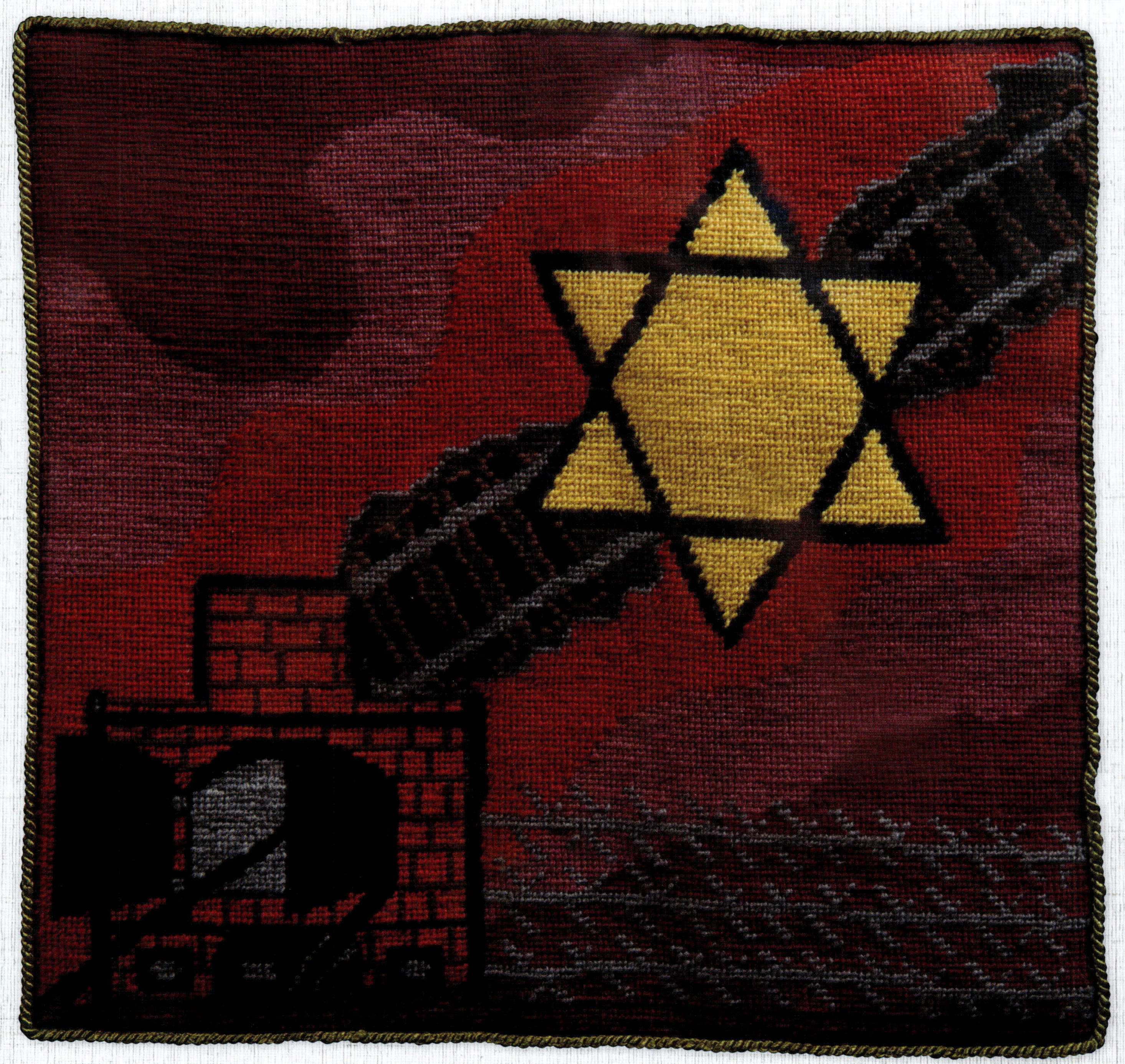

PANEL FIVE: ***Holocaust—The Horrifying Years***

PANEL SIX

In marked contrast to "Holocaust," "Israel" uses myriad stitching techniques, whimsy, and a creative vision that practically dances with kinetic lines and color. Trudie writes, "The Israelites, having fled from slavery, now stand at the foot of the mountain to accept the laws." That is what happened in Egypt many centuries ago, and to Trudie, that is what happened when the survivors of the Holocaust returned to their Holy Land. Trudie writes, "Through the embattled years of the Jewish Kingdoms, the dispersions and suffering that exceeds understanding, finally, a people separated for centuries was brought back together to create a new country and a new life. Rebirth."

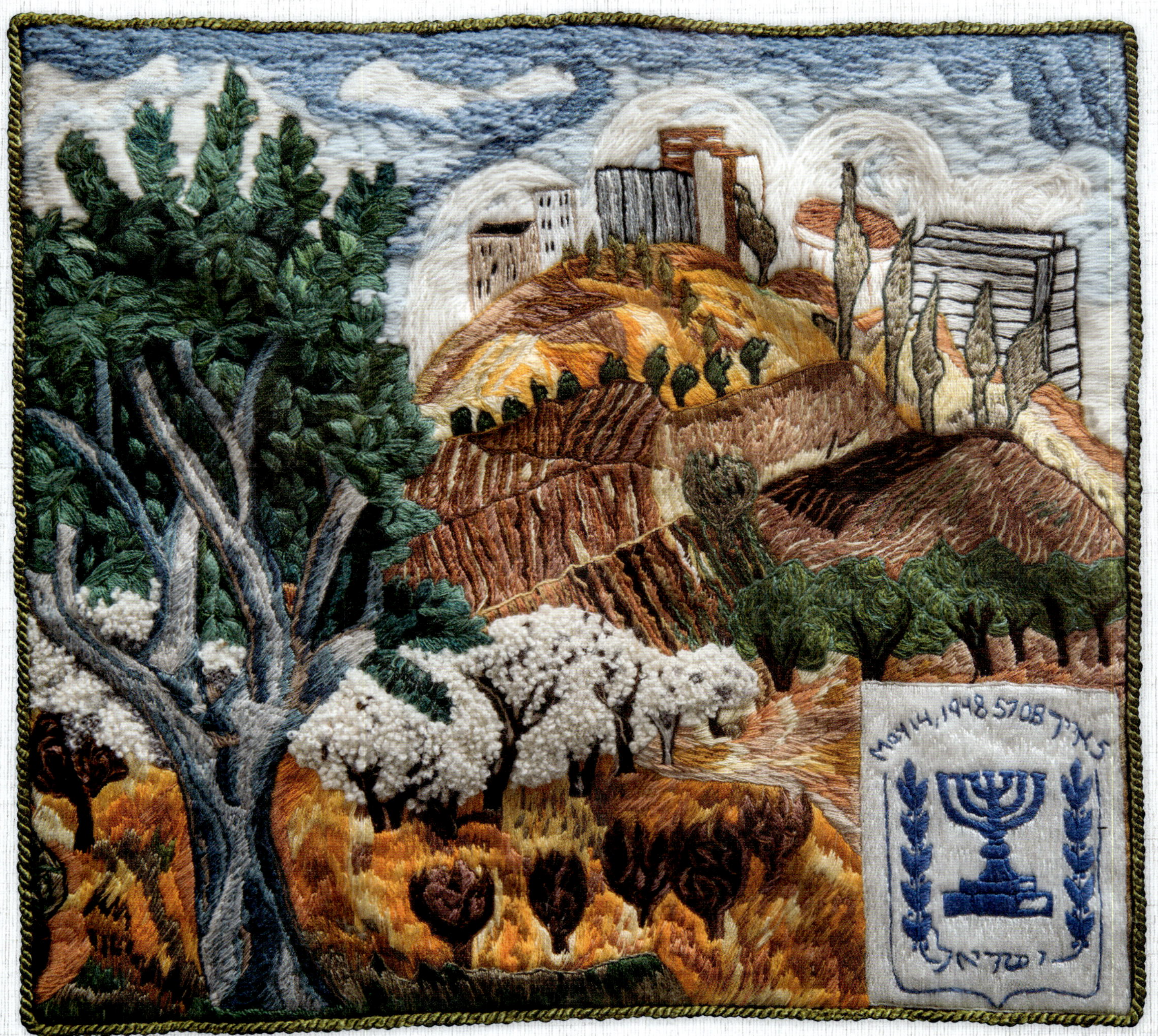

PANEL SIX: ***Israel***

PANEL SEVEN

"Circumcision" depicts a fundamental Jewish tradition. "As it is written in the law, he that is eight days old shall be circumcised among you, every male throughout your generations." Instead of a modern circumcision, however, Trudie reaches back in time. This panel depicts Moroccan Jews in 1830 CE. The woman wears a red silk kerchief and red slippers. The men, with closely shaved heads under black caps, wear their beards long. Traditional black slippers and a black wool cloak round out this classic wardrobe.

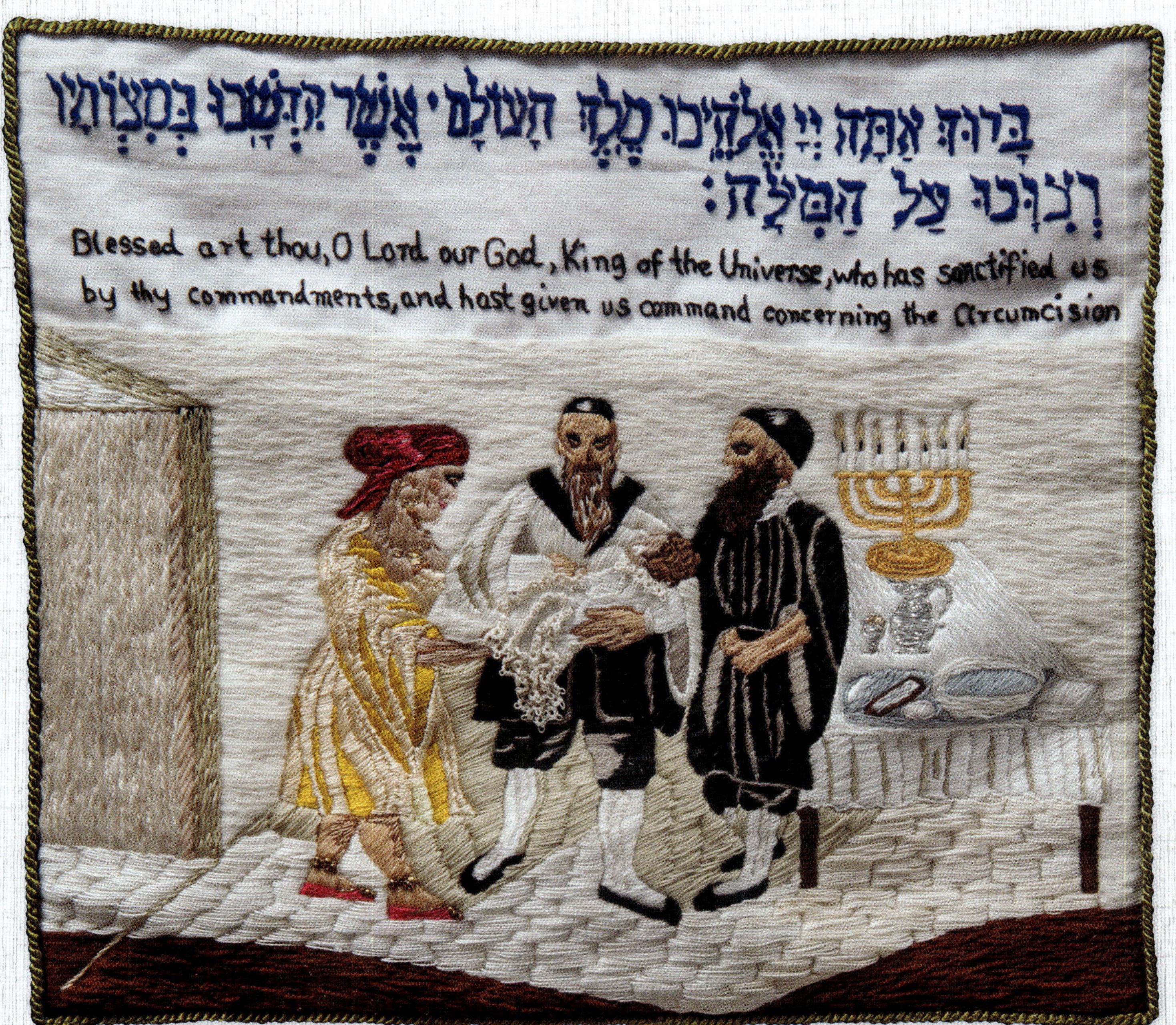

PANEL SEVEN: ***Circumcision***

PANEL EIGHT

Bar mitzvah is a Hebrew term meaning "son of the commandment." It is the moment a Jewish boy becomes a man and is henceforth duty-bound to observe the commandments of Judaism. It is thus one of the most universally celebrated events in Jewish life. Panel Eight depicts a traditional bar mitzvah. Trudie is having fun with this panel. The clapping hands invoke music and the feet communicate movement. The boy is about to read the "Haftarah." The other participants in the ceremony are dressed in full-length tunics, cloaks, and antiquated Jewish hats from another time and place, as if to say that this is a timeless ceremony, a ceremony pivotal to all Jewish life throughout all of history. An Ashkenazi Torah case with gold detail and silver *rimonim*[17] ornament the precious roller handles of Torah scrolls.

---

17 Torah filials or ornaments. Torah *rimonim* adorn both Sephardic Torah cases that house the Torah scrolls and the handles of the Torah rollers of Ashkenazic Torah scrolls. Often made of sterling silver and/or gold, *rimonim* can be simple or stunningly extravagant.

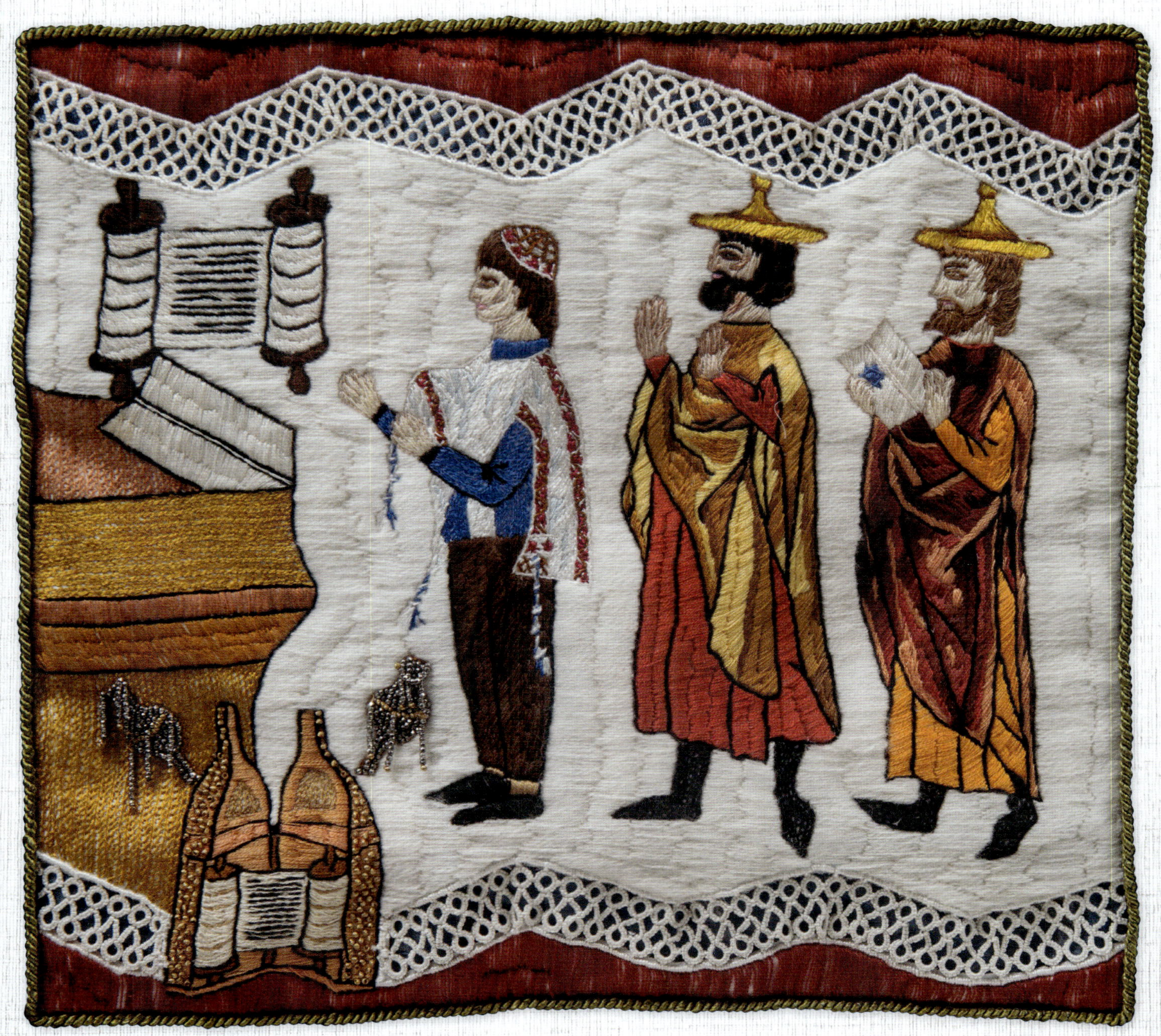

PANEL EIGHT: ***Bar Mitzvah***

PANEL NINE

Dedicated to her mother, whom Trudie interestingly refers to by her maiden name, Gansky, Panel Nine celebrates the observance of the Sabbath, the weekly foundational observance of Jews around the world. The Sabbath is frequently mentioned in the Bible, and specifically commanded in the Ten Commandments: "Remember the Sabbath day to keep it holy. Six days shalt thou labor and do all thy work, but the seventh day is the Sabbath of the Lord thy God." The powder-blue table appears to float in a cloud of tradition and comfort, untethered, its hint of a heart shape offering challah and grapes. The table is set with fine silver and the lit Sabbath candles send warm light. Pomegranates representing abundance, fertility, and life frame the scene in a kinetic vine of plenty.

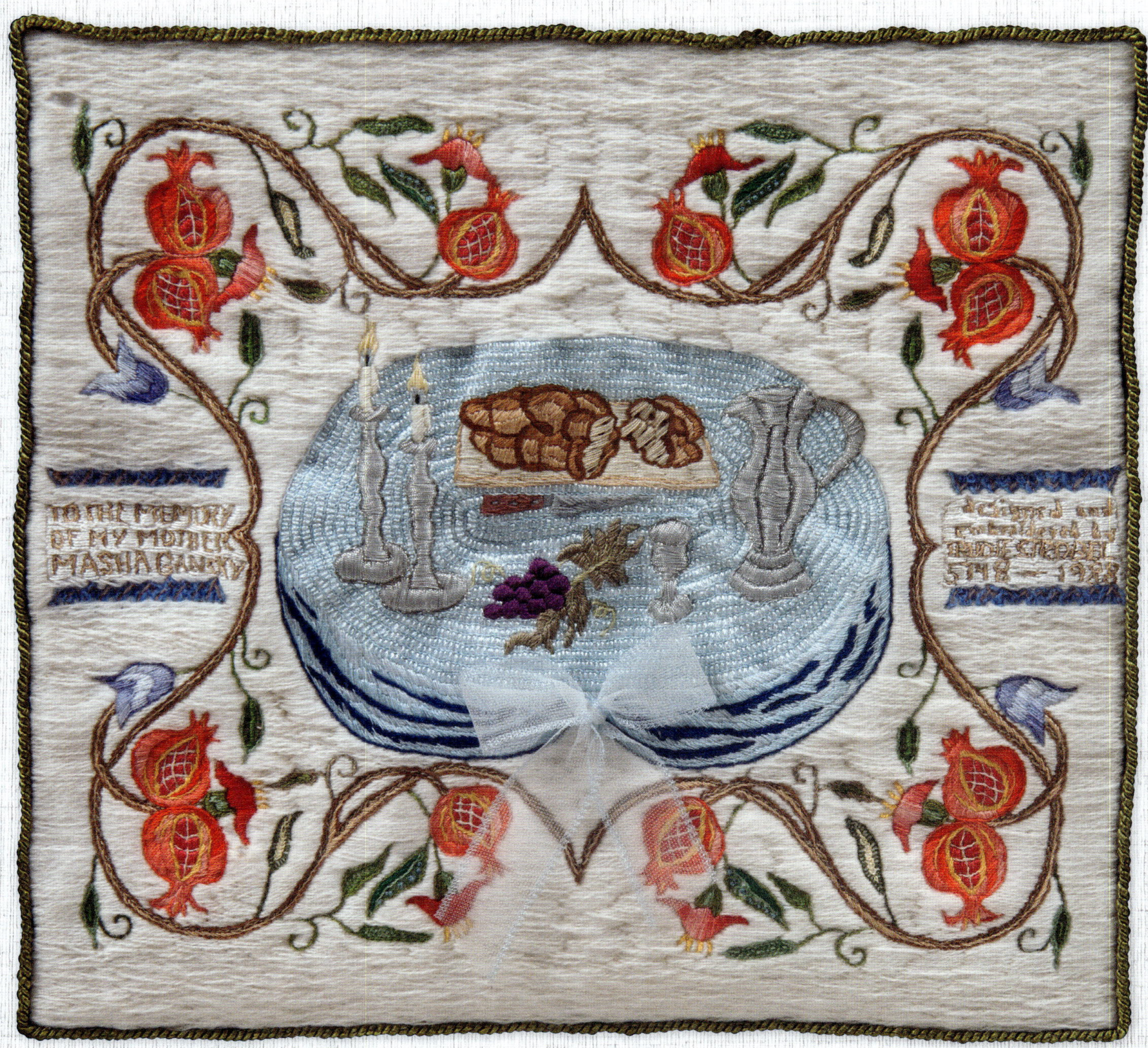

PANEL NINE: ***Sabbath***

PANEL TEN

Jewish tradition regards marriage as a sacred undertaking; accordingly, the Hebrew term for wedlock is *kiddushin*, which means sanctification. Jewish marriage customs, passed down from ancient ancestors, continue to be observed today. In Panel Ten, "Marriage," Trudie stitched two colorful pillars, Jachin and Boaz,[18] which are complementary but distinct. They represent the stability of the Jewish heritage; the connection at the base is embroidered in the Yemenite technique, which Trudie resurrected from the past. The marriage belt represents a gift exchange, a custom from Talmudic times. Traditionally Jewish marriages are solemnized under the open skies, and the chuppah is the dedicated enclosure for groom and bride, symbolizing the new home they will make together. The marriage is consecrated by a sip from a cup of wine by both bride and groom, thus the glittering cup of wine, stitched in gold and silver thread, is framed in a star of roses that rises above the flowing chuppah.

---

18 "And he reared up the pillars before the temple, one on the right hand, and the other on the left; and called the name of that on the right hand Jachin, and the name of that on the left Boaz." (II Chron. 17.) The two fabulous pillars are said to have stood on either side of the entrance to Solomon's Temple, the first temple in Jerusalem. *Jachin*, in Hebrew, means: He that strengthens; firm, stable, upright. The word *boaz* (or *baaz*) means strength, power, might, refuge, source of strength, fort.

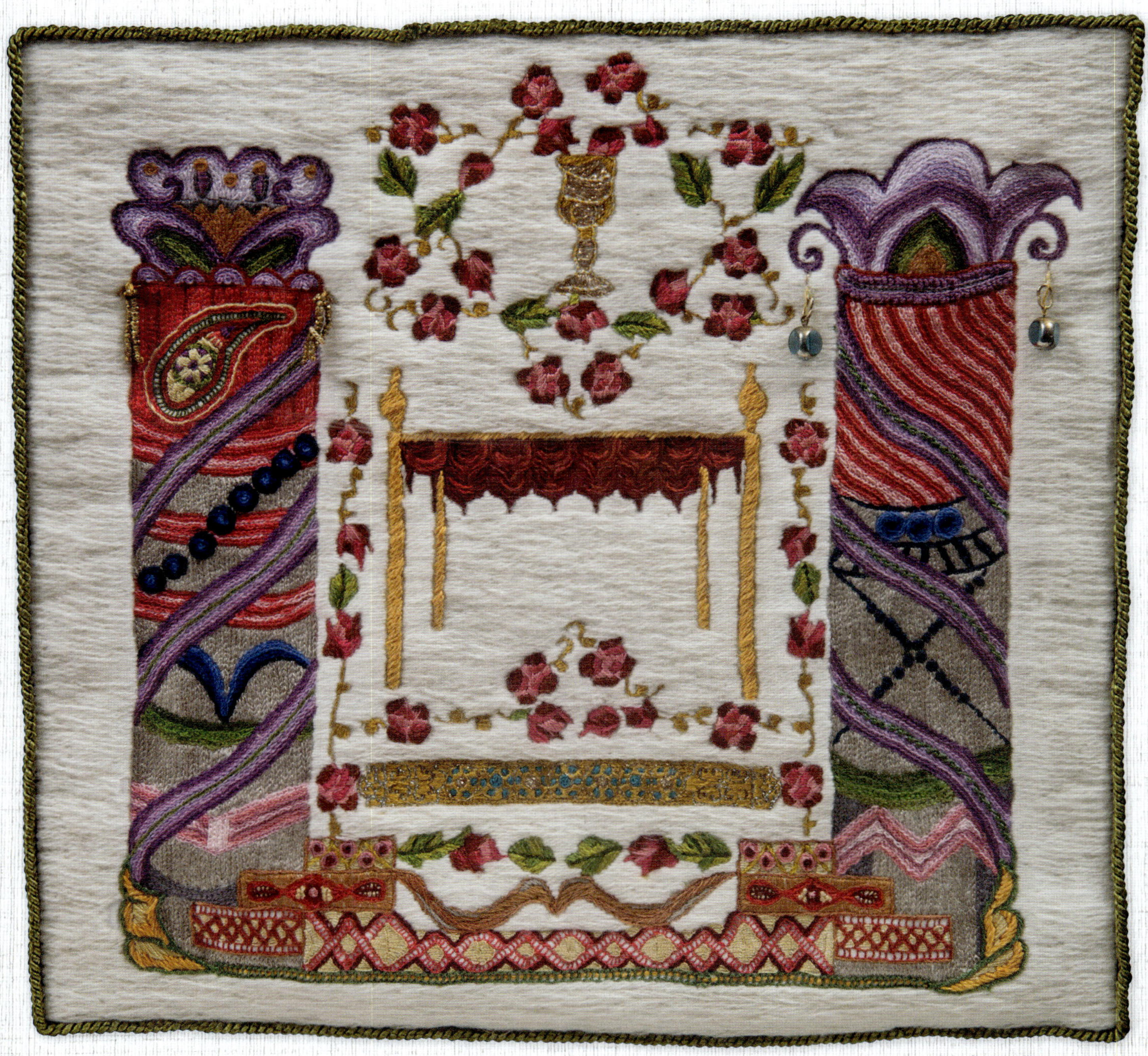

PANEL TEN: ***Marriage***

PANEL ELEVEN

Yom Kippur is the Jewish Day of Atonement, the holiest and most solemn day of the year. It falls on the tenth day of Tishre and marks the culmination of the ten penitential days that begin on Rosh Hashanah or New Year. The all-day services of Yom Kippur are concluded with the sounding of one blast of the shofar, or ram's horn. In Panel Eleven, "Yom Kippur," a rabbi blows the shofar on the highest of holy days. This veritable painting in thread communicates the effort, the joy, and the sadness in the complex facial expression of this temple leader. His flowing robes again convey a kinetic sense of life, heralding the joy of devotion of a race of people who persevered and survived.

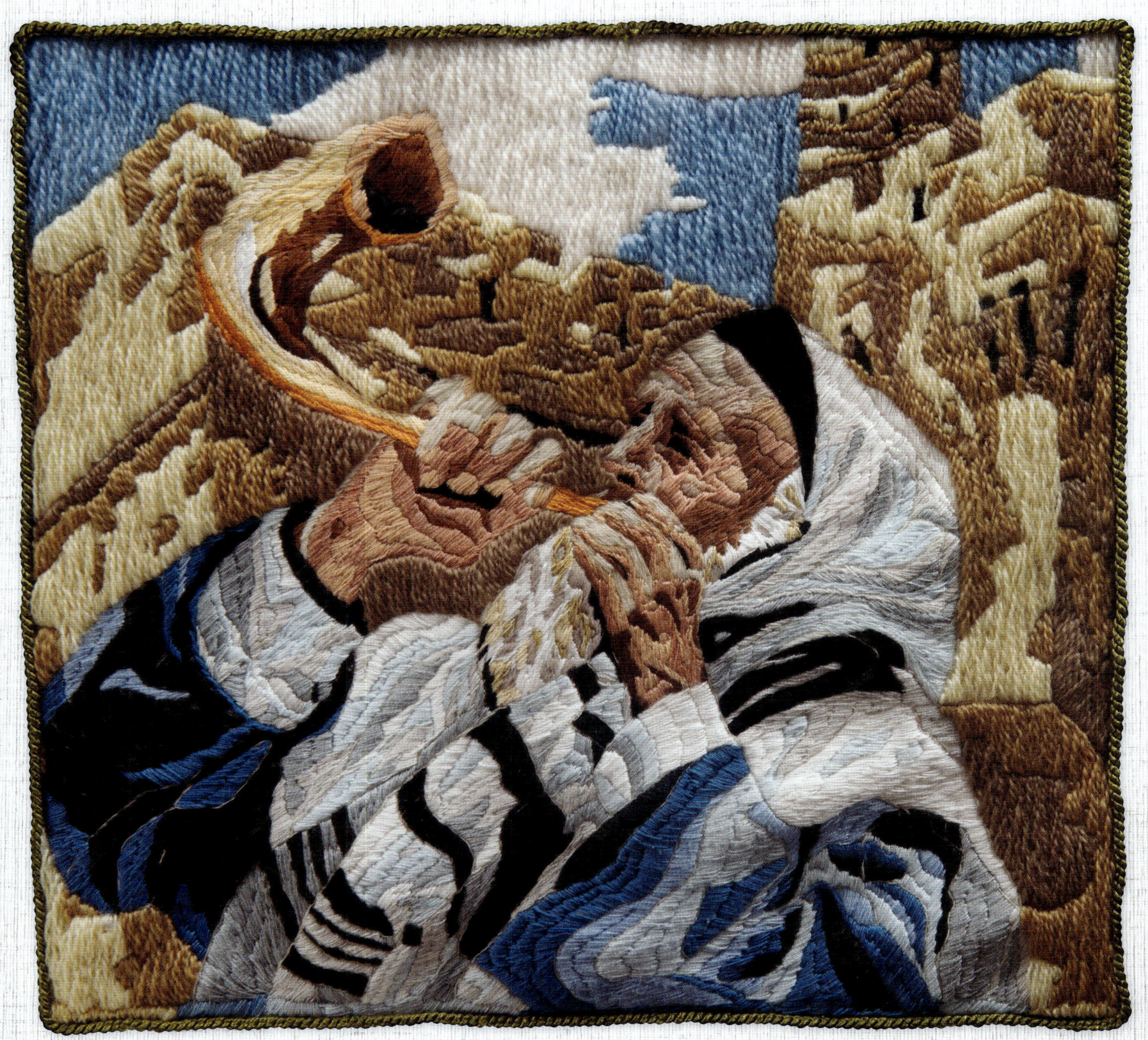

PANEL ELEVEN: ***Yom Kippur***

PANEL TWELVE

The final panel is fittingly titled "Funeral." It depicts a Jewish funeral in Italy in 1750 CE. As Trudie is always meticulous about compulsory wardrobe, the men in this panel wear the distinctive mark of red kerchiefs attached to their hats.

The rabbis teach that the self is the soul, not the body; the body will inevitably fail, but the soul is eternal. Early Jewish manuscripts associate the peacock with the human desire to fly free from the chains of mundane experience so as to reach spiritual heights. Hence, crowning this solemn scene, two magnificent peacocks preen decorously in blues and gold.

Taken together, the twelve panels that comprise "Moments in Jewish Time" represent an epic narrative of the Jewish people.

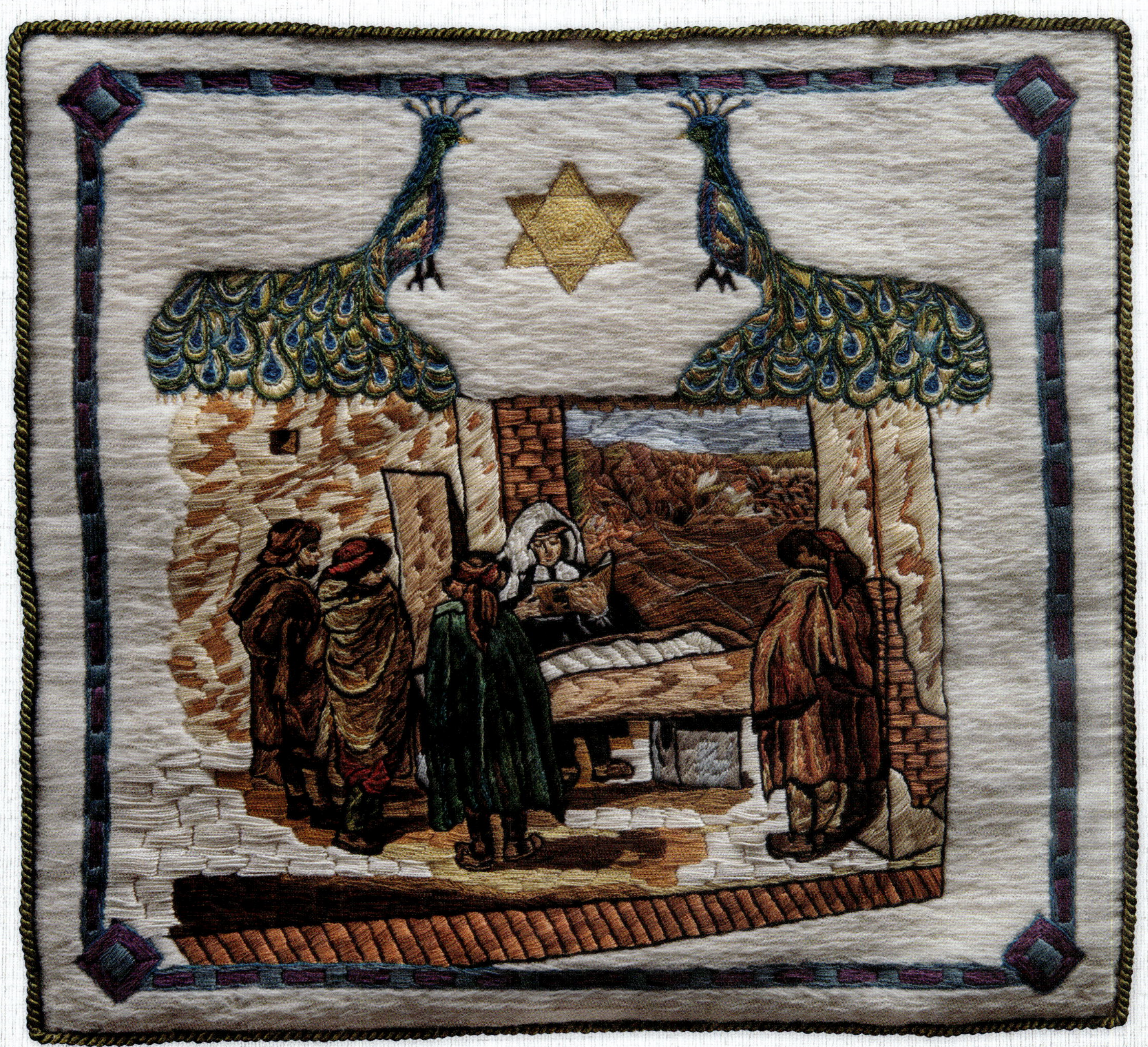

PANEL TWELVE: ***Funeral***

DISTINGUISHED JEWISH WOMEN OF ACHIEVEMENT

Trudie's second large-scale embroidery is called "Distinguished Jewish Women of Achievement." She selected the women depicted in this piece after much investigation and soul-searching. She studied such texts as H.E. Jacob's *The World of Emma Lazarus*; Edith Deen's *All of the Women of the Bible*; *Heroine of Rescue* by Friedenson and Kranzler; Trude Weiss Rosmarin's *Jewish Women Through the Ages*; *My Portion* by Rebekah Kohut; *Woman of Valor: The Life of Henrietta Szold 1860–1945* by Irving Fineman; *Rebecca Gratz: A Study in Charm* by Rollin G. Osterweis; *My Life* by Golda Meir; *Salon Sketches: Biographical Studies of Berlin Salons of the Emancipation* by Bertha Meyer; *Lillian Wald: The Nurse in Blue* by Sally Rogow; Mac Davis's *Jews at a Glance*, *They Are All Jews*, and *Jews Fight Too!*; Elma Ehrlich Levinger's *Great Jewish Women*; *Her Children Call Her Blessed* by Franz Kobler; and *The Szolds of Lombard Street* by Alexander Lee Levin.

Distinguished Jewish Women of Achievement · 1989
Read more about this work in Art Notes, page 178

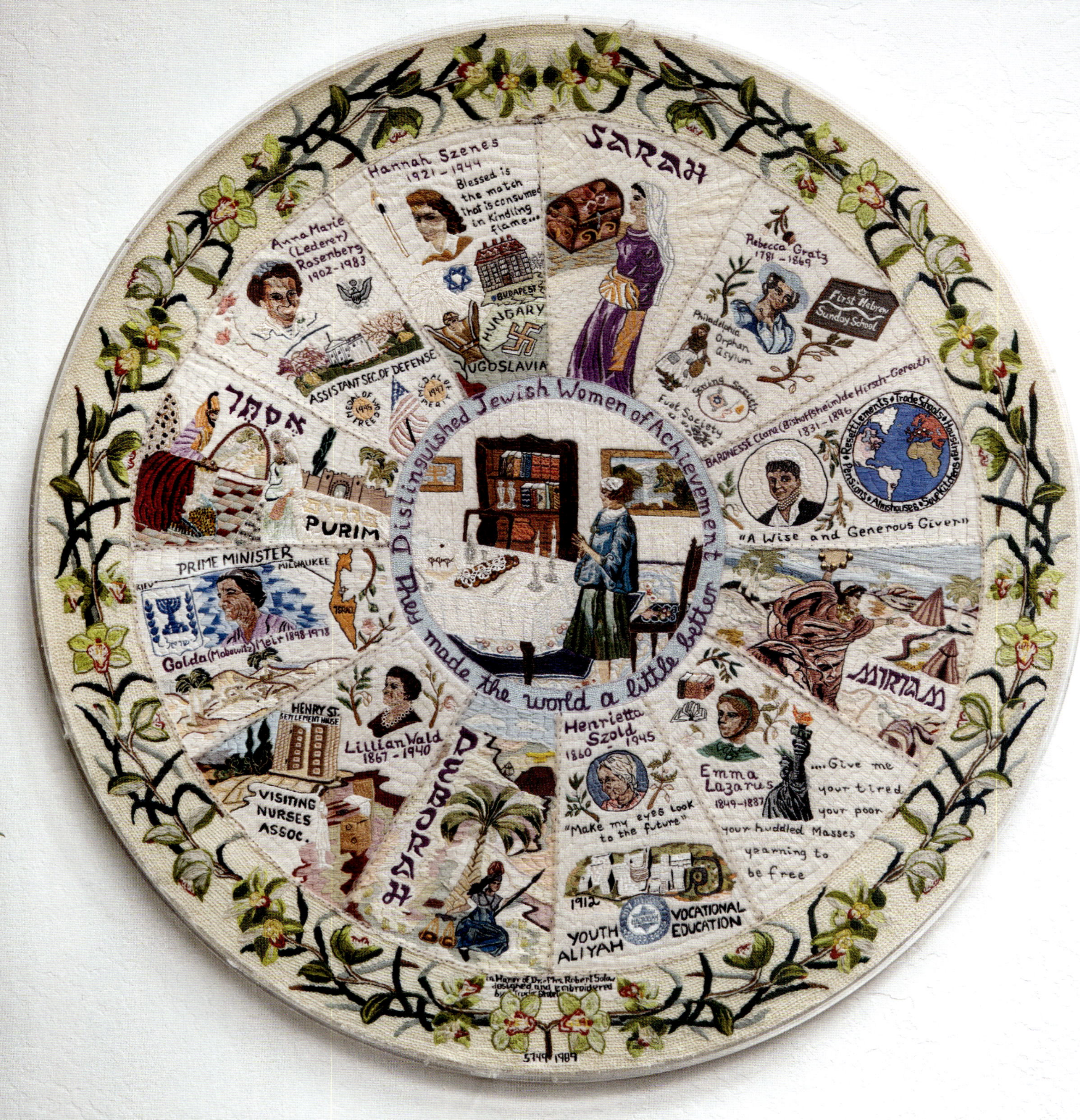
SARAH
Hannah Szenes
1921 - 1944
Blessed is the match that is consumed in kindling flame...
BUDAPEST
HUNGARY
YUGOSLAVIA
Anna Marie (Lederer) Rosenberg
1902 - 1983
ASSISTANT SEC. OF DEFENSE
Rebecca Gratz
1781 - 1869
First Hebrew Sunday School
Philadelphia Orphan Asylum
Sewing Society
Fuel Society
BARONESSE Clara (Bischoffsheim) de Hirsch-Gereuth
1831 - 1896
Resettlements • Trade Schools • Housing • Soup Kitchens • Almshouses • Pensions
"A Wise and Generous Giver"
The Distinguished Jewish Women of Achievement
They made the world a little better
אסתר
PURIM
PRIME MINISTER
MILWAUKEE
ISRAEL
Golda (Mabowitz) Meir 1898-1978
MIRIAM
HENRY ST. SETTLEMENT HOUSE
Lillian Wald
1867 - 1940
VISITING NURSES ASSOC.
DEBORAH
Henrietta Szold
1860 - 1945
"Make my eyes look to the future"
1912
YOUTH ALIYAH
VOCATIONAL EDUCATION
Emma Lazarus
1849 - 1887
...Give me your tired your poor your huddled masses yearning to be free
In Honor of Dr. & Mrs. Robert Solow
designed and embroidered
5749 1989

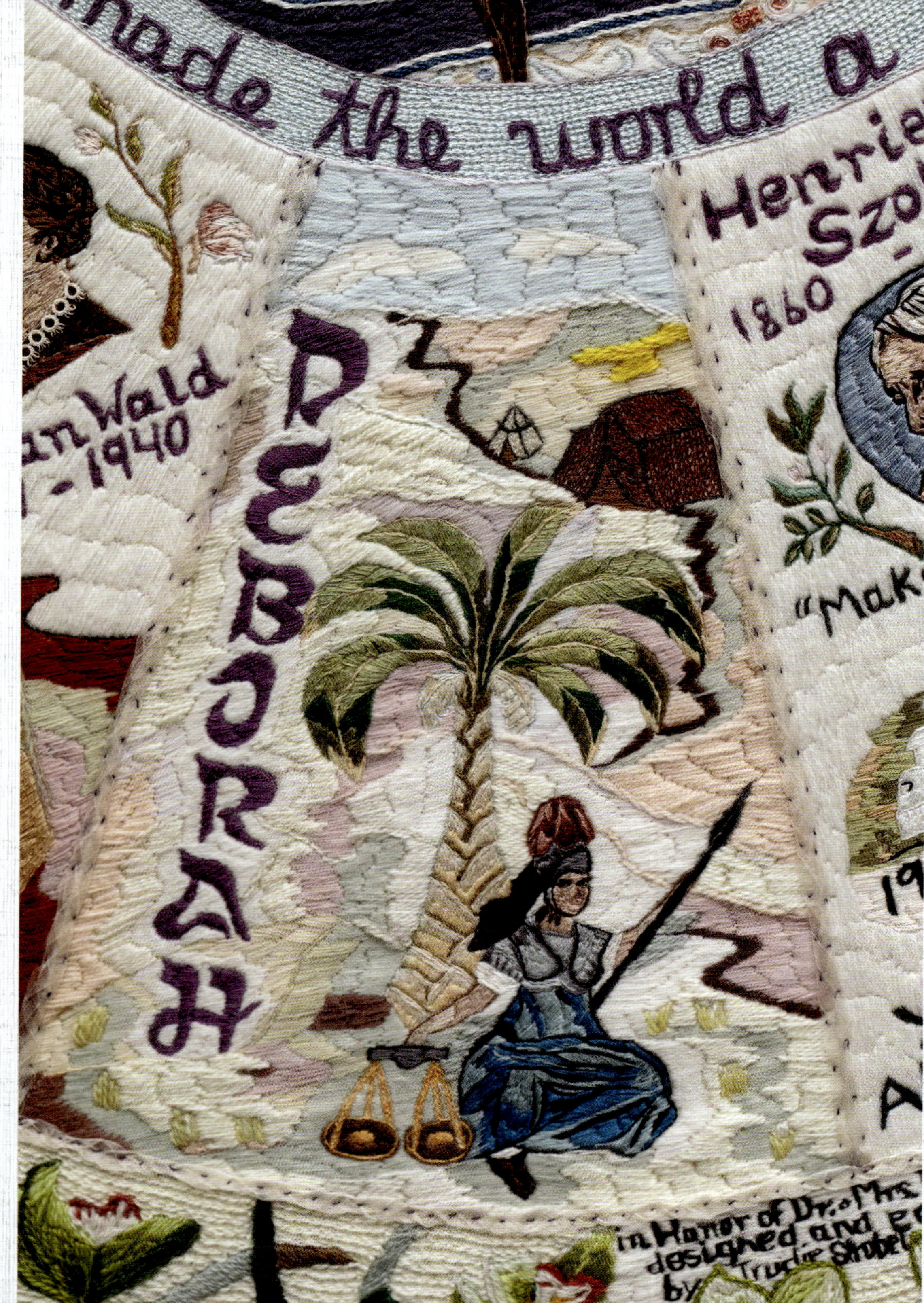

Detail of
Deborah

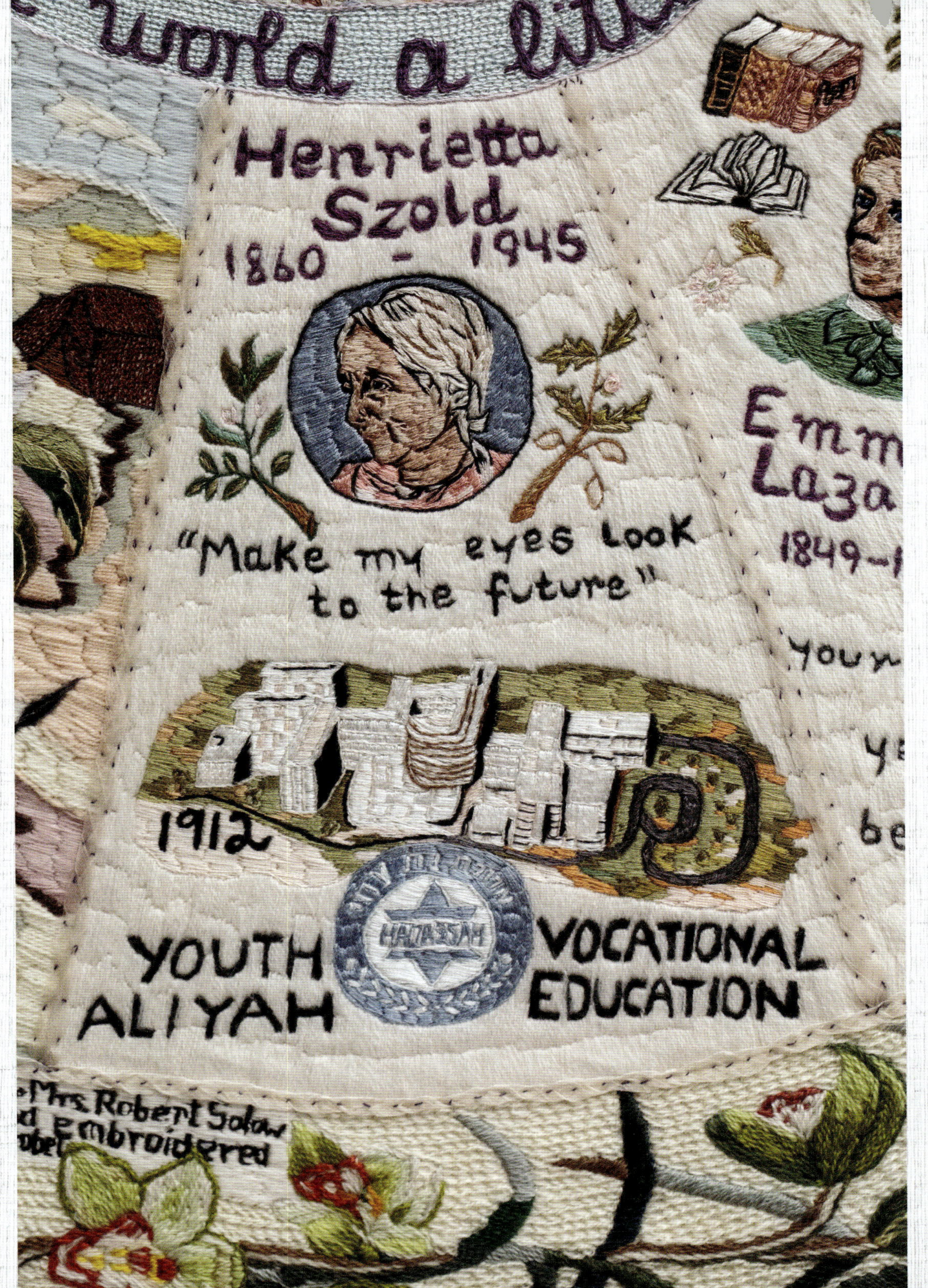

Detail of
Henrietta Szold

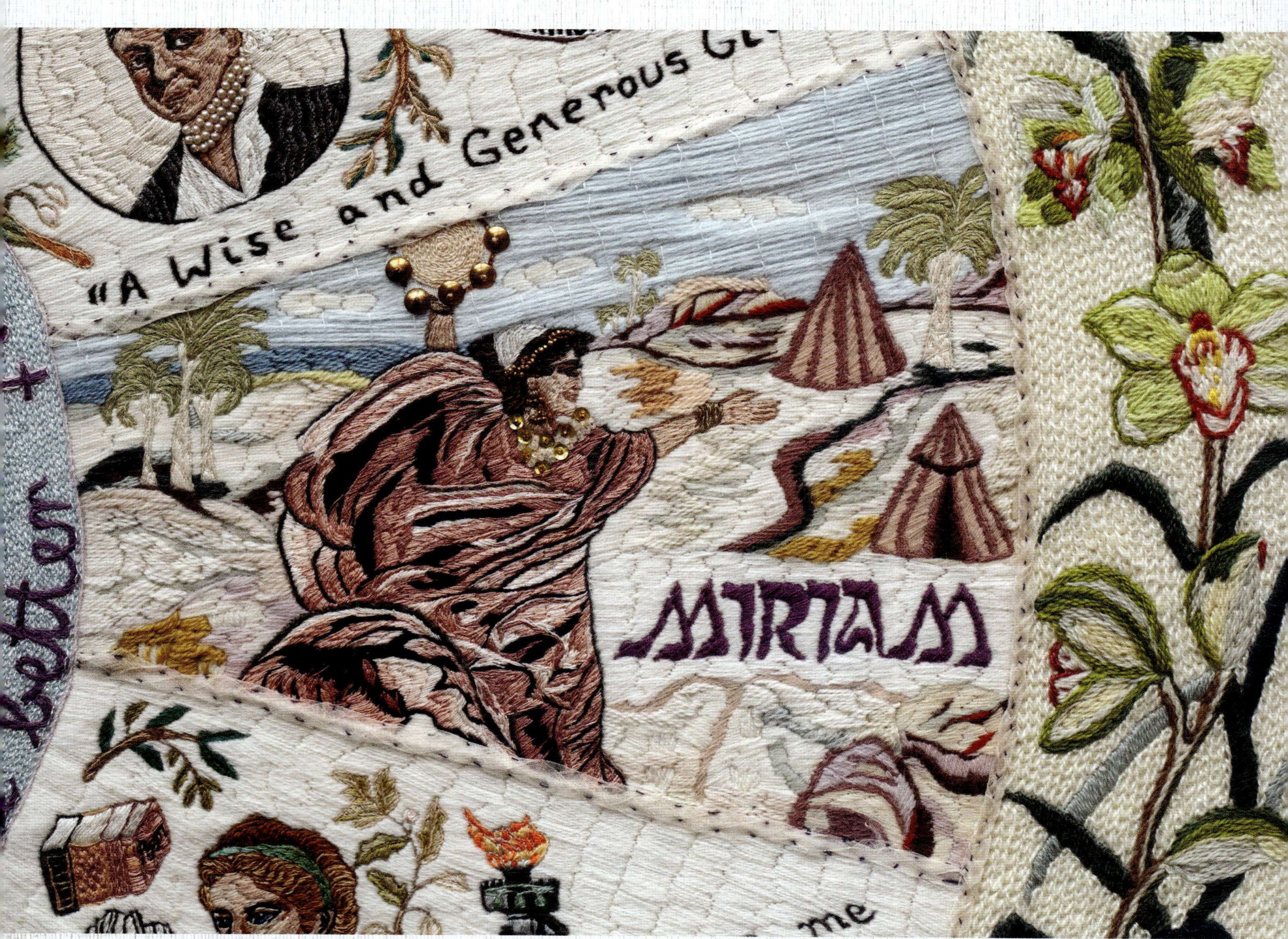

Detail of ***Miriam***

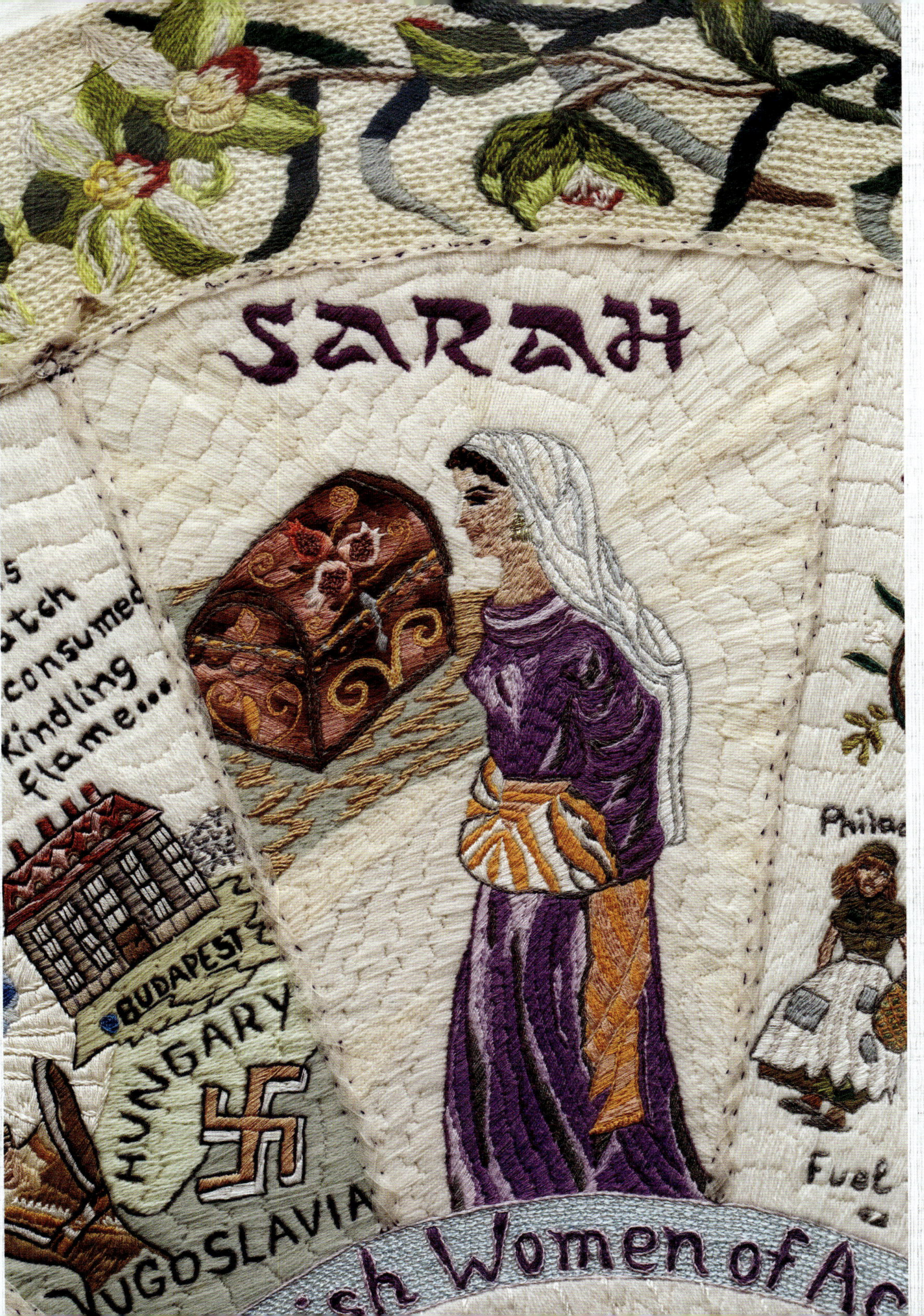

Detail of
Sarah

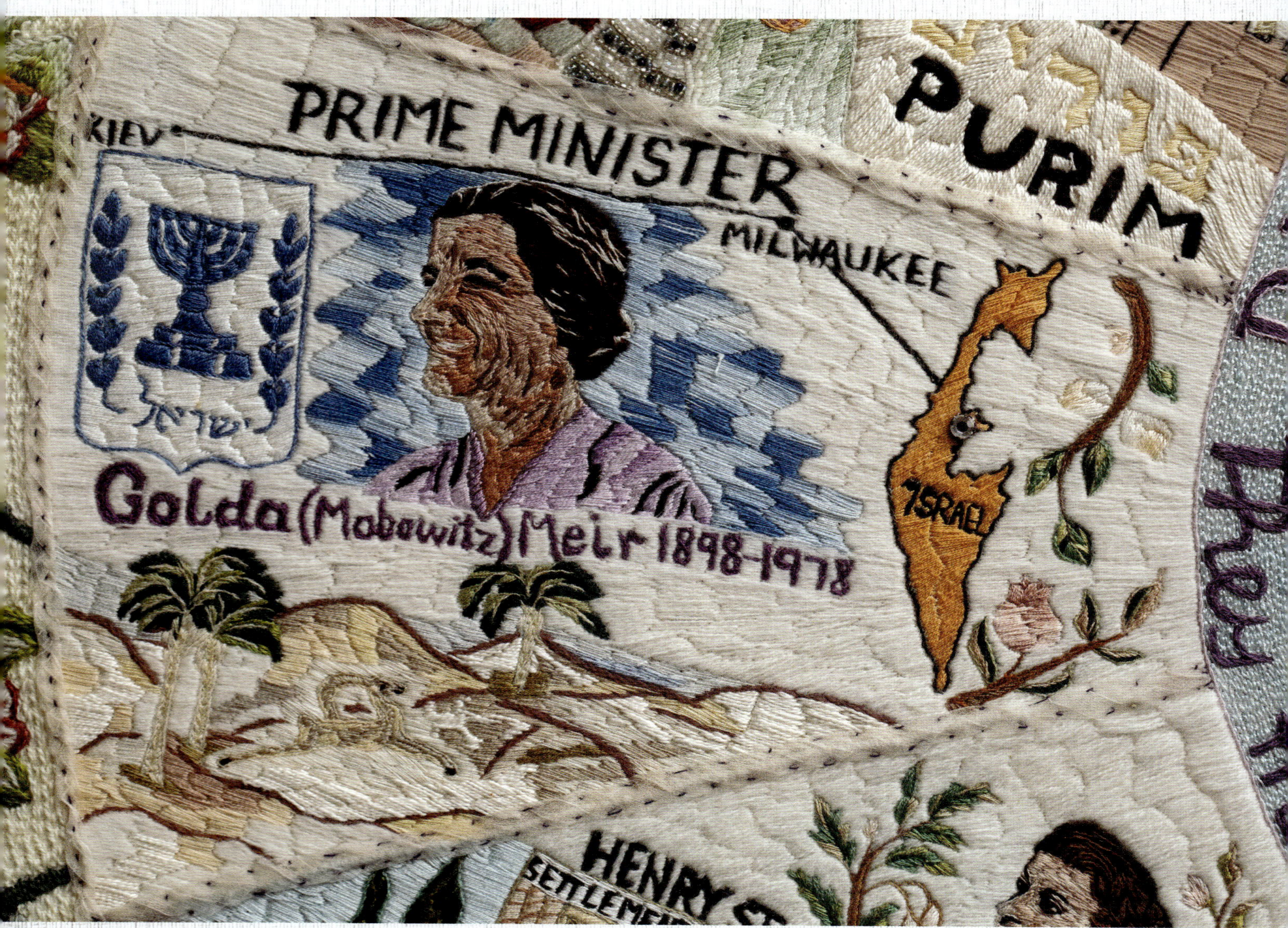

Detail of ***Golda Meir***

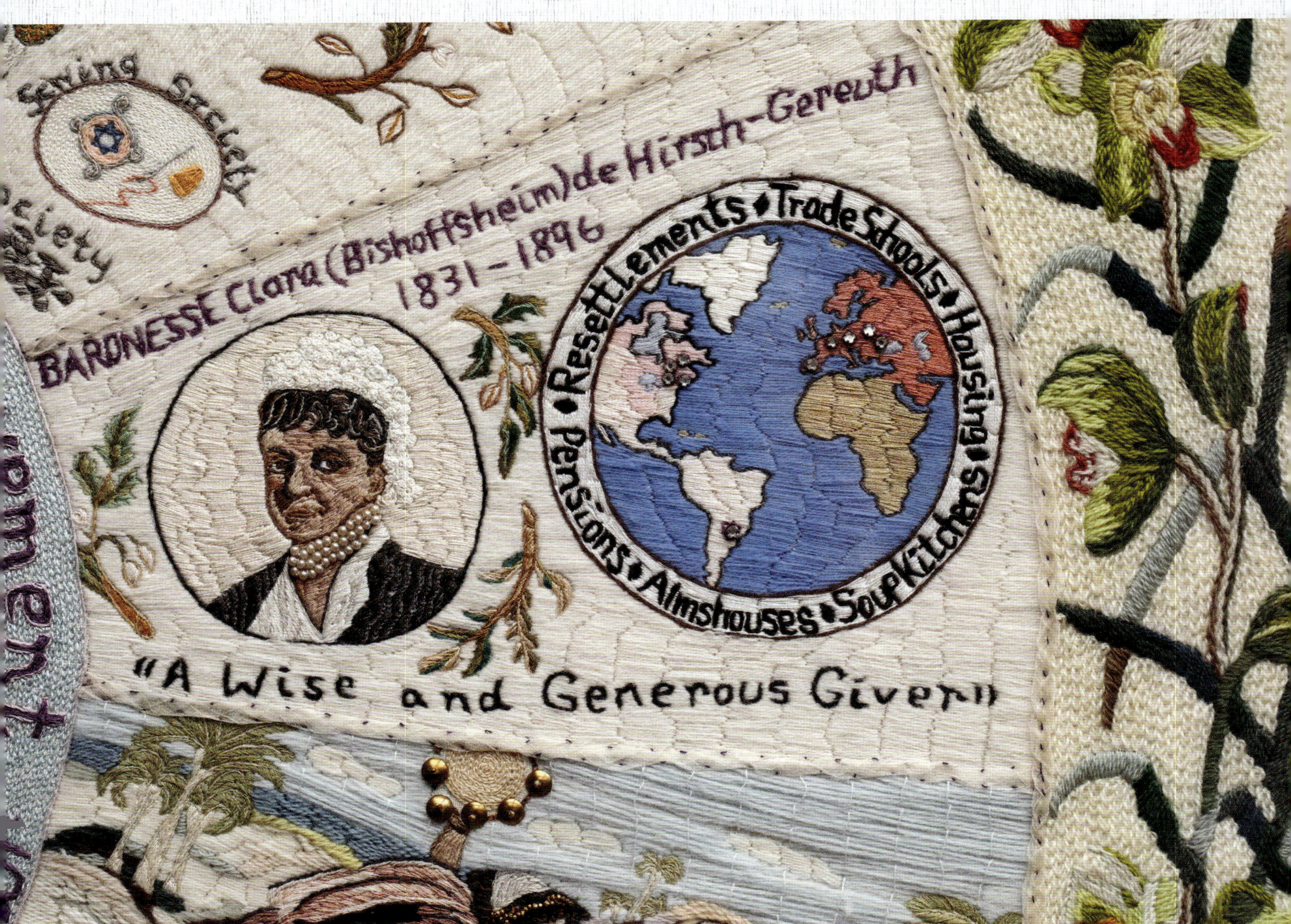

Detail of ***Baronesse Clara de Hirsch-Gereuth***

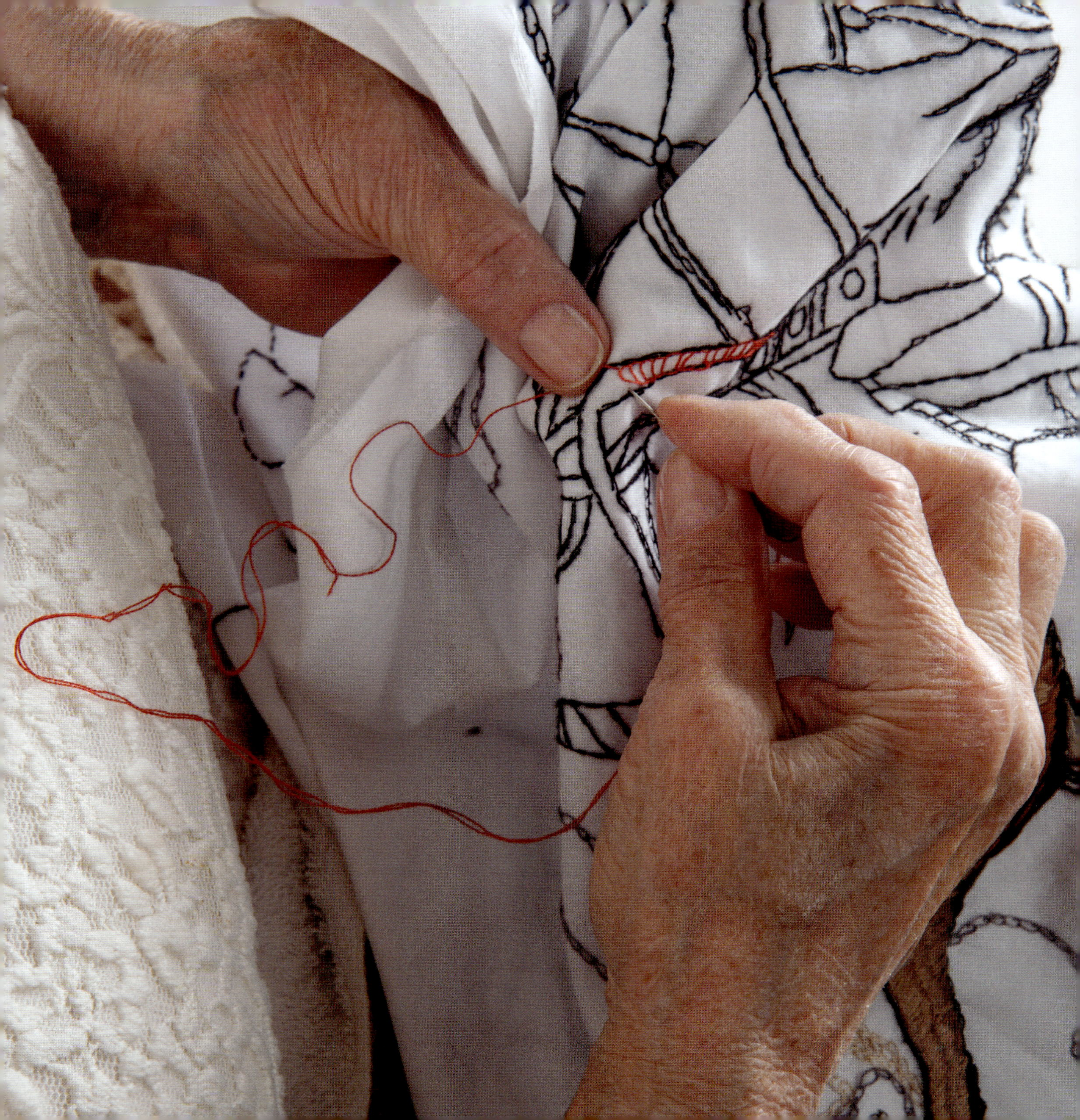

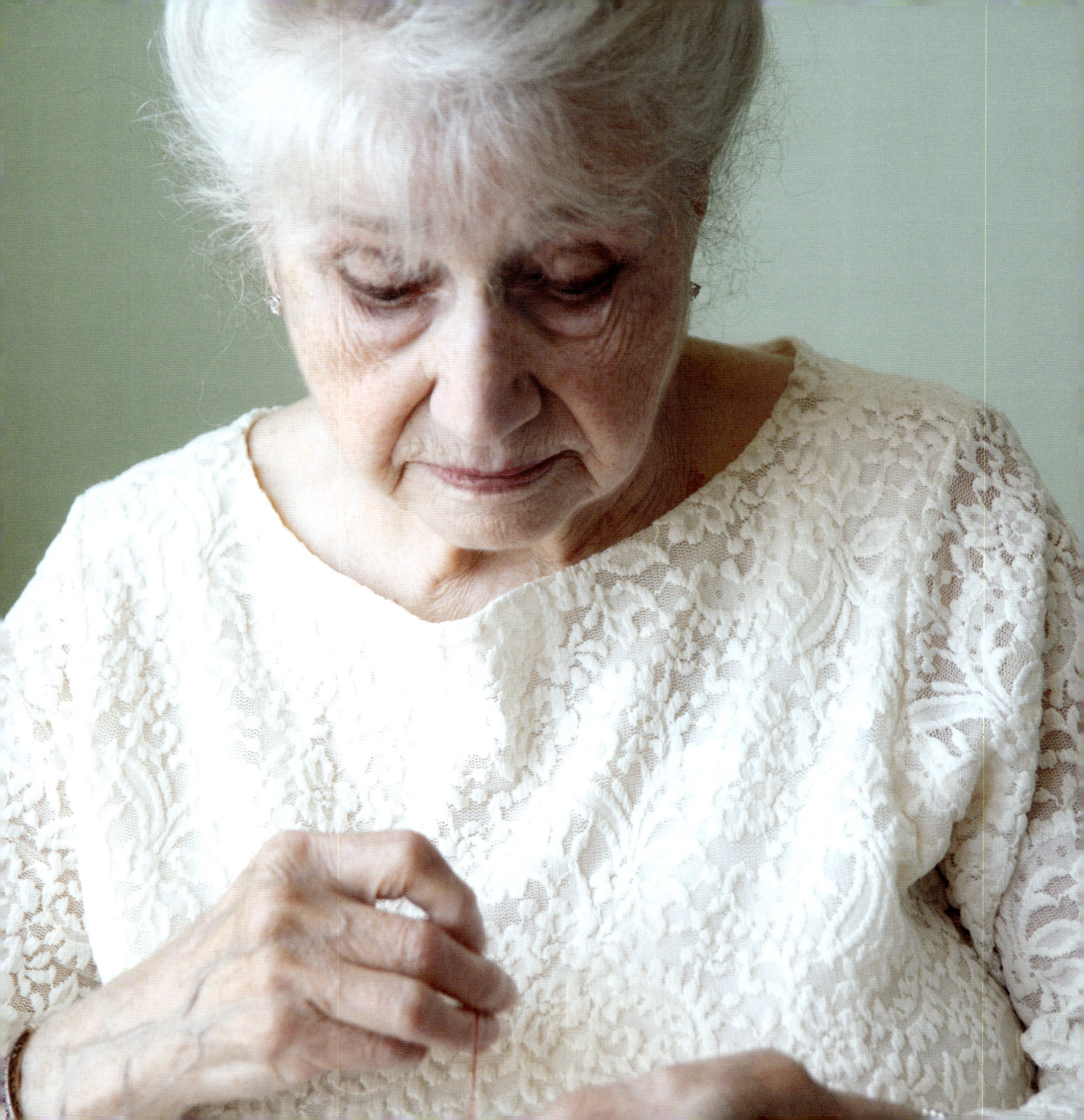

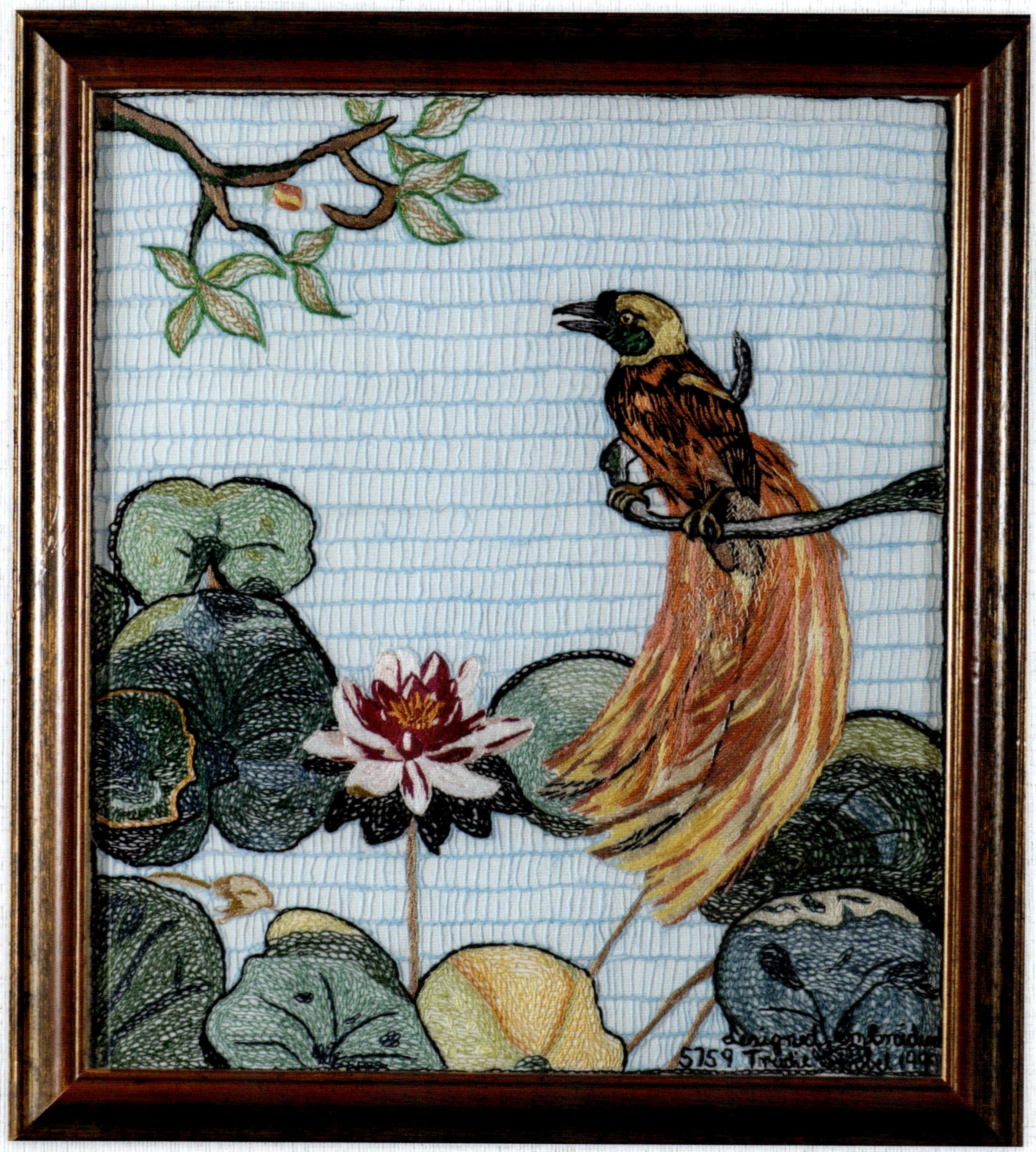

Bird of Paradise · 1999 · 12″ × 14″

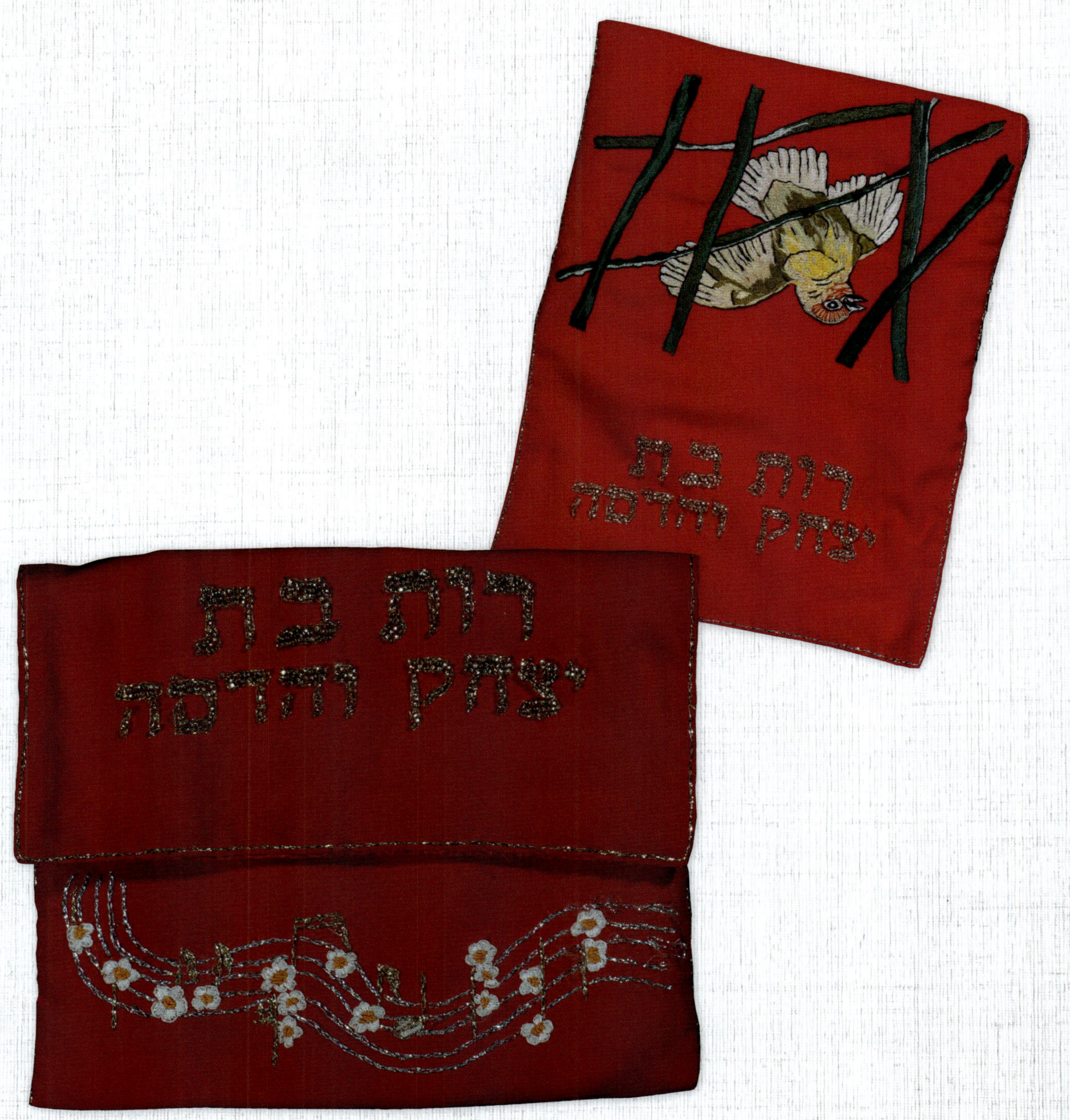

Cantor Ruth's tefillin bag · 2019

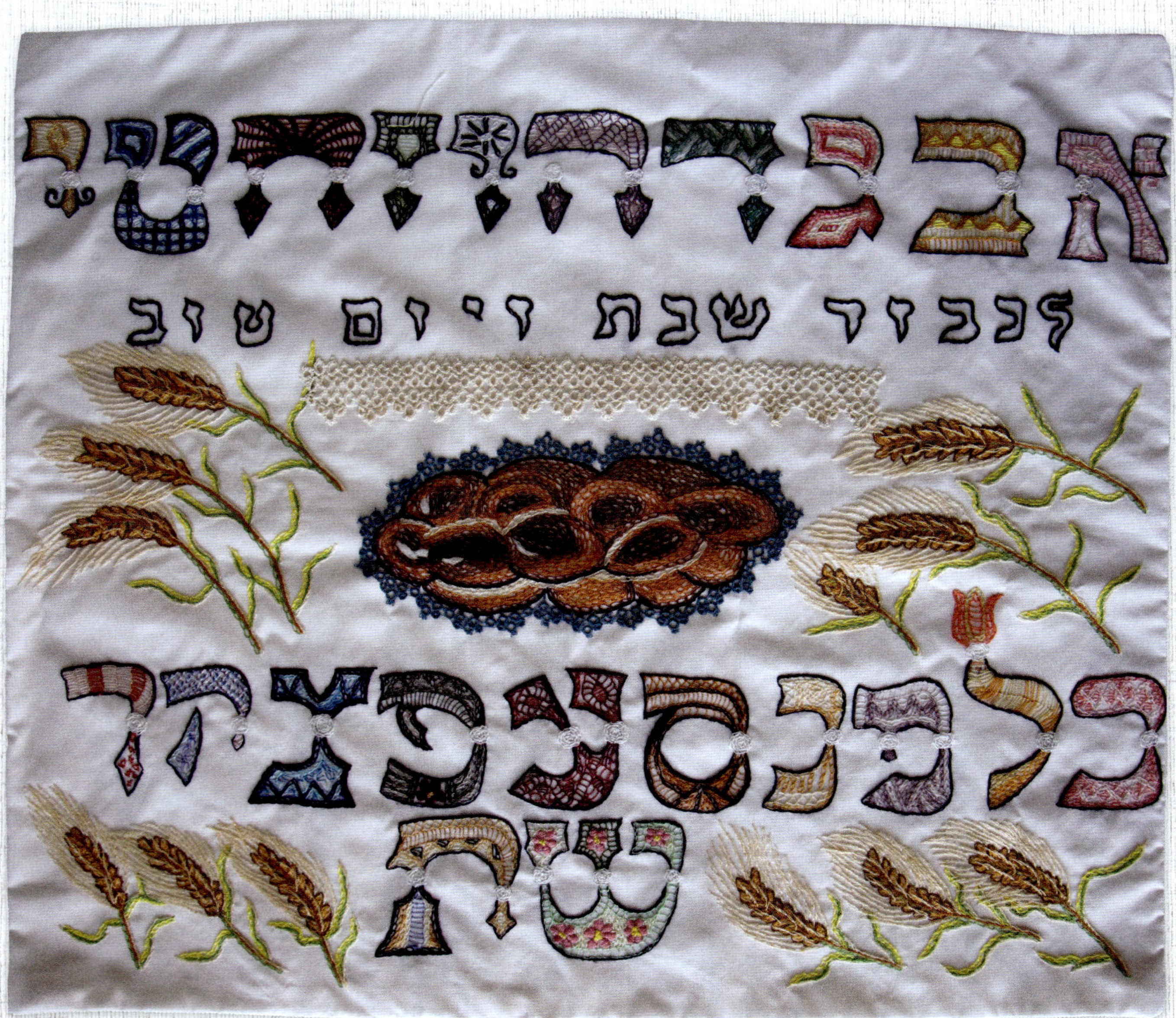

Challah cover · 2018 · 15″ × 19″

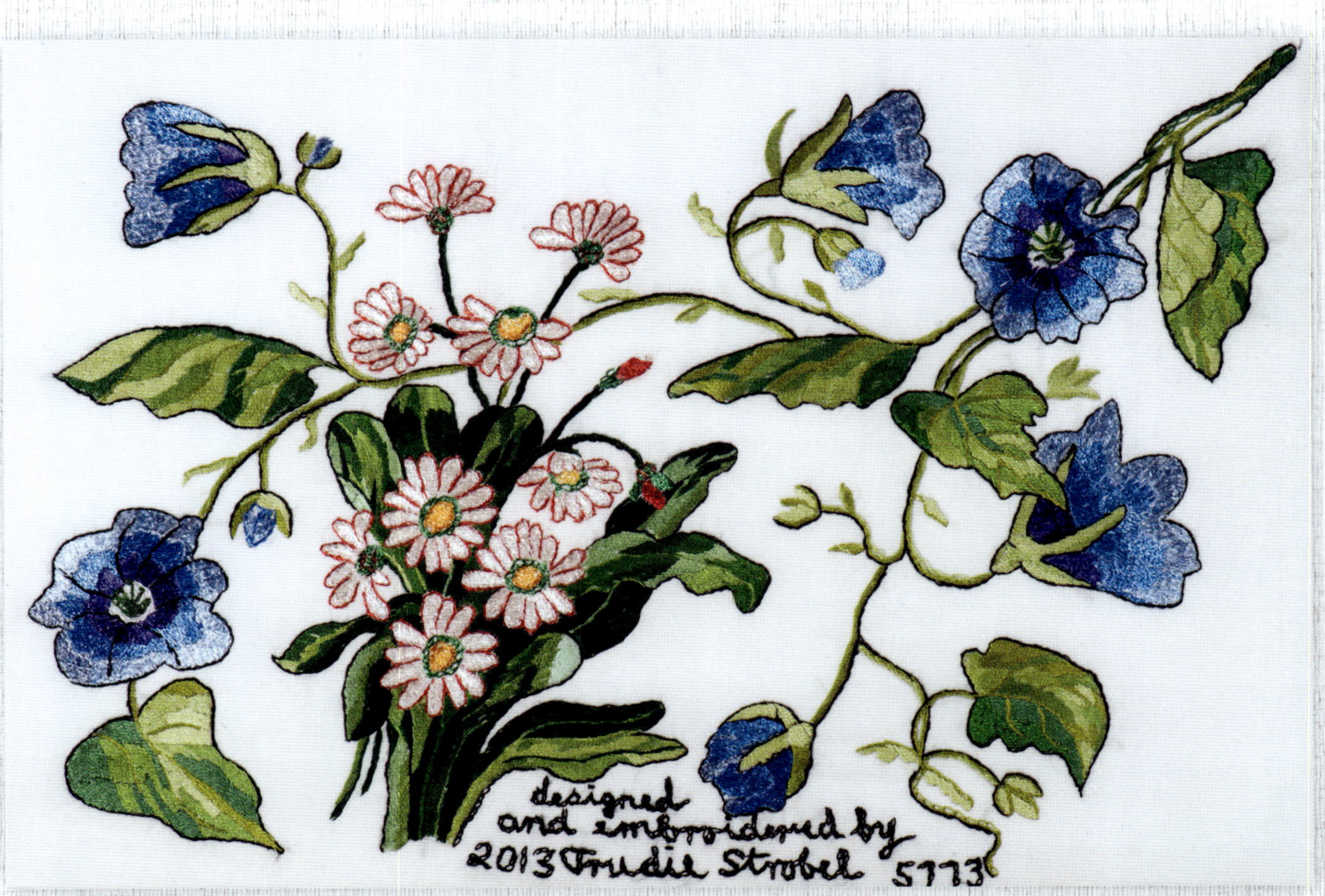

Morning Glories · 2013 · 11″ × 14″

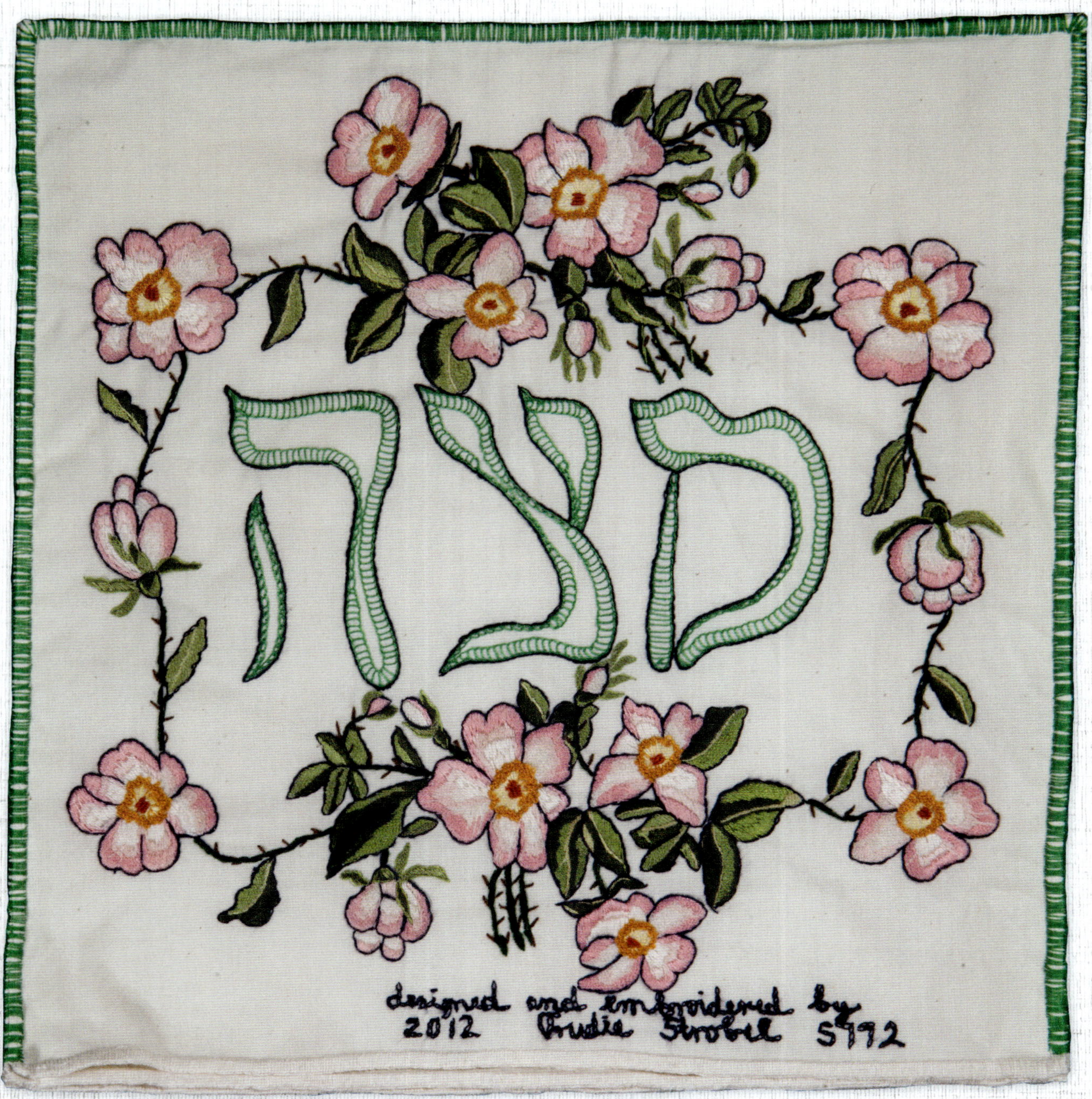

Matzoh cover · 2018 · 14″ × 14″

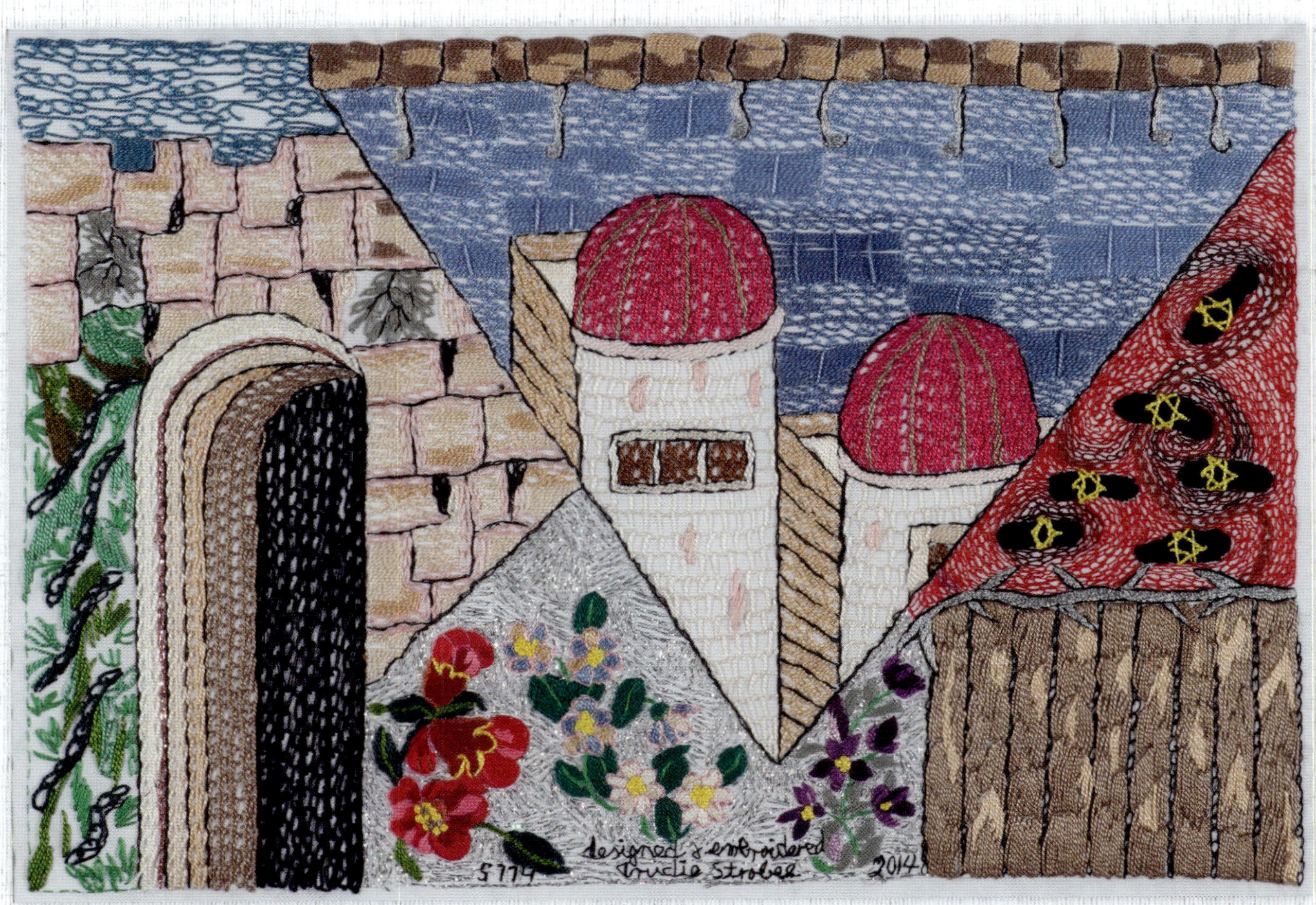

Gate of Jerusalem · 2014 · 12″ × 18″

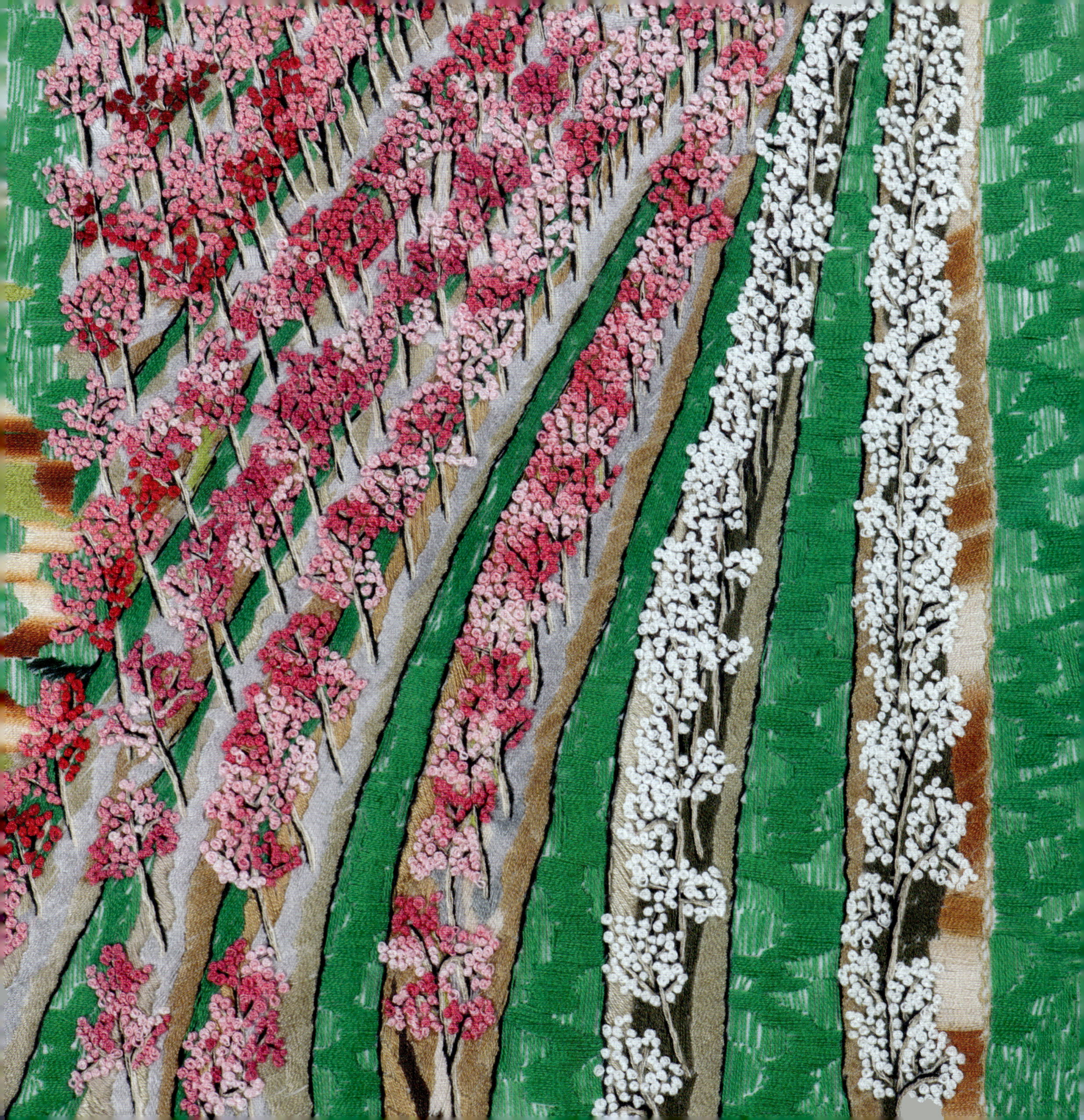

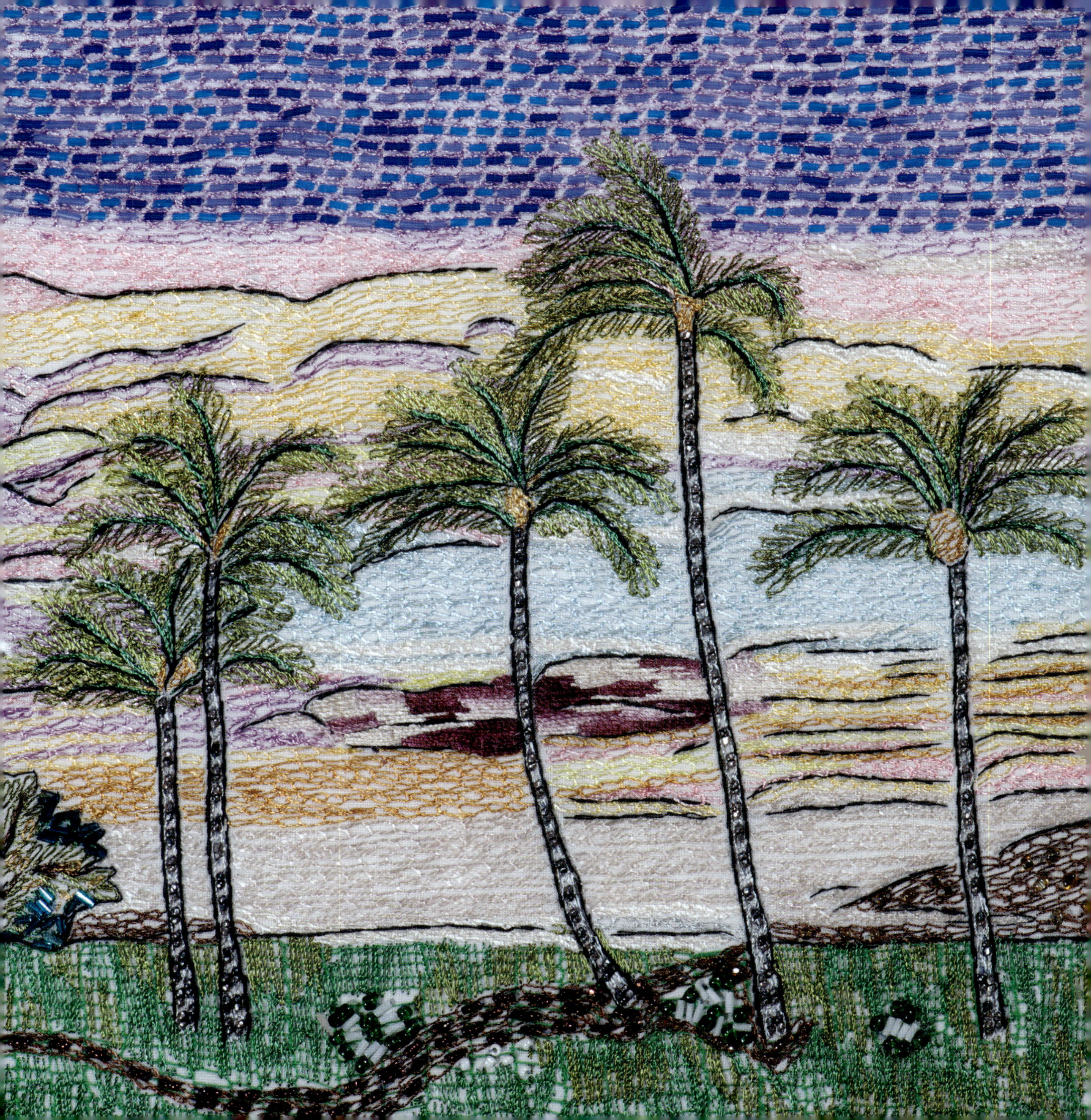

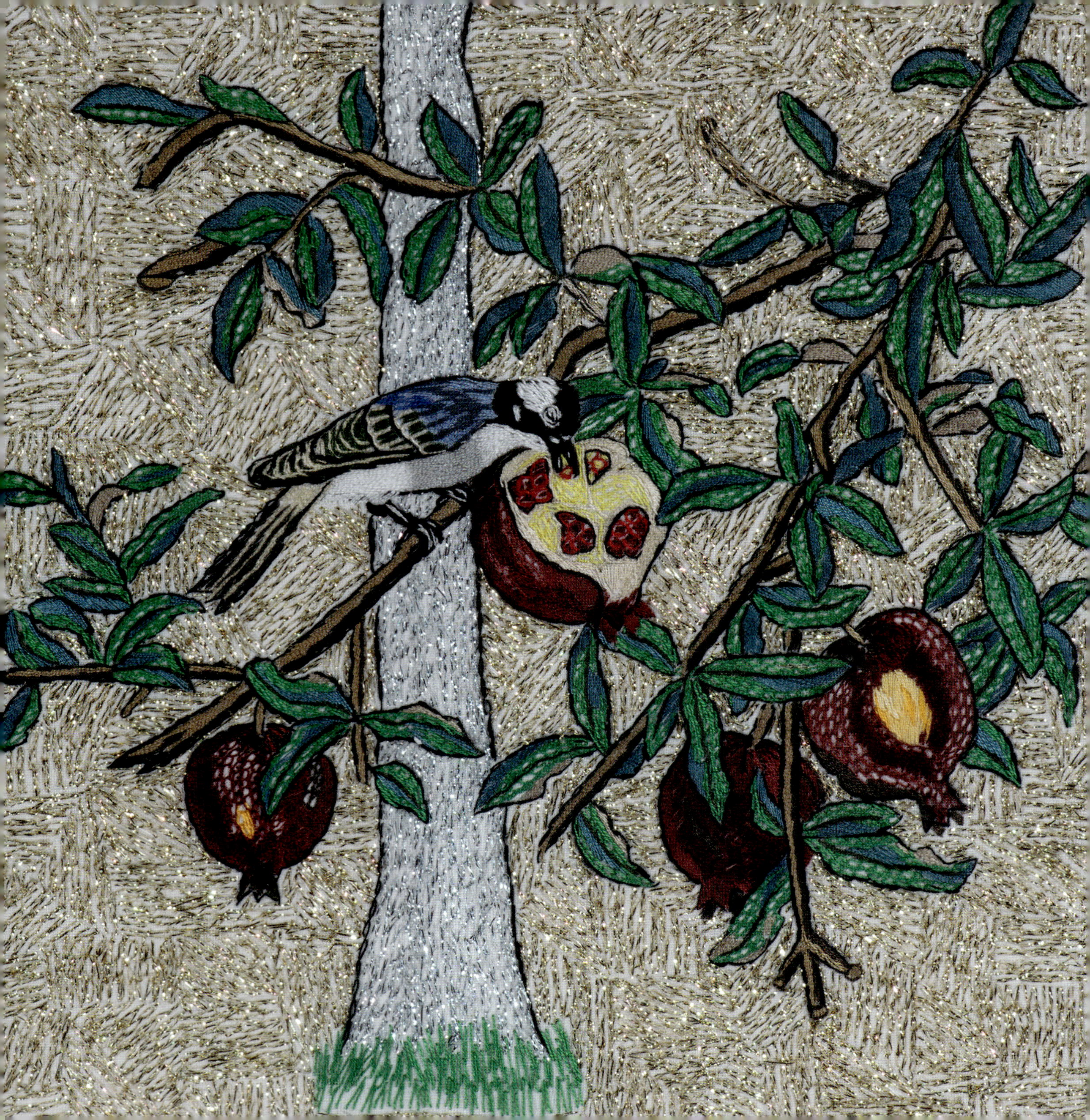

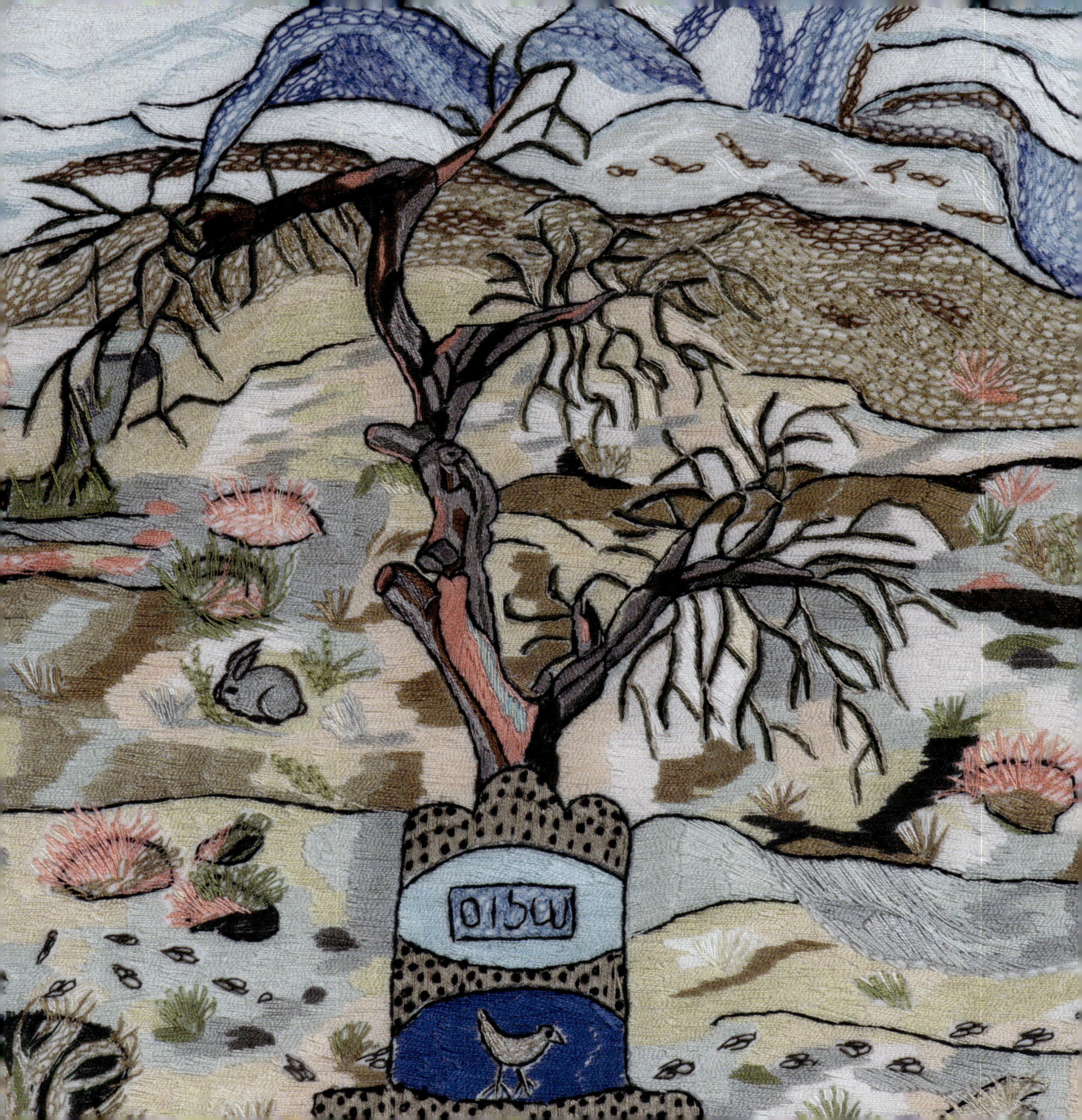

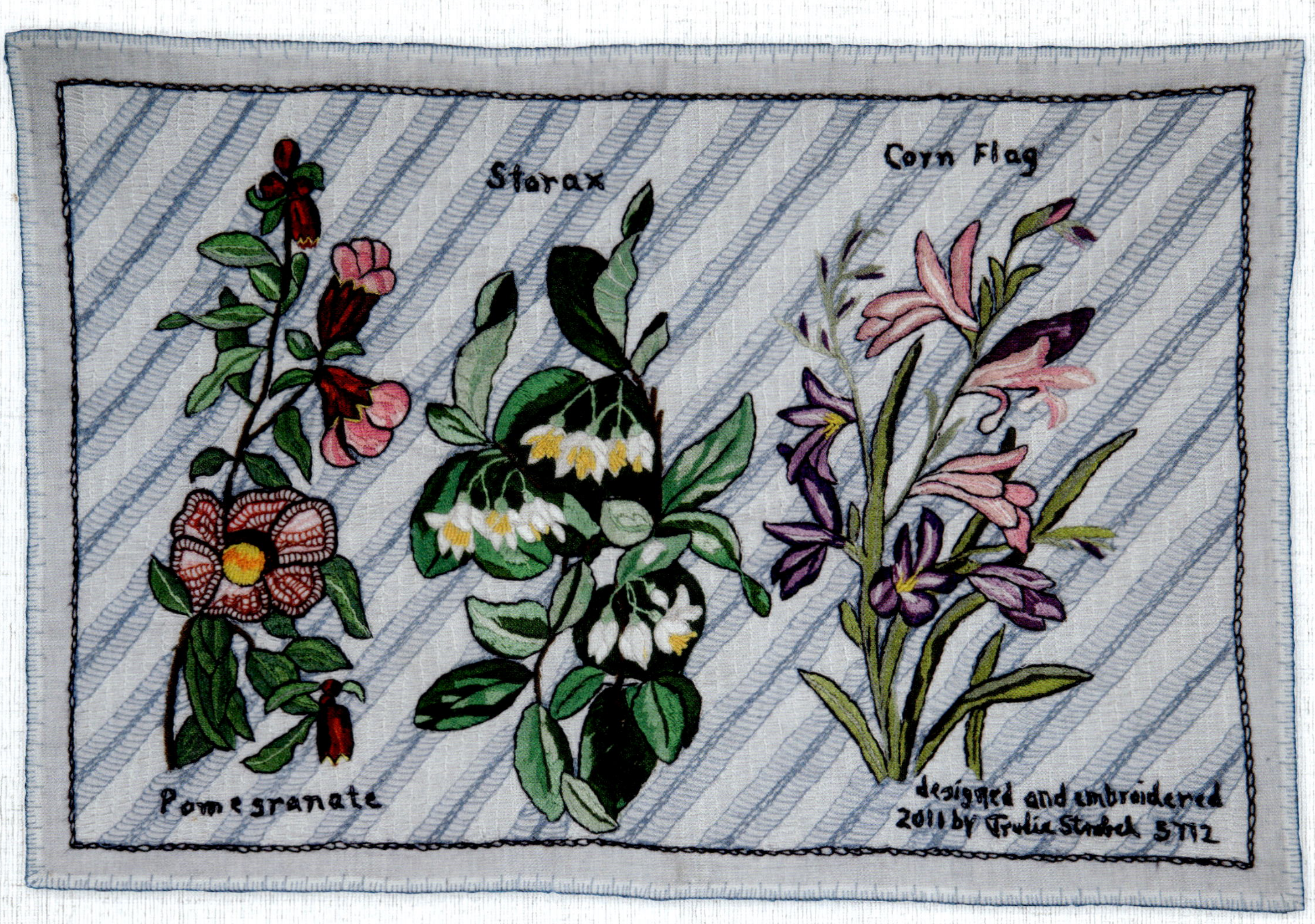

Above: ***Flowers*** · 2011 · 15″ × 19″
Page 150: ***Spring*** · Page 151: ***Summer*** · Page 152: ***Autumn*** · Page 153: ***Winter***

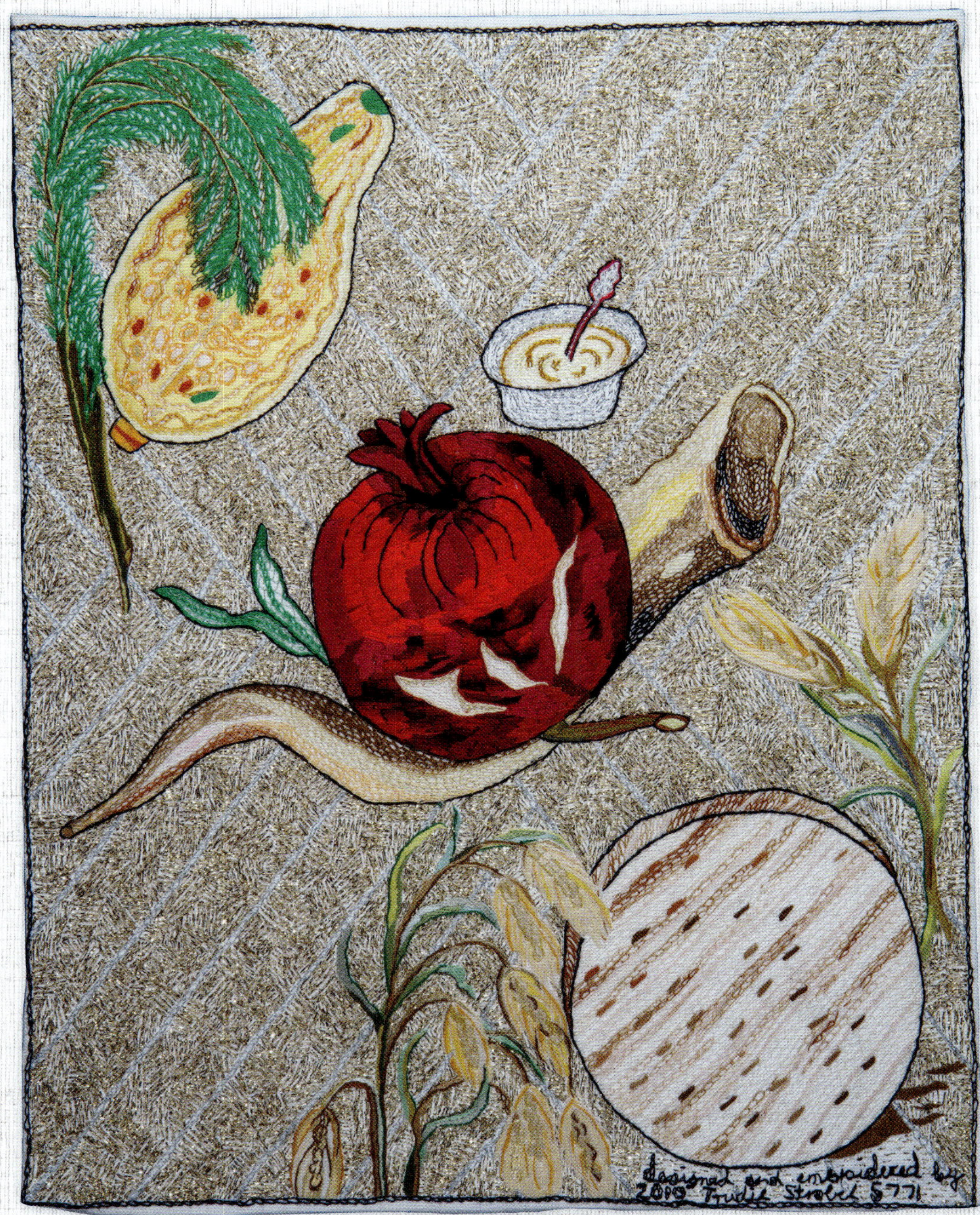

Three Holiday Symbols · 2010 · 17″ × 23″

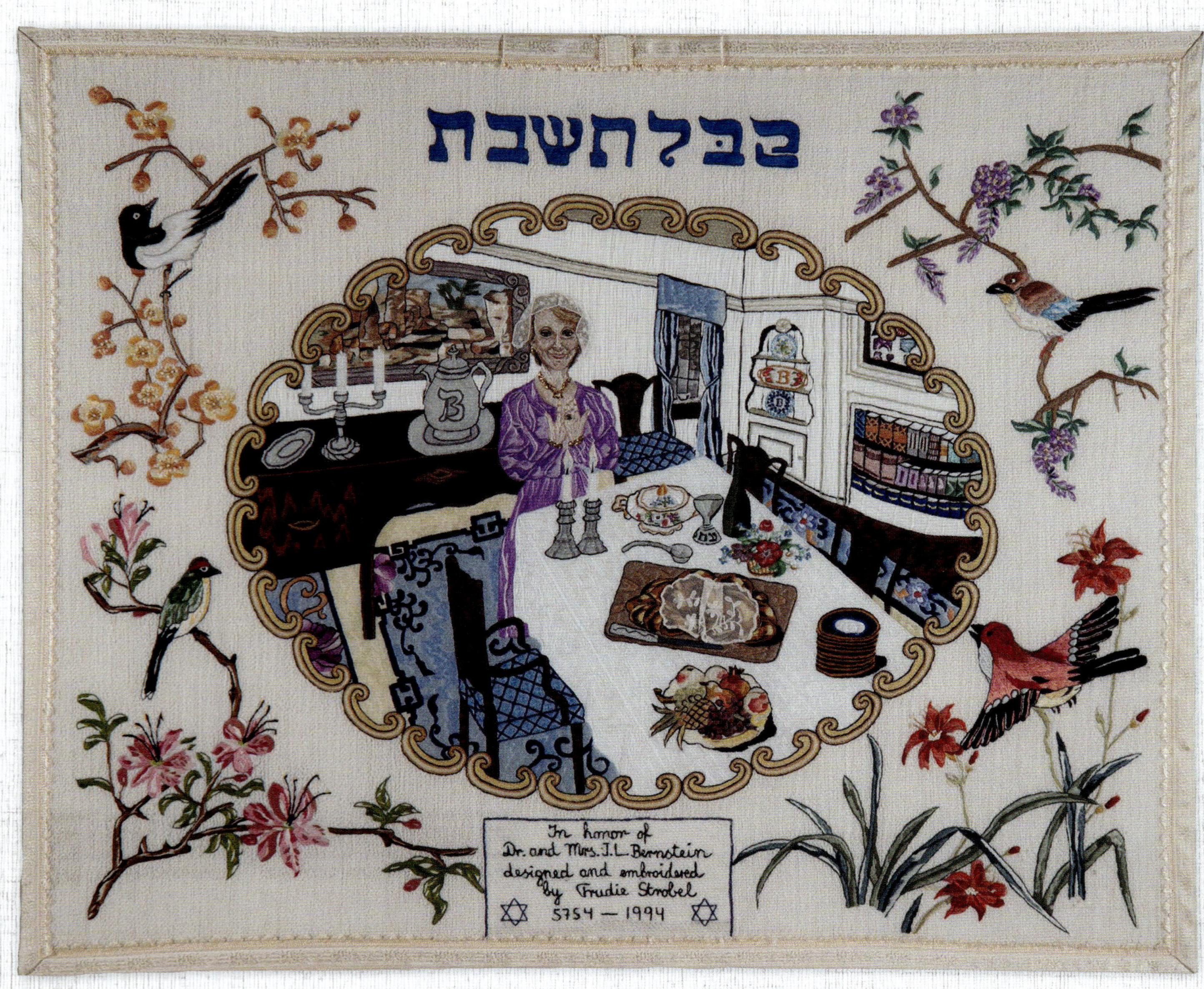

Blessings Over the Shabbas Candles · 1994 · 24″ × 30″

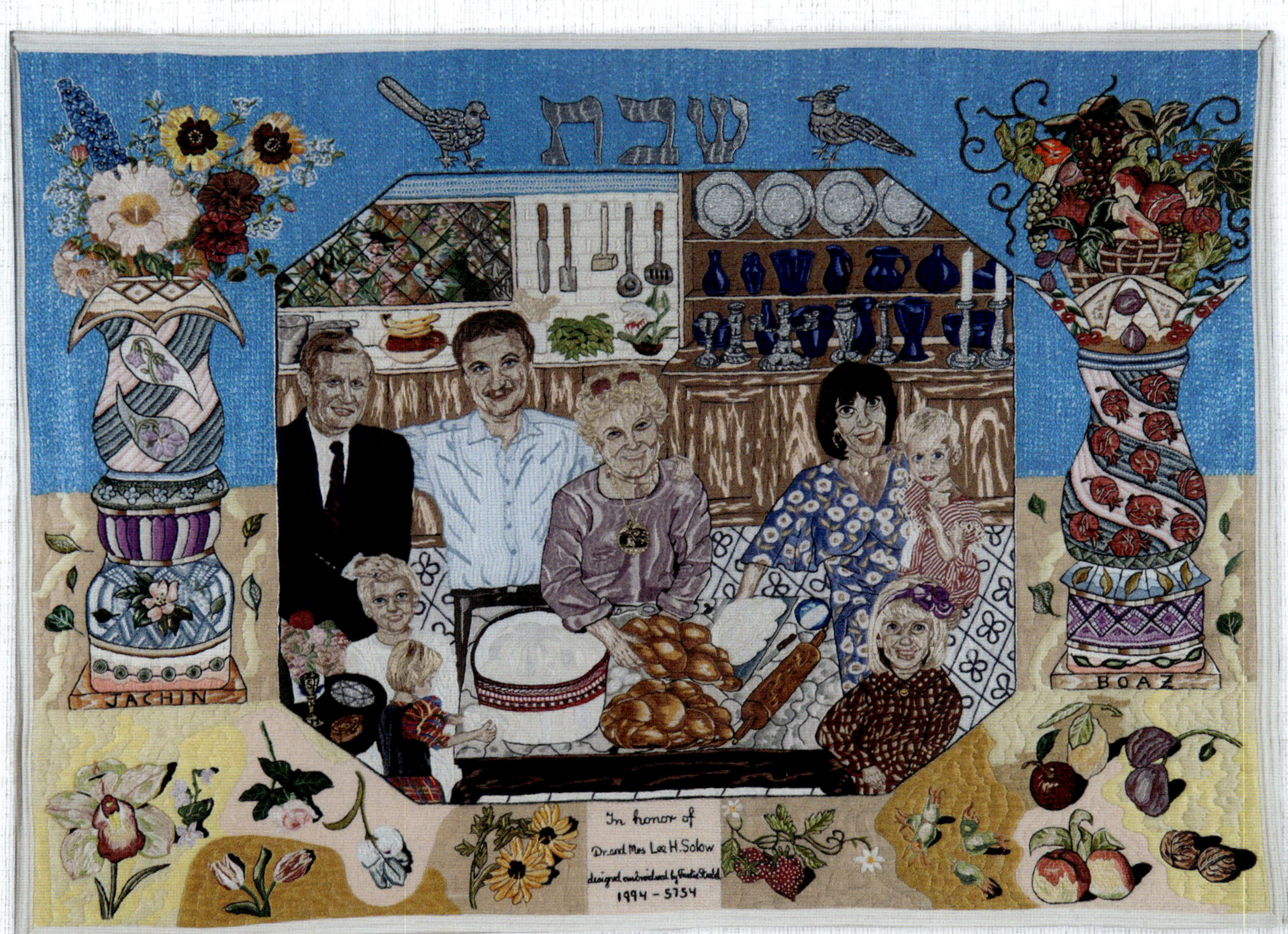

Shabbas · 1994 · 36″ × 42″

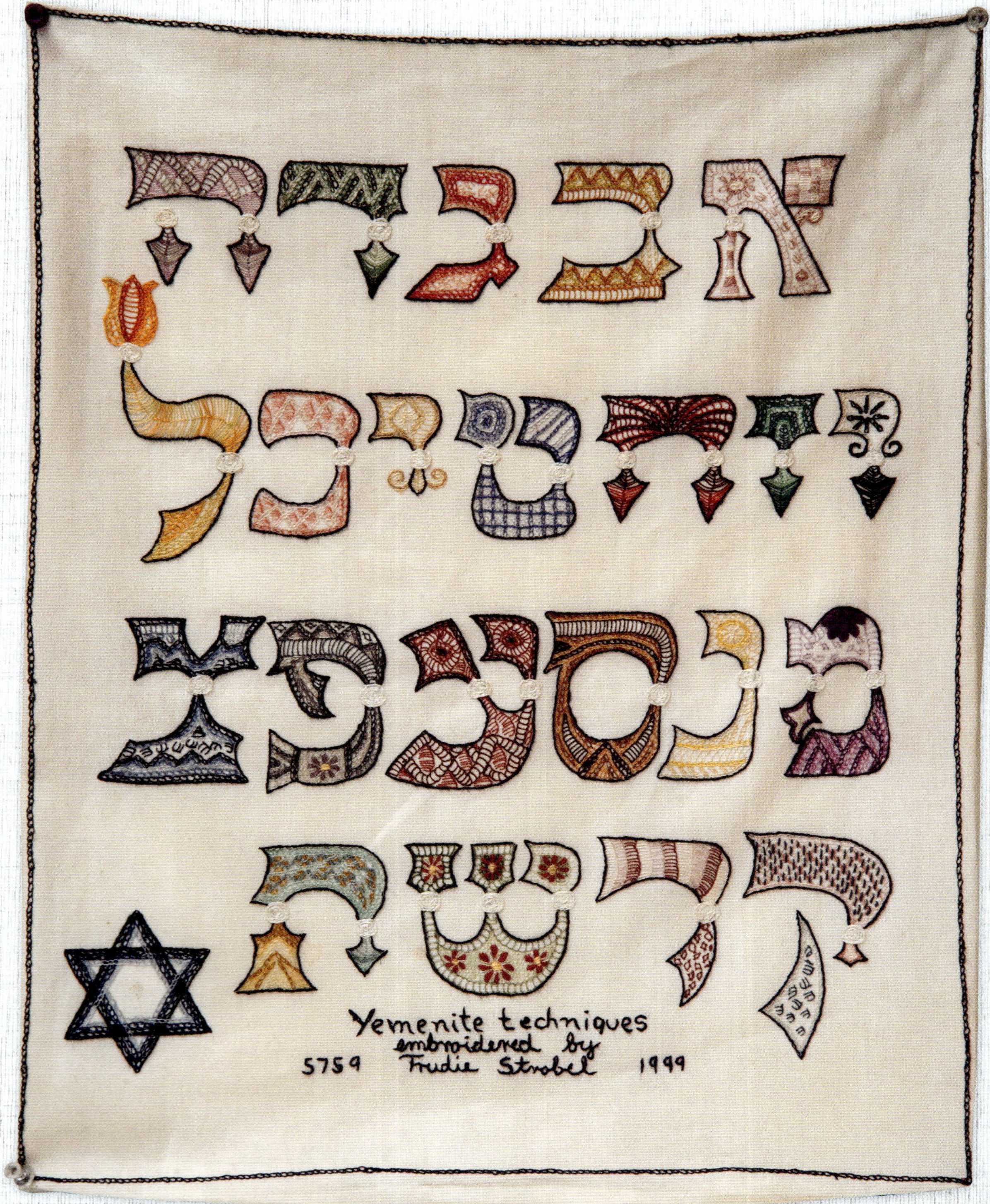

אבגדה
וזחטיכל
מנסעפצ
קרשת
Yemenite techniques
embroidered by
5759 Trudie Strobel 1999

STITCHES

The quintessential tapestorian, Trudie is a collector and practitioner of stitches. In the drawings on the next two pages, Trudie illustrates how the following basic stitches become traditionally Yemenite in their combinations and patterns:

1. Running stitch. A very basic Yemenite stitch. What identifies it as Yemenite is how it is used in combination with other stitches.
2. Closed chain stitch.
3. Open chain or ladder stitch.
4. Diagonal chain.
5. Double chain.
6. Detached chain and variations.
7. Fly stitch—"Very Yemenite."
8. Shallow fly stitch (also called "Roumanian" stitch).
9. Open herringbone stitch.
10. Closed herringbone stitch.
11. Blanket stitch.
12. Chevron stitch.
13. Buttonhole stitch (and fan pattern).
    **The fan pattern is emblematic of the Yemenite use of simple stitches in combination to create a typical Yemenite stitch pattern.
14. Laid Work stitching is also quintessentially Yemenite in execution because it involves multistep stitching that is borderline weaving on a minute scale.

Hebrew Sampler · *Trudie has made many of these Hebrew samplers as gifts. They depict the letters of the Hebrew alphabet using ancient Yemenite stitching techniques that she is determined to preserve for the future.*

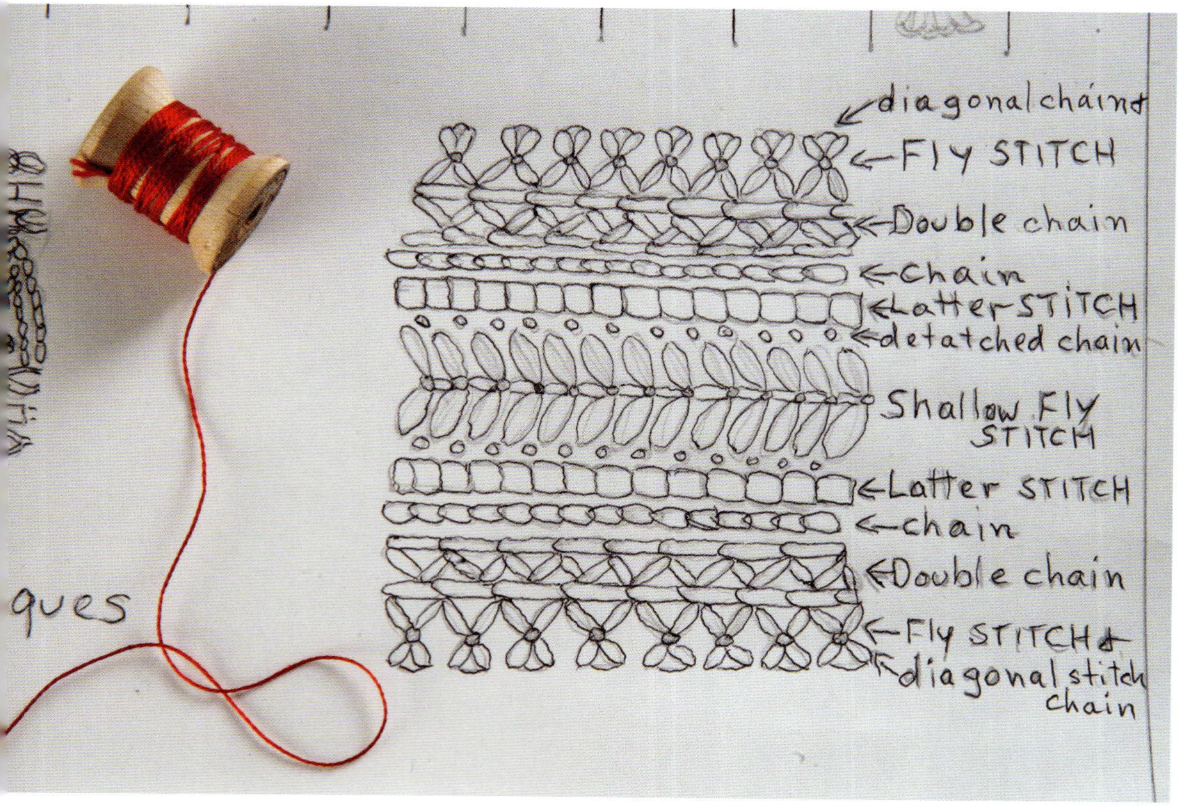

ques
diagonal chain &
FLY STITCH
Double chain
Chain
Latter STITCH
detatched chain
Shallow Fly STITCH
Latter STITCH
chain
Double chain
Fly STITCH &
diagonal stitch chain

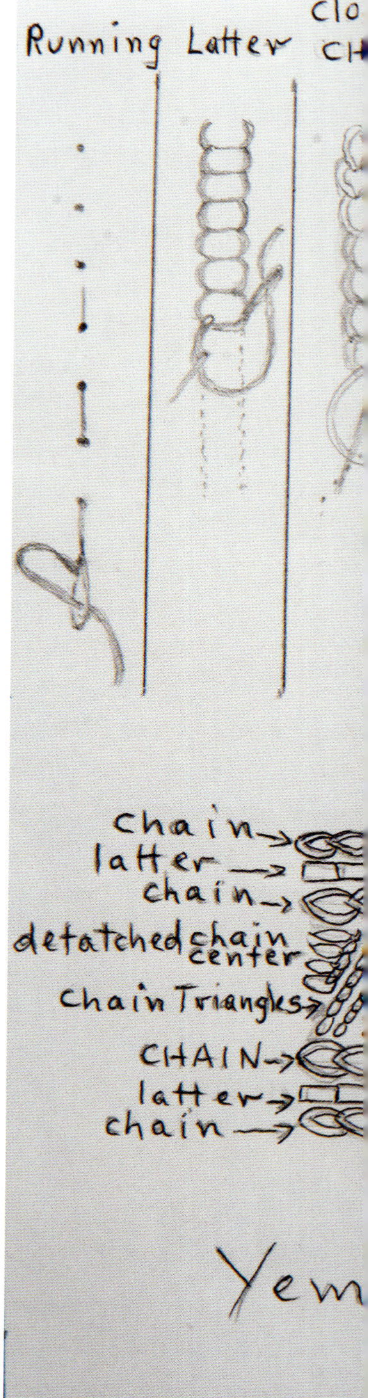
Running
Latter
chain
latter
chain
detatched chain center
Chain Triangles
CHAIN
latter
chain

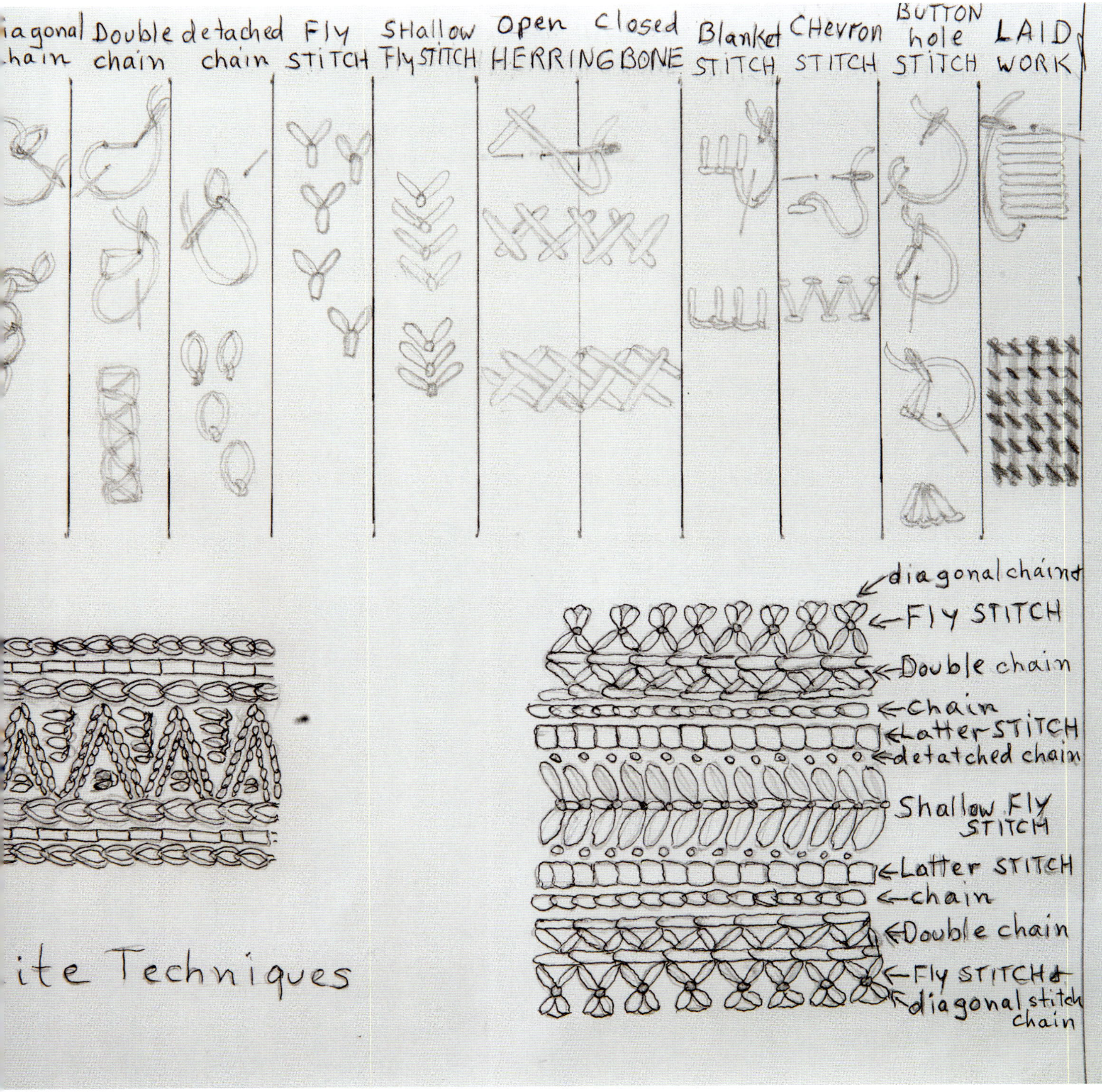

iagonal chain | Double chain | detached chain | FLY STITCH | SHallow Fly STITCH | Open HERRINGBONE | Closed HERRINGBONE | Blanket STITCH | CHevron STITCH | BUTTON hole STITCH | LAID WORK

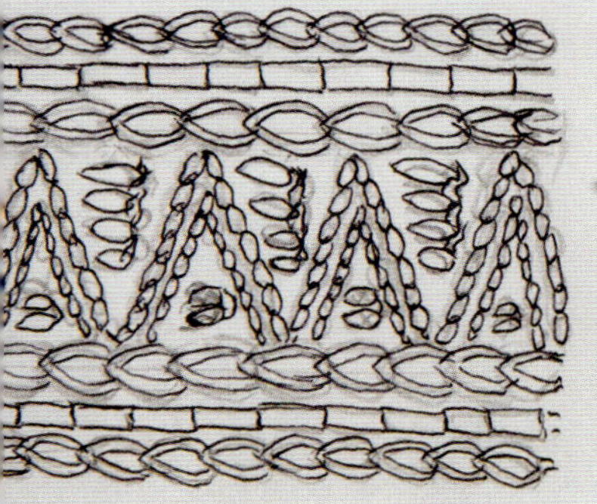

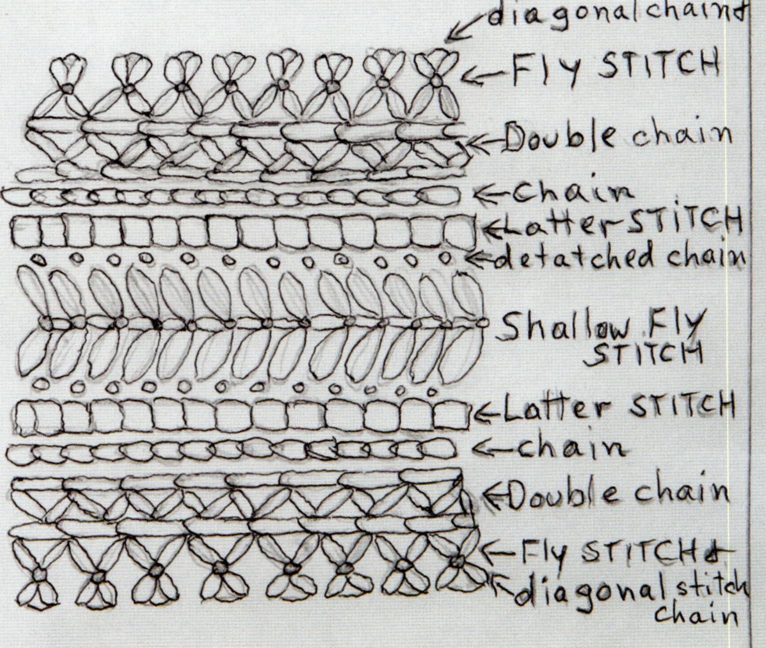

ite Techniques

The pieces that Trudie had completed at this point in her life were historical and biblical, and in that sense, they conveyed an element of the fabulous. But Trudie's own story, the story of her young life, the story still fiercely confined to the crypts of her memory, was foul, tragic, and painful. There was nothing fabulous in the starving of concentration camp prisoners, in the ubiquitous barbed wire, in the torture and killing of men, women, and children. There was nothing fabulous about the swastika and the mortal fear it evoked. The time had come for Trudie to design and stitch her own narrative.

She would do it in two powerful tapestries. She decided to call the first "1942." It would illustrate the defining moment in Trudie's childhood when the Nazi tore Papa Doll from her arms. It was the moment that had haunted her for so many years, the end of life as she had known it, the final rupture of paternal ties, an untethering that would catapult her into the dark ocean of evil. From what inner well of resolve did she find the strength to stitch the Nazi monster who had haunted her dreams for decades? In this tapestry, she allows herself the tears she could not shed as a child. The expression on her mother's face tells an entire story of its own. Behind Trudie and Masha, Jews are being herded into cattle cars, carrying suitcases, obeying orders, not knowing or believing they were being sent to the death camps, where everything would be taken from them, including any gold in their teeth. Children stand, confused, the Nazi's rifle trained on them; they are incapable of comprehending the potential depravity of man. "1942" is Trudie's intimate narrative, framed in Jewish stars strung on barbed wire.

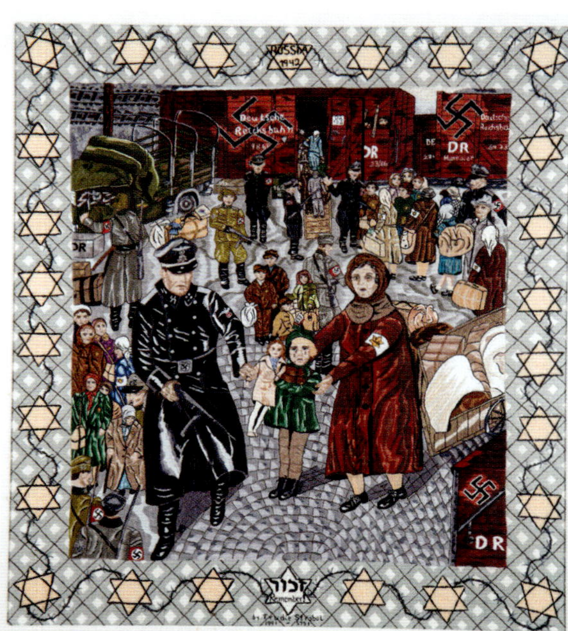

Russia 1942 · 1991 · 36″×37″

"1942" had been a sort of exorcism, and Trudie was making progress. She was coping better with her depression, though she still spoke little and was easily unsettled. In the library, she had come across a book by Sholem Aleichem. She loved the book. With so little formal education, she had never been a reader. She did not know that Sholem Aleichem was a leading Jewish author and playwright. She did not know that the book she had found, *Tevye's Daughters: Collected Stories of Sholem Aleichem*, had become the basis for the wildly popular musical about Tevye the Dairyman called *Fiddler on the Roof*, which had opened on Broadway in 1964 and become the first musical in history to surpass 3,000 performances. What she did know is that the book warmed her heart and brought her to a distant place and time that felt familiar. Dr. Solow gave Trudie another prescription, one that sent her to the library to read all of the work of Solomon Naumovich Rabinovich, whose pen name was Sholem Aleichem ("Peace Among You" in Hebrew).

Born in 1859 in Pereyaslav, Aleichem grew up in the nearby shtetl of Voronko, in the Russian Empire (now in central Ukraine). His father, Menachem-Nukhem Rabinovich, had been a rich merchant, but a failed business affair plunged the family into poverty. When Sholem was thirteen years old, his mother died of cholera. His life and work inspired Trudie's next tapestry.

Now Trudie was ready to return to the telling of her own narrative. This time she would tell a bigger story. It would be called "Final Destination." Trudie says, "This is the Shoah."

This large-scale masterpiece stands forty-two by fifty-four inches. Stitch by tiny stitch, it tells a personal narrative of the Shoah, depicting the administrators of evil and the victims of evil, as Trudie remembered them. The face of each character is stitched in detail, sculpted in thread, the expressions ranging from despair to horror to the smug visages of the Nazis. The garments are meticulously rendered to reproduce everything from the gleam of the Gestapo's boots to the ragged disrepair of the prisoners, all wearing the yellow Star of David. That Trudie Strobel, who had received little formal education and no art education, no drawing lessons, no instruction in shading or perspective, could render such detail in thread is nothing short of miraculous. The stark juxtaposition of life and death in this axis of evil is powerfully communicated in the border that marries barbed wire and marguerites, horror and beauty in a painterly dance of irony and tragedy with a tiny pinch of hope. "Final Destination" took almost a decade to complete. It is Trudie Strobel's Sistine Chapel.

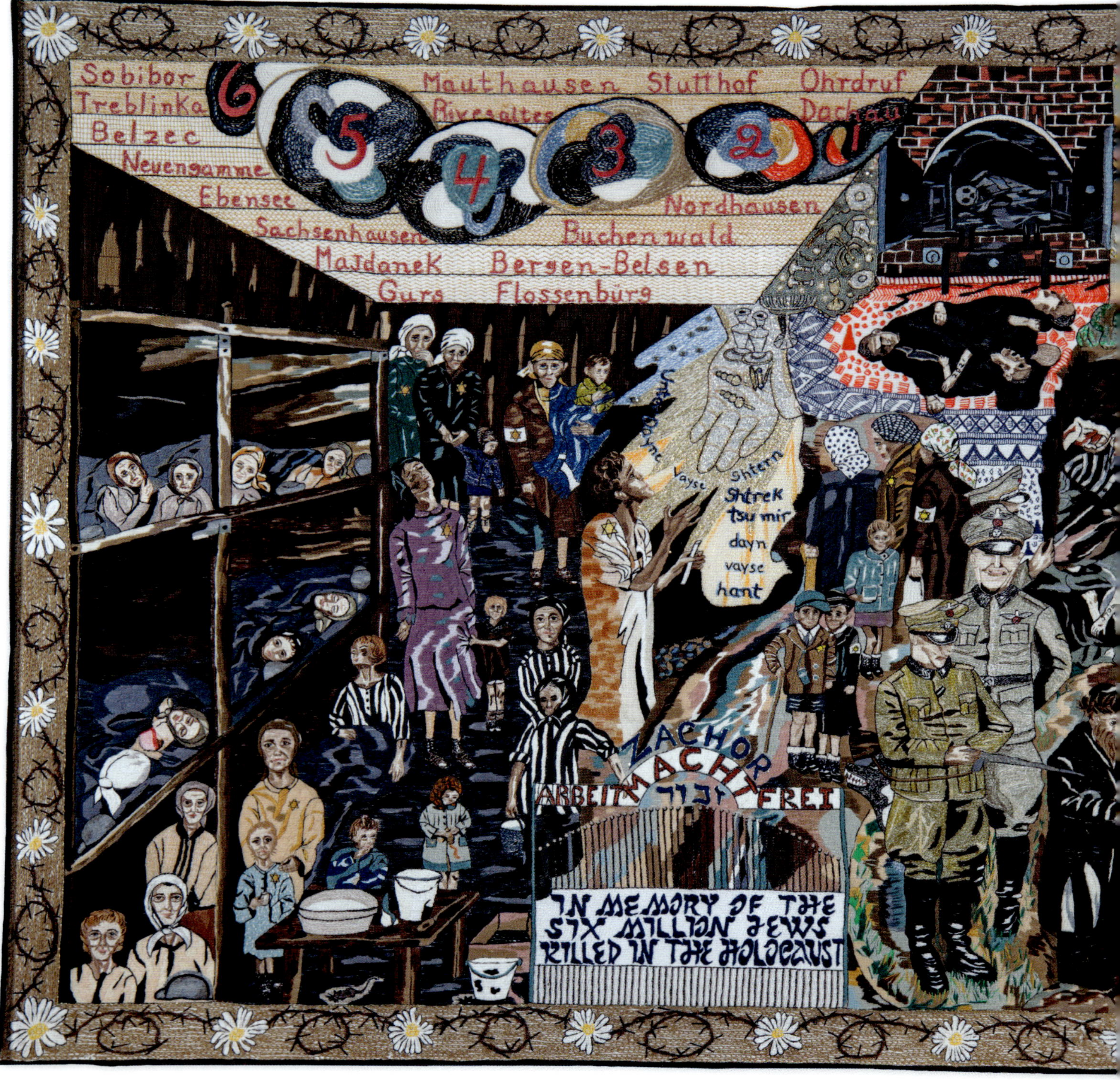

Sobibor
Treblinka
Belzec
Neuengamme
Ebensee
Sachsenhausen
Majdanek
Gurs
6 5 4 3 2 1
Mauthausen
Stutthof
Ohrdruf
Rivesaltes
Dachau
Nordhausen
Buchenwald
Bergen-Belsen
Flossenbürg
Unter Dayne Vayse Shtern
Shtrek tsu mir dayn vayse hant
ZACHOR
ARBEIT MACHT FREI
זכור
IN MEMORY OF THE SIX MILLION JEWS KILLED IN THE HOLOCAUST

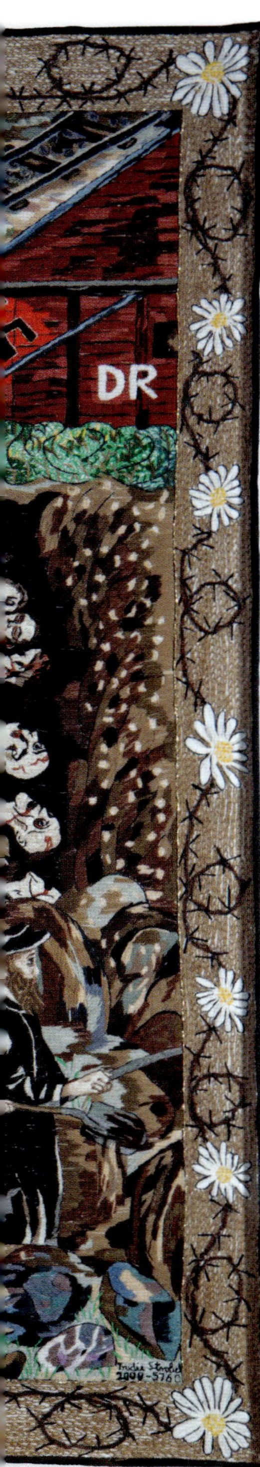

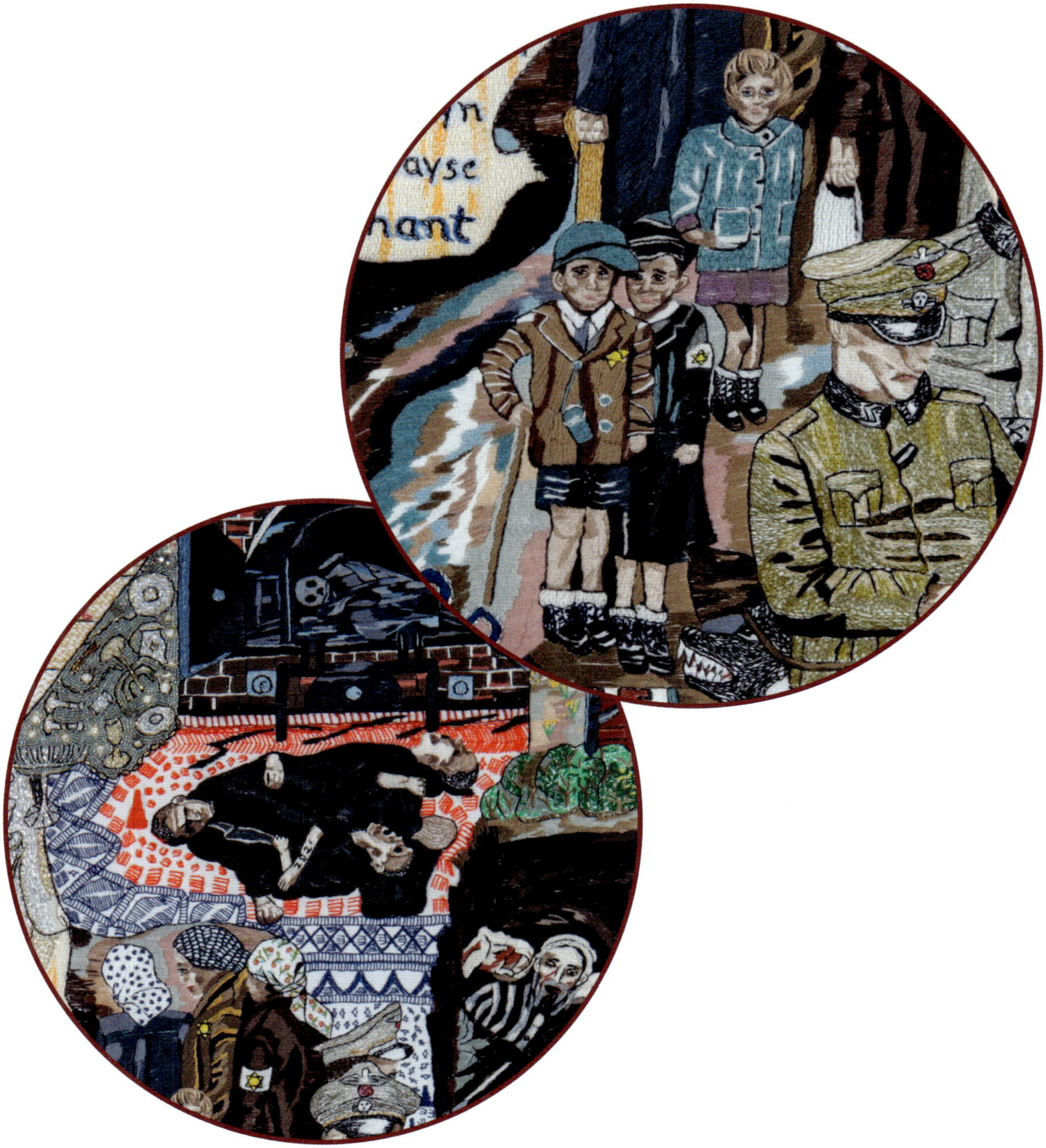

Final Destination · 2000 · 42″ × 54″ · *Learn more about this piece in Art Notes, page 187*

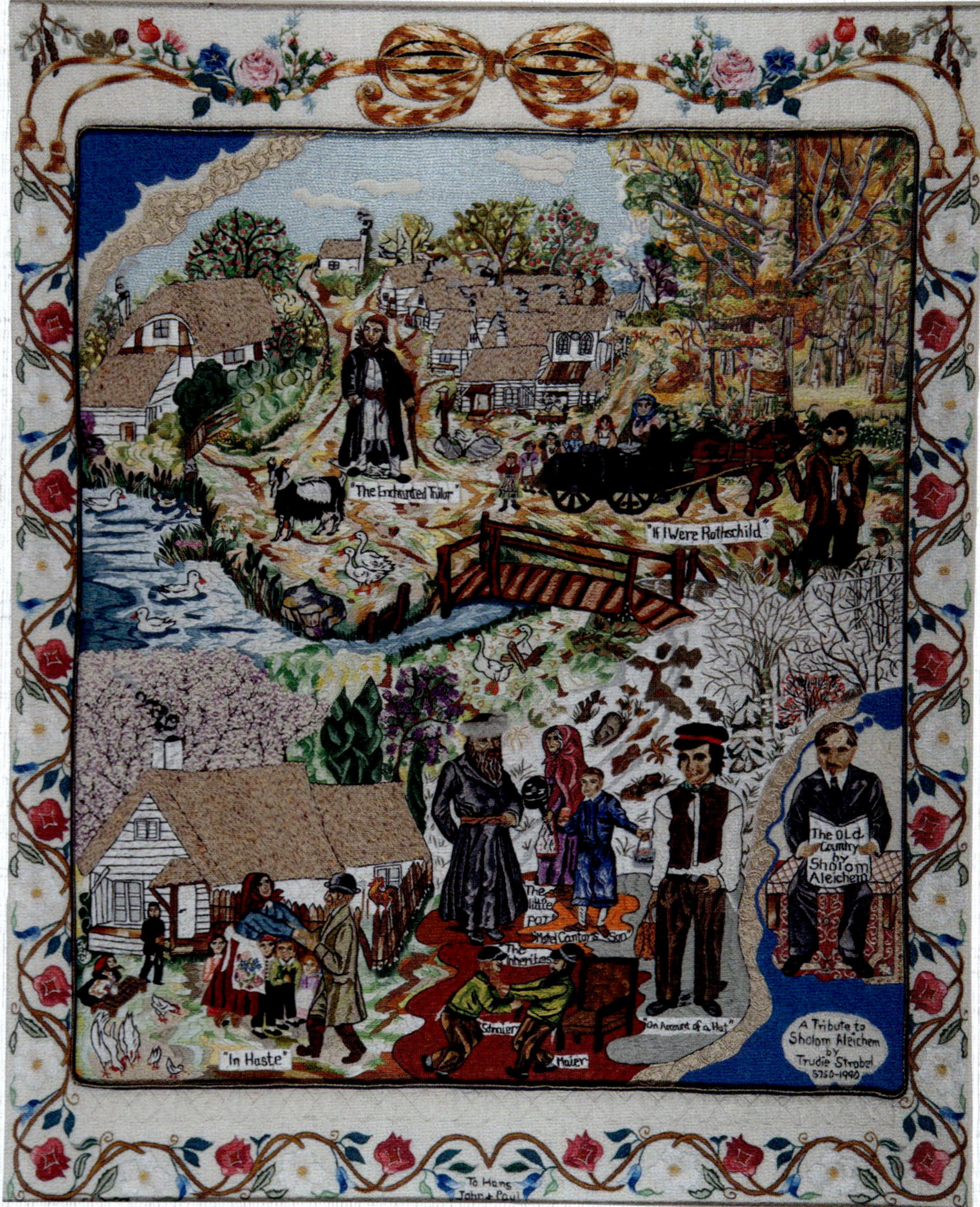

A Tribute to Sholem Aleichem · 1991 · 44″ x 57″

Sholem Aleichem, the pen name adopted by Solomon Rabinovich, has been called the Jewish Mark Twain and is indeed probably the greatest Yiddish humorist. His writings conveyed a comprehensive picture of Jewish life in Russia during the latter part of the nineteenth century and early part of the twentieth century. *Read Trudie's comments on this work in Art Notes, page 173.*

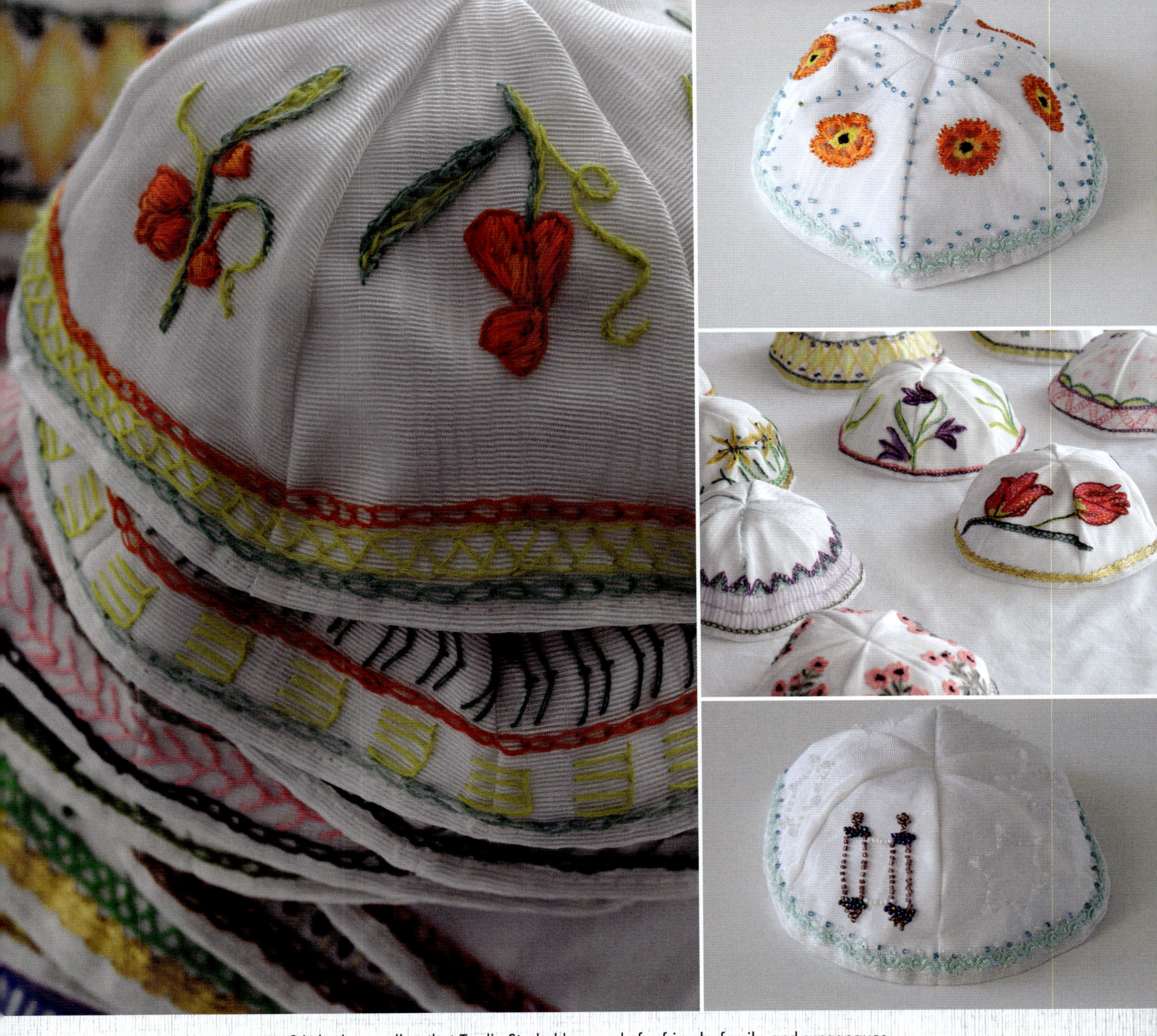

Stitched yarmulkes that Trudie Strobel has made for friends, family, and synagogues

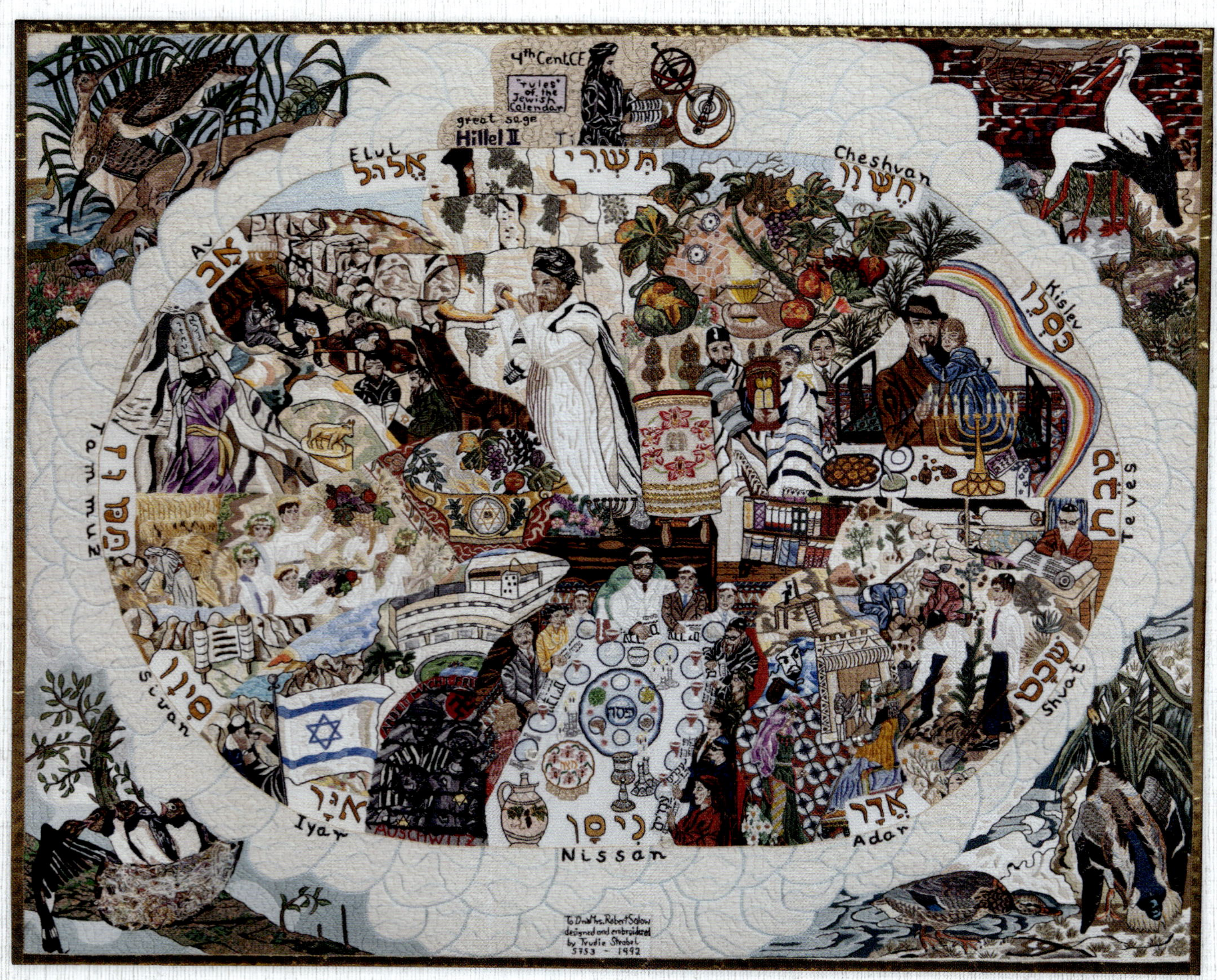

The Jewish Calendar · 1992 · 42″ × 64″ · *Learn more about this work in Art Notes, page 175*

AFTERWORD

Chana Zgierski, a child, was murdered in Auschwitz. Trudie never knew Chana. It was Chana's father, Leo Zgierski, who left the memory of his daughter with Trudie shortly before he died, the only member of the Zgierski family to have survived the death camp, to have lived on in testament to the horror. Those who survive must remember. Those who remember must share. And it is thus that we pass the memories forward, candles whose flickering flames must never be extinguished.

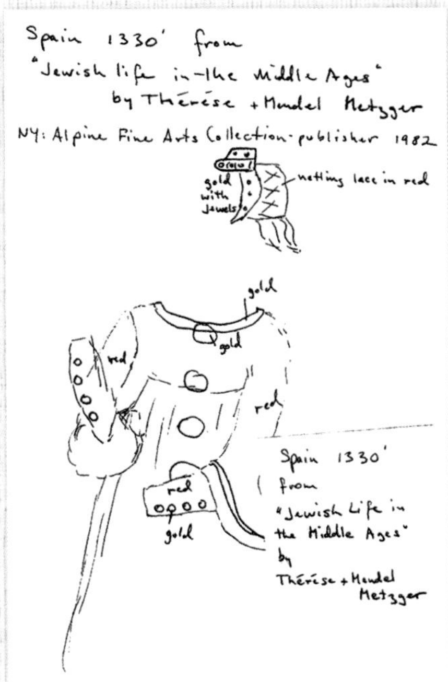

When my daughter, Maya, was preparing for her bat mitzvah, Samara Hutman, then the director of the Los Angeles Museum of the Holocaust, arranged for Maya to meet Trudie so Maya could accept and carry forward the memory of Chana Zgierski, through a program named Remember Us: The Holocaust Bnai Mitzvah Project. Maya would share her bat mitzvah with Chana; she would dedicate the bat mitzvah to the young girl who was beaten to death before she could experience her own special day. Serendipitously, Maya's Hebrew name is also Hanna, though spelled differently. There is something elliptical about that, like the round Rosh Hashanah challah, like the spiraling currents of our community of lives.

This is how the journey of this book began. As I sat in Trudie's living room, surrounded by her astonishing body of work, I realized that it must be shared. We started by cataloguing, and

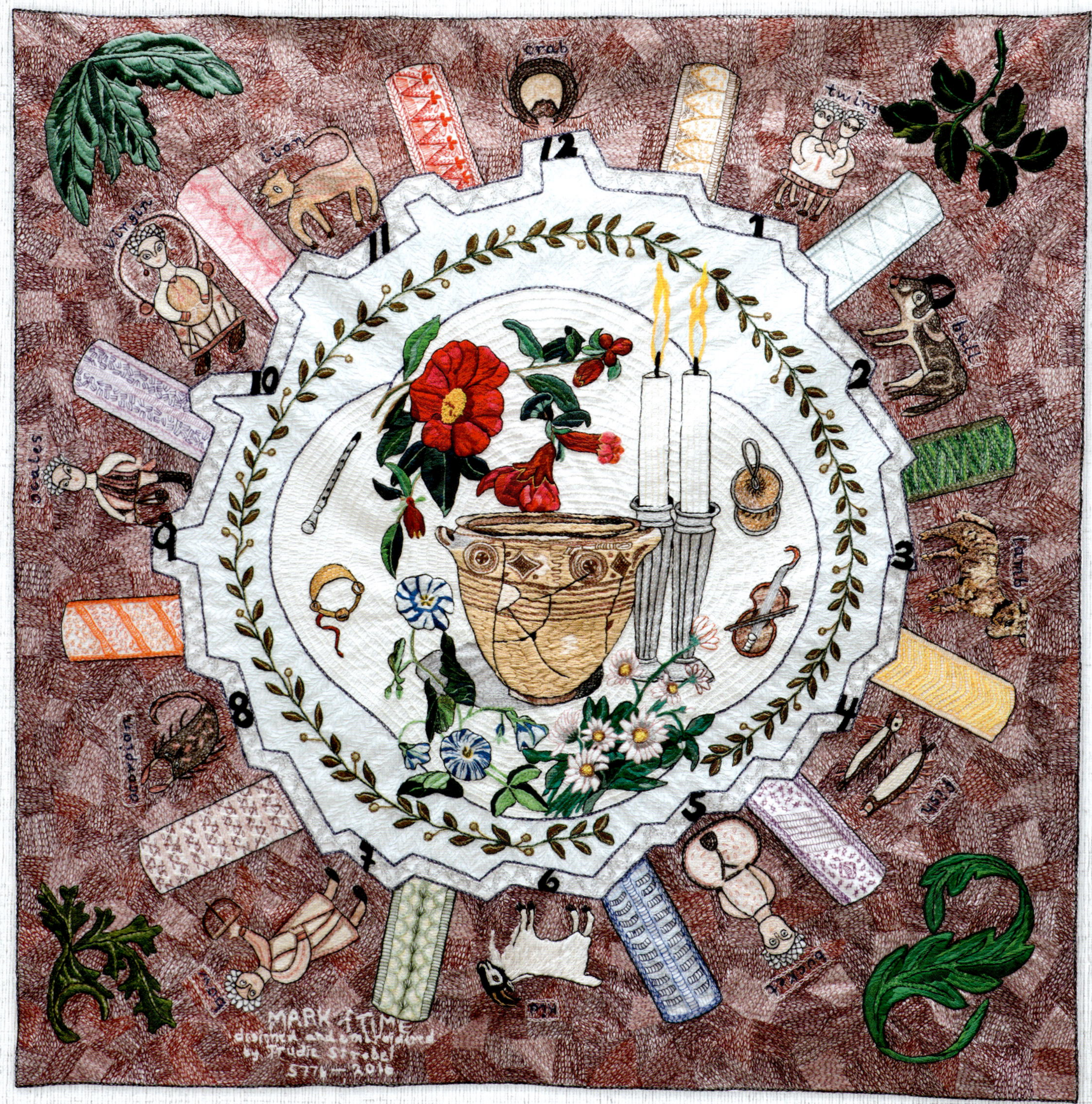

Mark of Time · 2016 · 36″ × 36″ · *Read more about this work in Art Notes, page 189*

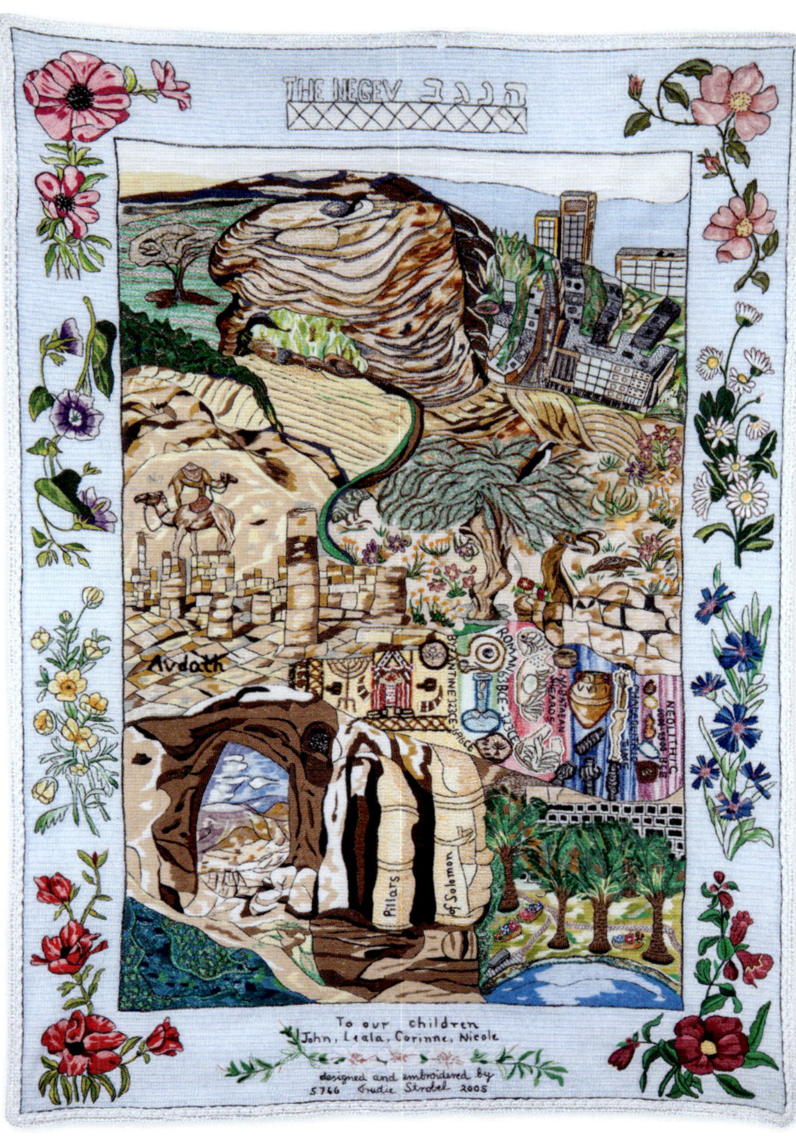

The Negev · 2005 · 28″ × 44″
Learn more about this work in Art Notes, page 187

as we worked, I came to realize the magnitude of what she had created. The catalogue very quickly listed more than one hundred works, many of them enormous and intricate, each one detailed and stitched with a goal of perfection.

Trudie gave so much away. She gave many pieces to her doctors; she gave to her temple; she gave to museums; she gave to her friends; she gave to friends of her friends. She kept notes and letters, and going through her files, we were able to reach most of the beneficiaries of her work. Many still lived in the Los Angeles area, but some had moved away. Pieces had been passed down to children, ferried off to Israel, New York, Carmel, Tacoma. Some were lost, though we continue to hold out hope that they will one day be found. Many of the pieces are large and intricately framed, so shipping them was tricky. In some cases, we traveled to them. In other cases, they traveled to us. For Trudie, seeing the works again after so many years was like a homecoming.

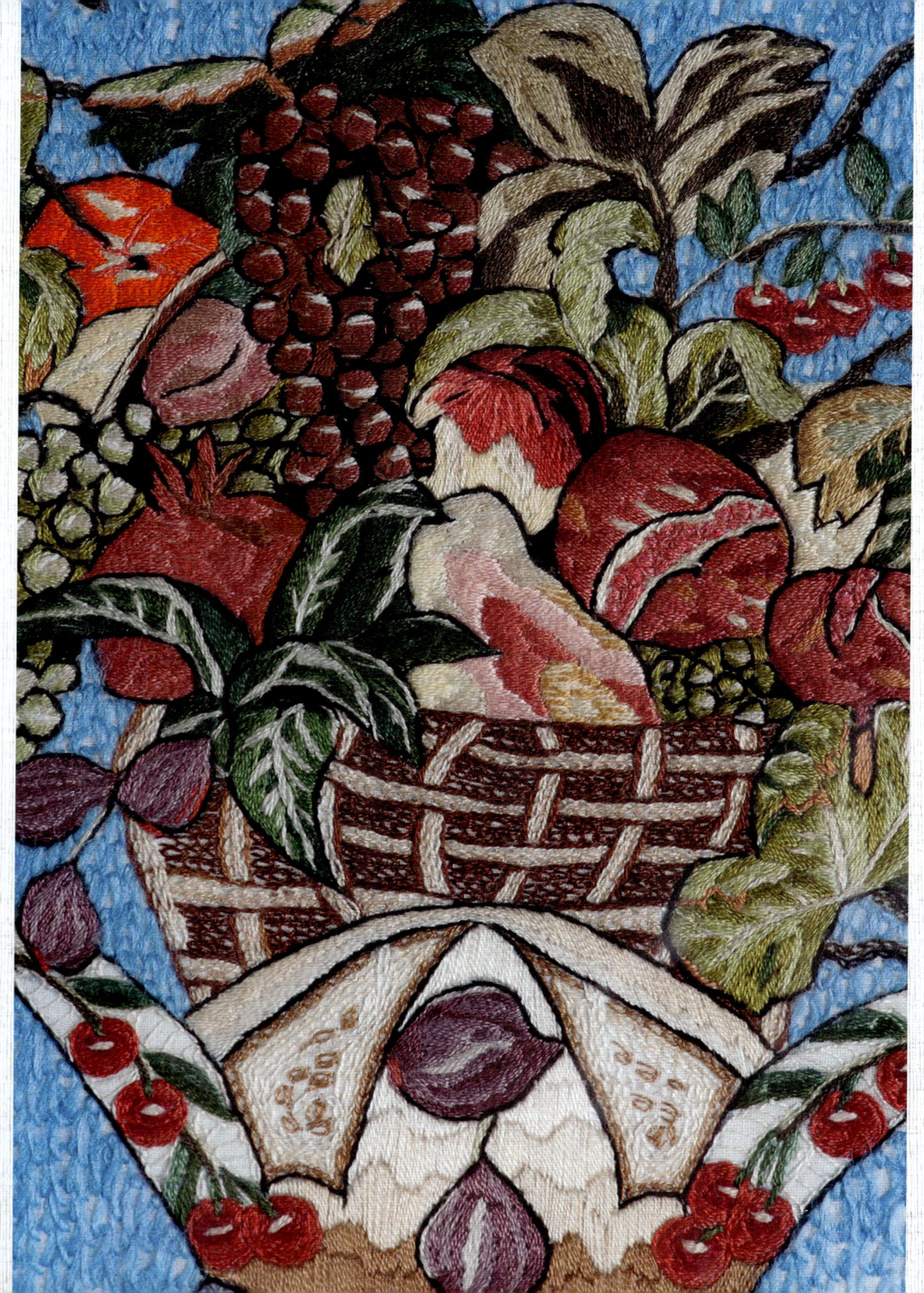

ART NOTES

In the pages that follow, Trudie shares thoughts and notes about some of her works.

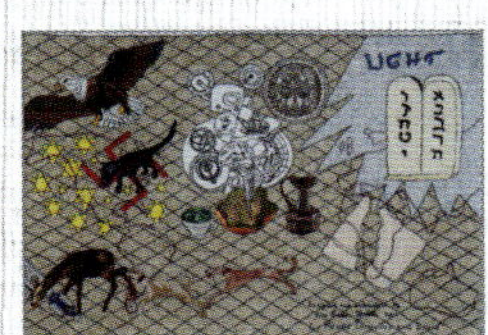

See page 62

Light #2: In Trudie's Words

Our dear son John gave us a book, *The Jews of Europe in the Middle Ages.* It fascinated me from cover to cover. It's the history of Judaism from the eleventh to the sixteenth century. My eyes were opened even wider as to what the Jewish people accomplished then and now. We are such a small group.

I hit my fist on the table and said, "We are not the vermin the Nazis called us."

Our tablets brought conscience to the world. Our temple was twice destroyed. Our persecution went on for centuries, all over the world. The Nazi rat killed so many millions of our beautiful yellow stars.

It is the center of this piece that illustrates our accomplishments that makes me proud to be a Jew. Dogs hunting deer is a visual metaphor often found in Jewish manuscripts; in this case the deer is protecting the Torah crown, which I embroidered with semiprecious beads.

A Tribute to Sholem Aleichem: In Trudie's Words

As I was reading one of Sholem Aleichem's vivid and animated stories about shtetl life, my heart was captured with his humor. I decided to make an embroidery of his stories of shtetl life, depicting

Detail from ***Shabbas*** · 1994

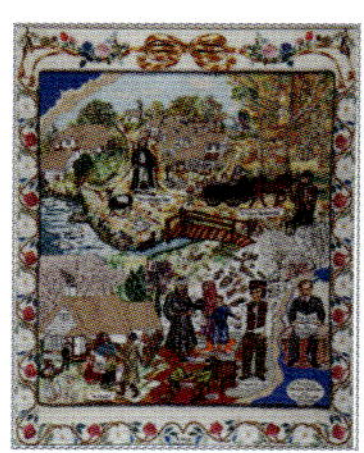
See page 166

the characters, themes, and symbols of Sholem Aleichem's work. Since his stories took place on different holidays and in all seasons of the year, I depicted the four seasons with a centered bridge connecting them. Wrapped in borders of pomegranates and almond blossoms, the tapestry is crowned by a Victorian ribbon bow, strewn roses, figs, and carob branches. On the ribbon are selected flora of Israel.

The characters that I wove into the tapestry begin with Tevye, from "If I Were Rothschild." The eternal dairyman, he professed his endless faith in God and his desire to be rich, with his horse and wagon, his six daughters and his wife, Golda (characters who were to become even more famous in *Fiddler on the Roof*). Menachem Mendel, from "In Haste," the luckless marriage broker who comes home to reunite with his family on Passover eve, is depicted with his derby hat and galoshes. Shimmen-Eli, "The Enchanted Tailor," is shown on a hot summer day with the goat he had proudly purchased in yet another poor business venture. Character details I was determined to capture are the threads in his beard, the pins in his coat, and "in his walk a little dance." The twins of "The Inheritors," Maier and the redhead Schnaier, are fighting to the point of pulling their beard hairs out; the fight is over the right to the one seat along the Eastern wall in the old Kasrilevka Synagogue that their father had left them. In *Motl the Cantor's Son*, the poor young orphan boy is selling the Kvass drink that his brother invented to make ends meet. Yenta, the Poultry-woman from the story "The Little Pot," is making the Rabbi dizzy with her nonstop gossiping and complaining. Sholem Shachnah Rattlebrain from "On Account of a Hat" is so absentminded that he unknowingly absconds with the red-banded Conductor's Cap on his trip home, arriving late for Passover. The characters are larger than life in comparison to their shtetl surroundings. Meager circumstances, rich tradition.

In the lower right corner of the tapestry sits the master himself: Sholem Aleichem, whose stories felt as if they were written for me.

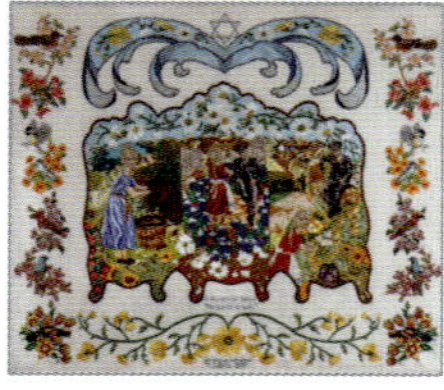
See page 74

***Margarit-g-lach*:** In Trudie's Words

The first time I met Margaret Solow, a Yiddish song, "Margarit-g-lach," came into my mind. In the song, a young student observes a girl named Hava picking daisies. He tells her she is the most beautiful daisy there is, but then he leaves.

Brokenhearted, she waits for him.

I depicted the two characters in a field of bluebonnets. The ribbon effect at the top and the yellow-gold daisies at the bottom are inspired by the title of the song, and they complement the old-fashioned three-paneled screen in which the embroidered story unfolds. The border of birds and flower clusters underscores the romance in this pastoral setting.

See page 168

The Jewish Calendar: Notes

Temporal customs, observances, and history of Judaism are on full display in the wonderful piece that graces the home of the Neumann Solow family.

While the Gregorian calendar we use today, named after Gregory XIII in 1582, is determined by the revolution of the earth around the sun, the Jewish calendar embraces both moon and sun. The months are fixed by the movement of the moon, and the days by the movement of the sun. The ordinary Jewish year has twelve months composed of thirty or twenty-nine days each, with "Leap Months" being added seven years out of each nineteen. The ordinary months of the Jewish calendar are Tishrei, Cheshvan, Kislev, Tevet, Shevat, Adar, Nissan, Iyar, Sivan, Tammuz, Av, and Elul. In this tapestry, the twelve months and the Jewish holidays are logically arranged clockwise in an oval.

The beginning of the Jewish New Year is celebrated the first day of Tishrei. The days of Rosh Hashanah are devoted to prayer, solemn festivities, and rest from work. *Shana Tovah* cards are sent to greet one another. The holiday is also named Yom Tevuah, the day of the blowing of the ram's horn (or shofar), which is a symbol of God's summons to the people for self-judgment, self-improvement, and atonement. The calendar depicts the blowing of the shofar in the background of the Western Wall (the Wailing Wall) of the Temple in Jerusalem. The period is concluded on the tenth day of Tishrei by Yom Kippur, the Day of Atonement, the solemnest of Jewish holidays.

When the summer crops are gathered from the fields of Israel, Sukkot (the fifteenth of Tishrei) is the earliest thanksgiving festival. It is one of the most colorful of Jewish festivals. In memory of the harvests, Jews build a Sukkot, which is depicted with a grape-leaf roof. The

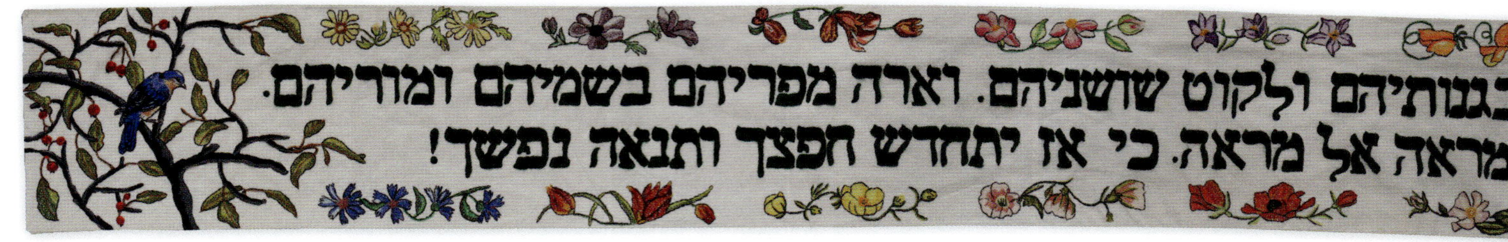

Banner for Peter Kahn Library

lulav (palm branches) and *etrog* (citron fruit) are the ancient symbols of Sukkot. The rabbi pronounces a blessing while holding the etrog and waving the lulav in all directions to symbolize God's omnipresence.

Just following the festival of Sukkot (twenty-third of Tishrei), a Torah festival, Simchat Torah takes place, during which the last Torah portion of the year is read and the new portion for the coming year begins. The calendar shows the traditional march around the synagogue with the Sefer Torahs.

The festival of Hanukkah (twenty-fifth Kislev) celebrates the time when Matisyahu and his five sons led a tiny Jewish army against the Hellenist-Syrian King Antiochus, driving his troops out of Jerusalem and Eretz Yisrael. There was only enough oil for one day when they lit the menorah, but miraculously that one bit of oil lasted for eight days. The calendar depicts a father and a child lighting a candle (which is done each night for eight nights), along with the traditional gifts of money (Hanukkah gelt) and the dreidel. The four Hebrew letters on the dreidel (nun, gimel, hey, and shin) stand for the initials of the phrase "Nes gadol hayah sham" ("A great miracle happened there"). The tapestry also offers the traditional dish, latkes with applesauce and sour cream.

On the eighth of Tevet, King Ptolemy II of Egypt forced seventy-two geographically disparate Jewish sages to translate the Torah into the Greek language. The king assumed that each would write something different, but all the sages translated the Torah in exactly the same way. Each year on this day, Torahs are inspected, cleaned, and repaired. The tapestry portrays a scribe writing a letter of the Torah.

The fifteenth of Shvet, the New Year of the Trees or Tu BiShvat, is celebrated by the planting of trees. The Bible warns against destroying trees, so trees are planted in honor of the

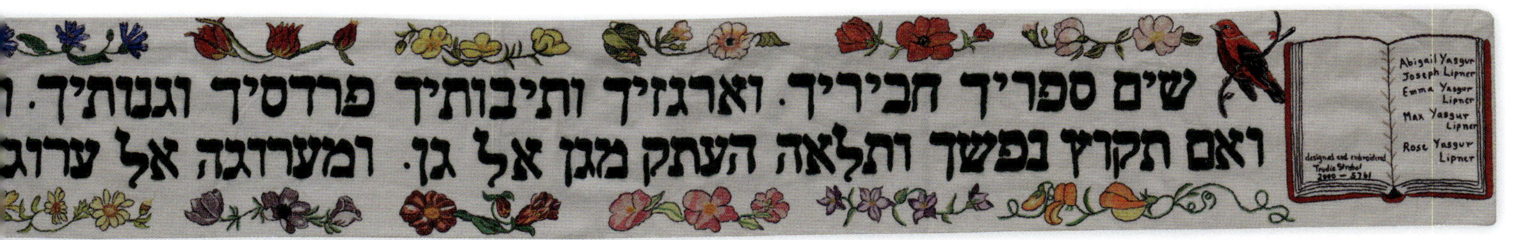

birth of children, a cypress for a girl and a cedar for a boy. The calendar shows children planting trees in Israel, making it a more verdant, fruitful country.

Purim, which occurs the fourteenth of Adar, commemorates the miracle of survival from the vizier Haman's plot to kill all the Jews of Persia. The calendar depicts Queen Esther pleading with her husband, the Persian King Ahasuerus, to save her people, and the villainous Haman being hanged on the gallows. The mask and grog grinder symbolize the joy and festivities of this holiday.

The first day of Passover falls on the fifteenth of Nissan and lasts for eight days. It commemorates the deliverance of the Israelites from Egypt and is celebrated as "the Season of our Freedom." On the first night, a special home ceremony known as the seder (order) is observed. The youngest participant asks the Four Questions, and the head of the household, accompanied by the other participants, responds to the questions by reading the Passover story from the Haggadah. Matzoh (unleavened bread) is eaten during the eight days of the holiday. This is done in commemoration of the unleavened bread that the Israelites baked in haste as they were led by Moses in their flight from bondage. The calendar picture shows some of the essential ingredients of the seder: the reading of the Haggadah, the bitter herbs, the traditional wine, the shank bone, the roasted egg and salted water, the green vegetables and the charoset.

Yom Hashoah, or the Day of Remembrance, occurs on the twenty-seventh of Nissan. The Day of Remembrance honors the 6 million Jews who were victims of the Holocaust.

The fifth of Iyar commemorates the establishment of the State of Israel on May 14, 1948, in the Hebrew year 5708.

Lag B'Omar, celebrated on the eighteenth of Iyar, is a day of weddings and picnics, playing games and singing songs. Bonfires are lit all over Israel, especially at the grave of Shimon bar Yochai, the revered Kabbalist and student of Rabbi Akiva, which sits on Mt. Meran, the highest point in Israel. On Lag B'Omar, it is tradition for young boys to get their first haircut, which is depicted in the tapestry.

The sixth of Sivan depicts the giving of the Torah at Har Sinai. Shavuot, the festival of the wheat harvest, is celebrated with depictions of children carrying baskets of such harvest offerings as figs, barley, wheat, grapes, pomegranates, olives, and dates. Note the rendering of the biblical heroine, Ruth, who is collecting the grain. The story of Ruth is read at this time of the year.

Trudie dramatized the seventeenth of Tammuz, the day Moses descended from Mt. Sinai with the two stone tablets of the Ten Commandments, saw the golden calf, and threw the tablets to the ground.

On the ninth of Av, the First and Second Temples were destroyed. The calendar depicts those ruins alongside men in prayer, as Tisha B'Av is a day of fasting and prayer.

The shofar is sounded throughout the month of Elul after the morning service in order to inspire a mood of penitence for the Day of Judgment.

The great Sage Hillel II authored the "rules" of the Jewish calendar. Trudie shows Hillel on top of an oval shape surrounded by clouds. Trudie explains, "All of the calendars that have ever been in use have been derived from studies of the skies."

The bird scenes in the four corners of the tapestry emphasize the four seasons of the year. The stork in the autumn scene is a migrating bird. Winter is represented by the mallard duck. The common Mediterranean swallow, a bird beloved by the ancients, celebrates spring. A native North American bird, the long-billed curlew, heralds summer. Trudie has always been a student of birds.

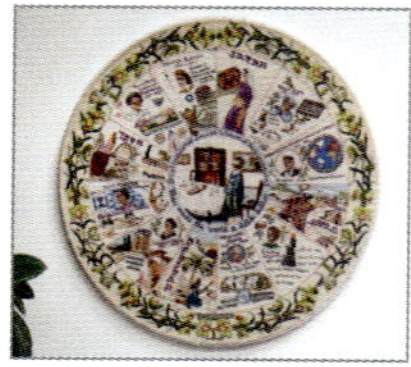

See page 135

***Distinguished Jewish Women of Achievement*:** In Trudie's Words

As I was looking at photographs of Europe's oldest active synagogue in Prague, Czechoslovakia, I became enchanted by the beautiful Hebrew letters on the face of the clock that is situated on the gabled roof. I suddenly saw Sarah, Queen

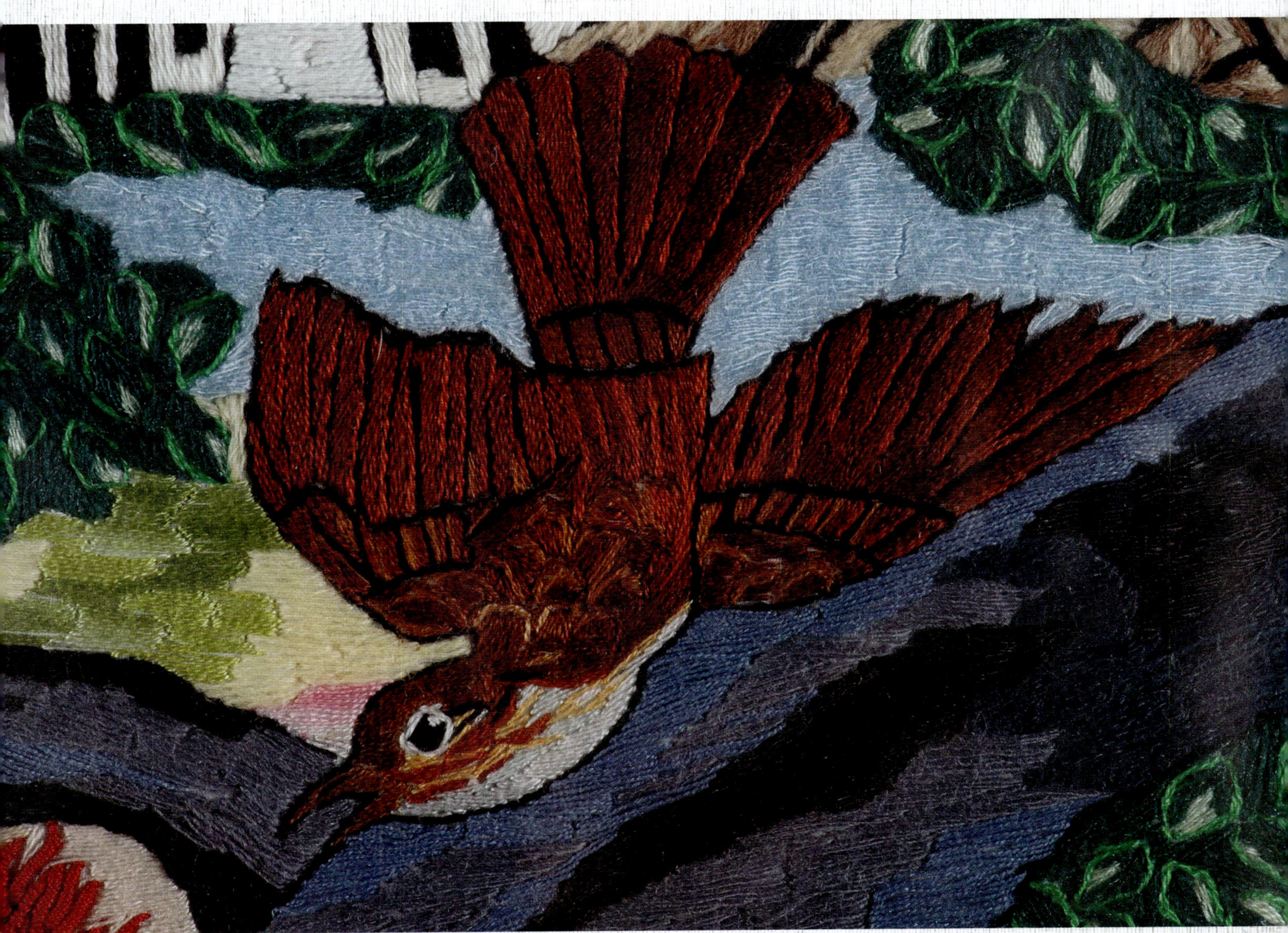

Detail from ***Bruce Solow and Family*** · 1996 · 28″ × 40″

Esther, Henrietta Szold, and Golda Meir as a chain in time of Jewish women who courageously helped shape our world. I imagined twelve women in a clock-like design. I arranged my Heroines by chronological age, interspersed by our biblical heroines into twelve sections, just as one would find on the face of a clock.

I placed a mother in the center, blessing the candles, the pulse of time radiating to the surrounding heroines.

It was very difficult to select only twelve Jewish women of achievement, for we have a tremendous reservoir of Jewish women who have accomplished gigantic feats. The heroines depicted in my circle achieved their historic goals despite insurmountable odds and by persistent hard work, empowered by their love for Judaism and mankind. I chose the cymbidium garland to surround these beautiful treasures, for the cymbidium orchid flower is the queen of all flowers.

Each woman depicted is surrounded by her symbol of achievement.

Mother Sarah is shown as rising up from a treasure chest of the Pharaoh, her beauty filling the whole room.

Rebecca Gratz is surrounded by olive, almond, and pomegranate branches. Her accomplishments include founding the first Hebrew Sunday school, the Philadelphia Orphan Asylum, the Sewing Society, and the Fuel Society. Legend has it that it was Gratz's great beauty that inspired Sir Walter Scott to write *Ivanhoe*, the historical romance set in England at the time of Richard I.

The portrait of Baroness Clara de Hirsch (Gereuth Bischoffsheim) is ringed by almond, olive, and lemon branches. Her philanthropic deeds continued after the death of her husband, Baron de Hirsch. She used her vast fortune to support Jewish resettlements in Galicia, America, Canada, and Argentina, and she established trade schools, housing, pensions, almshouses, and soup kitchens all around the globe.

The first woman to be named prophet, Miriam Ha-Neviah (Miriam the Prophet), the sister of Aaron who is the brother of Moses, led a chorus of women in song and dance. A strong female leader, Miriam was a teacher, healer, poet, musician, dancer, and midwife. Exodus 15:20 reads: "And Miriam, the prophetess, the sister of Aaron, took a drum in her hand; and all the women went out after her with drums, dancing." In the tapestry, she is depicted striking a timbrel high above her head to make joyful music.

The poet Emma Lazarus is surrounded by almond and olive branches and the many books of poetry and stories that she wrote. Who can forget her famous poem "The New Colossus" on a tablet in the main entrance to the pedestal on the Statue of Liberty? It reads in part:

> Give me your tired, your poor
> Your huddled masses yearning to breathe free,
> The wretched refuse of your teeming shore.
> Send these, the homeless, tempest-tost to me,
> I lift my lamp beside the golden door!

Henrietta Szold's portrait is framed with olive and almond branches. She founded Hadassah in 1912 which, among myriad other charitable endeavors, helped fund the Hadassah-Hebrew University Medical Center. She was a Jewish scholar, a working editor, a pioneer Zionist, and a defender of democracy. Her ideals and programs still enrich the lives and work of the hundreds of Hadassah members in the US and Puerto Rico. She was also the first director of Youth Aliyah in Jerusalem and was instrumental in establishing Hadassah vocational education.

Deborah, the prophetess and judge who ruled over Israel, lived in a tent under a lofty palm tree, from which she administered advice to those who came before her with their quarrels.

Lillian Wald's portrait is bordered by an almond and rose branch. A social worker, she developed the first visiting nurse service in New York City, and she campaigned successfully for the establishment of the United States Children's Bureau. A guiding light in the leading social reform organizations of the day, she worked to change child labor laws and the welfare system.

Golda Meir (Mabowitz) is encircled by depictions of the critical points in her journey from Kiev, her birthplace, to Milwaukee, where she spent her youth, to Israel, where she immigrated as a young woman. Lemon and pomegranate branches meet the desert, culminating with the emblem of Israel. Meir was a Labor Zionist leader who became Israel's first ambassador to Russia, then Israel's foreign minister, and eventually the country's prime minister (from 1969 to 1974).

The scene depicts Queen Esther having an audience with King Ahasuerus. Through her intercession, Haman, the grand vizier, was exposed and hanged on the very gallows he had built for Mordecai. Haman's plan was to exterminate all the Jews in the Persian Empire because they were disloyal and subversive and might prove a menace to the power of the king.

Anna Marie Rosenberg (Lederer) is surrounded by the White House, where she served as

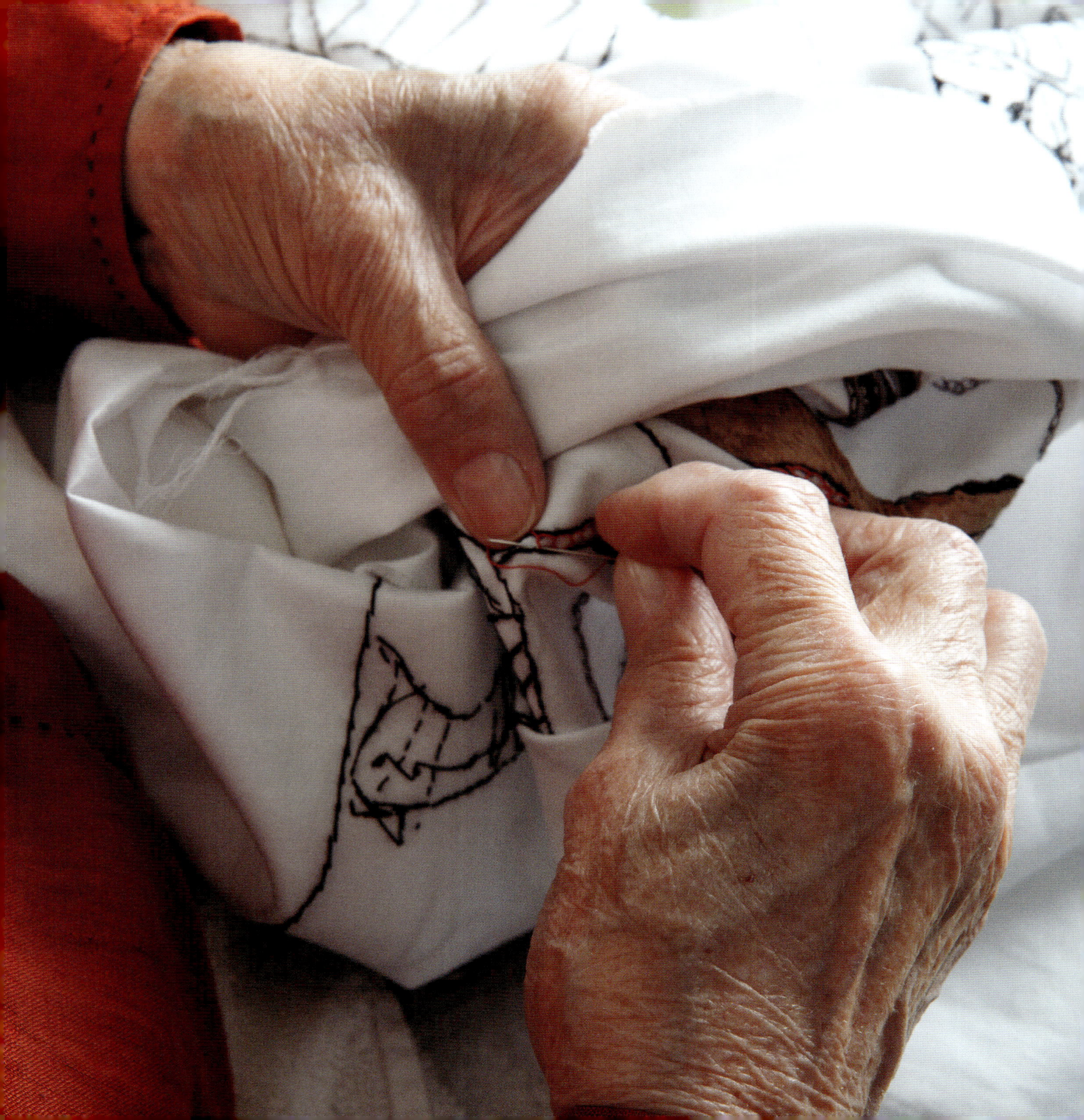

Assistant Secretary of Defense. She was the first woman in United States history to hold such a high federal and military post, as well as the first woman to be honored with the US Medal for Merit and the US Medal of Freedom.

Hannah Senesh is framed by words from her poem "Blessed Is the Match" and is shown parachuting into Nazi-occupied Europe. Senesh had volunteered for this mission so she could help her fellow Jews, and was trained by the British for the Haganah. Captured soon after she crossed into her native Hungary, she was tortured and executed at the age of twenty-three as a British spy. Her gesture of heroism was symbolic, and according to Abba Eban, "A whole generation came to see her as a symbol of vast martyrdom... She bequeaths to her survivors, especially the youth among them, the lesson of inescapable responsibility."

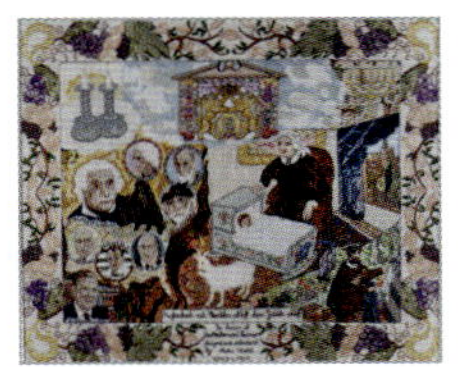
See page 24

Rozhinkesh mit Mandelen**:** In Trudie's Words

As I work on my embroideries, I listen to Yiddish music. I was listening to one of our beloved lullabies, "Rozhinkesh mit Mandelen," and as I sang along with Jan Peerce, suddenly the idea for this new work came with such visual intensity that I had to stop embroidering so I could put the idea down on paper.

Jewish leaders in health, education, medicine, finance, and science have given so much to humanity. Sleep is the symbol for peace in this prayer rendered in thread.

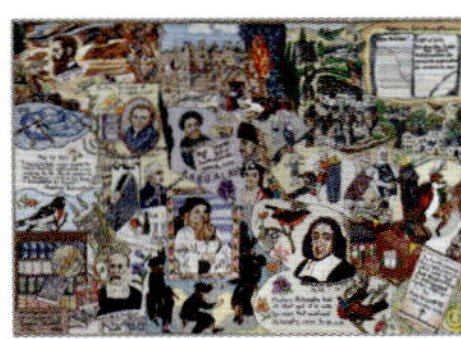
See page 18

European Ashkenazi History: Notes

An ambitious undertaking. How to depict all of European Ashkenazim history in one tapestry? Trudie began, as usual, with research. She read Abba Eban's 1968 book, *My People*, as well as his 1984 *Heritage: Civilization and the Jews*. She consulted Chaim Potok's *Wanderings*, and *Pictorial History of the Jewish People* by Nathan Ausubel, updated by David Gross, along with Stewart C. Easton's *The Heritage of the Past*. And she topped her research off with *The Encyclopedia of the Jewish Religion* and Bridger's *The New Jewish Encyclopedia*.

There are many chapters in this stitched historical narrative, including these:

- **The Crusades.** When the Crusaders reached Jerusalem, the Jewish population of the Holy City was herded into the synagogues and burned alive.
- The Crusades were followed by other dark centuries of blood accusations, **"black-death"** massacres, and expulsions, during which German Jews sought refuge in the Slavic countries, particularly Poland.
- At this time, the Jews in Rhenish provinces began to develop their own Judeo-German language, which later became known as the **Yiddish** language, the spoken and written tongue of most Eastern European Jews.
- The great seventeenth-century rationalist philosopher **Baruch Spinoza**, who propounded modern conceptions of the individual and the universe, laid the groundwork for the Enlightenment.
- As the persecutions of the Middle Ages increased, some Jews turned to Jewish mysticism (Kabbalah) to explain the sufferings of a faithful people. One of the self-proclaimed "redeemers" was **Shabbetai Zevi**, who proved himself to be a false messiah and charlatan. Also depicted are Jacob Frank and his daughter Eva Frank who similarly proved to be false messiahs and charlatans. They repudiated both the Bible and the Talmud, establishing in their stead the revelations of the Zohar (a commentary to reveal the hidden meaning of the Torah).
- The Hasidic movement began as a revolt of the *unlearned* against the strict rule of the rabbis. Its first leader, **Baal Shem Tov** (Master of the Good Name, abbreviated Besht), was born in Podolia in 1700. Hasidism acted as an equalizing influence on Eastern European Jewry, which had hitherto been dominated by an upper class made up of the wealthy and learned. **Hasidism**, which emphasized the emotions as opposed to the intellect, answered a deeply felt need in Jewish religious life; it endorsed a poetic and human element, and led the marginalized Jewish masses back to the mainstream Jewish values and the dream of universal peace.
- France, 1791. **Napoleon** granted the Jews of France the right to citizenship. In response, the renunciation by the Sanhedrin (Jewish rabbinical court system) of the quest for separate Jewish nationhood marked an important turning point in Jewish history and set the tone of Western Jewish life for the next century and more.

- With citizenship, the European Jews were quick to absorb European culture, but they found social acceptance slower in coming.
- Powerful Jews such as the **Rothschilds** consistently refused loans to governments oppressing Jews, and they worked discreetly but effectively to change public opinion about their fellow Jews.
- **Moses Mendelssohn** led the movement to achieve complete legal and political emancipation for the majority of Jews in Western Europe. Yet Mendelssohn's greatest achievement was probably his translation into German of the Pentateuch, which provided a bridge to the German language and to a life beyond the ghetto.
- Mendelssohn's work greatly contributed to the Haskalah, or Enlightenment, the movement that sought to broaden the intellectual and social horizons of the Jews to enable them to assimilate into Western Society. Haskalah spread to Austria, Poland, Lithuania, and Russia
- The scholar **Nachman Krochmal** was the Galician leader of Haskalah.
- Linguist **Isaac Baer Levinsohn** took up the cause, translating these writings into Russian.
- **Moses Leib Lilienblum** encouraged Jews to publicly assimilate. They could practice Judaism safely in private. But after the pogrom of 1881, Lilienblum recognized that the only way to truly protect the Jews was to establish a Jewish national home in Palestine.
- **Theodor Herzl**, born in Budapest, took up the cause. The "Dreyfus Affair" in Paris brought about a wave of anti-Semitism that Herzl knew could be remedied by the establishment of a legally recognized Jewish State. Herzl advocated that Jews cease to passively endure and that they instead proactively shape their own lives and the future of Judaism.

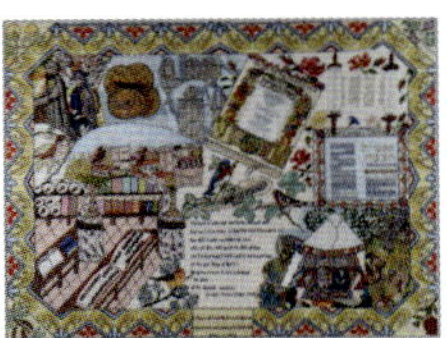

See page 86

Golden Age of Spain: In Trudie's Words

Judah Halevi was a physician, poet, and merchant. He was known as the singer of Zion. In 1140, he left Spain for the land of Israel. He died a few months later in Cairo, never having reached Jerusalem. We are blessed to have 800 of his poems passed down to us.

I was reading one of Judah Halevi's poems, a poem of Zion entitled "My Heart Is in the East":

...A trifle would it seem to me to leave all the good things of Spain—
Seeing how precious in mine eyes to behold the dust of the desolate sanctuary.

Reading the words, I felt burning ideas, and as I started to draw them, the ideas all connected.

The tapestry is, in itself, a visual poem that stitches together Sephardic history from its early times of peaceful coexistence with Muslims to Ferdinand and Isabella's 1492 edict expelling all Jews from Spain. The Golden Age of Spanish Jewry, in which the arts, poetry, and science flourished, lasted roughly from 900 to 1200 CE, from the birth of Hasdai ibn Shaprut, the Jewish leader and statesman in Andalucia, who paved the way to a flourishing of Jewish life in Moorish Spain, to the death of the great Maimonides. Moses ben Maimon (aka Maimonides) wrote the Mishneh Torah (repetition of the law) in 1180; it is a systematic arrangement, topic by topic, of the whole of Jewish law. Devoid of personal judgments or opinions, it provides the reader with a clear and organized summary of Jewish law in accordance with the recognized principles of the halakhah, the body of Jewish religious law. In 1190, Maimonides completed *Guide for the Perplexed*, his greatest philosophical work, which sought to reconcile the teachings of Judaism with the philosophy of Aristotle. The town of Cordova bloomed with scholars, poets, and grammarians during the Golden Age of Spanish Jewry. Learning centers taught not only Bible, Mishnah, and Hebrew grammar, but also poetry, logic, music, and medicine.

The scroll pen in the center of the tapestry is the tool of transference of knowledge; children were taught not only to write, but to write beautifully. The birds and the flowers herald a golden age. The featherlike design of the border incorporates the notion of scroll pens, which are separated by fertile clusters of pomegranates. The corners are laced with the bounty of Palestine—pomegranates, figs, carob, and citron.

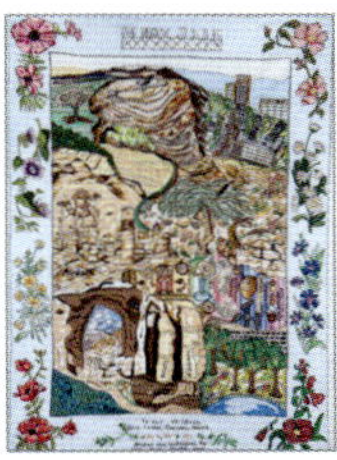

See page 171

The Negev: In Trudie's Words

I used to dream of a Negev with golden hills and a constellation of sparkles on a pristine desert. Nelson Glueck's *Rivers in the Desert: A History of the Negev* taught me that our Negev is something different: bare landscapes, bold colors, and bright light. That is how I chose to depict the Negev in this tapestry.

In the early period, the Neolithic peoples of the Negev had the ability to make excellent tools out of stone, and they introduced pottery making. Then, during the latter part of the Chalcolithic period near the end of the fourth millennium BCE, people of the Negev wove cloth, fired pottery, and carved ivory images.

The 1,000 years that began with the Nabataean Kingdom in the fourth century BCE was the longest period of continuous civilization in the history of the Negev. Commerce thrived and the population grew. The Nabataeans invented means to harvest water in the dry lands by building hundreds of miles of terraces and digging thousands of cisterns to collect every possible drop of the rare rainwater. This ancient skill is now imitated by modern settlers in the region. The majestic ruins of Avdat, set atop a hill, dominate the scorching desert plain. Avdat was a Nabataean city dating to the third century BCE. The citizens of Avdat controlled the caravan routes from the Persian Gulf to Eilat and Gaza. Along the road that leads to Eilat, I have drawn the natural arch in the valley of Timna and the so-called "pilasters of King Solomon," which was a mining center of considerable importance.

Our Negev is home to many animals. The wild goat is feasting on an acacia tree in a luxuriant oasis.

The tapestry is bordered with flowers native to Israel.

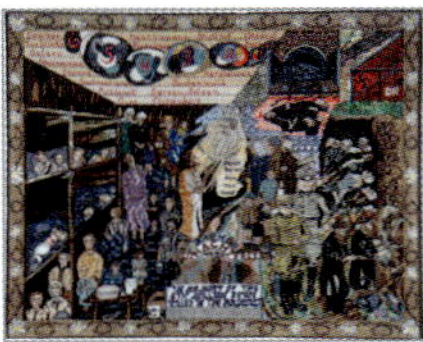

See page 165

Final Destination: In Trudie's Words

The train tracks brought us to this hellish place; for many, straight to the ovens. Others were shot into holes of mass graves.

The bodies lying by the ovens rest on a detail of Yemenite embroidery techniques, the oldest Jewish techniques that I still use. The only small treasures we had were our tears. The Nazis with their vicious dogs with large teeth frighten mothers and children entering the camp. The slow movement of time in these concentration camps, the waiting for death.

We have a very touching and very sad song, "Unter Dayne Vayse Shtern" ("Under Your White Stars"): "My words are the tears that rest in your hand." That song is a glimmer of hope and comfort. The mountain of confiscated religious objects, candlesticks, and Torah wimpels[19] roll off God's hands. On the left side at the top are six smoke clouds rising from the concentration camps, many of which are named.

In several camps, there was a sign on the entrance gate: ARBEIT MACHT FREI (Work Sets You Free). How cynical. When you were too weak to work, you were executed. The border of this tapestry is prison wire and marguerites. After liberation, the marguerite was the first joy I remember; I picked one in the grass to give to Mama.

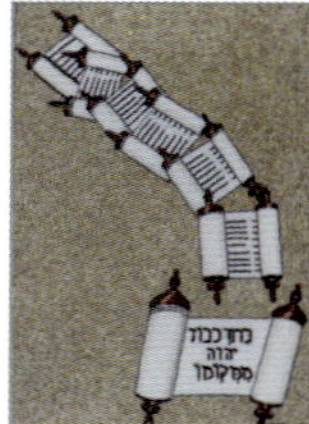

See page 54

***Floating Torahs*:** In Trudie's Words

As I was listening to Rabbi Grater's reading of the Haftarah, I suddenly saw myself holding one Torah while other Torahs, one after another, slipped from under my Torah and floated away. There were seven.

The gold background design of embroidery was inspired by Klimt's painting of Adele Bloch-Bauer I.

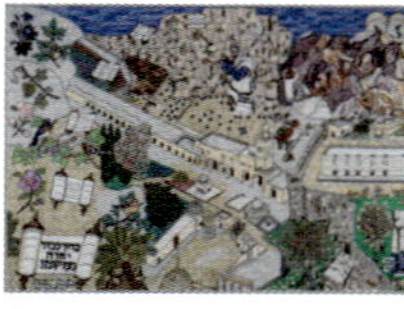

See page 76

***Floating Torahs Over Jerusalem*:** In Trudie's Words

My mind carries me over Jerusalem. I see Torahs floating. The ground is silver and gold, and as I look upwards I see a mountain range—a Torah within it. Mt. Sinai brings the Laws through Moses to us. Part of the old wall in Jerusalem coexists with the modern. From above, I see the part of Jerusalem that is our Kotel; it is not entirely visible because I view it from the West. The shofar is calling us to come. The blue stars are our people. The Torahs float up toward Mt. Sinai. Cypress, olive, mulberry, chestnut, and box trees. The yad, the feather pen, the ink pot, all to write the Torah.

---

19 A wimpel is a long linen sash used as a binding for the Sefer (sacred handwritten) Torah by Jews of Germanic origin.

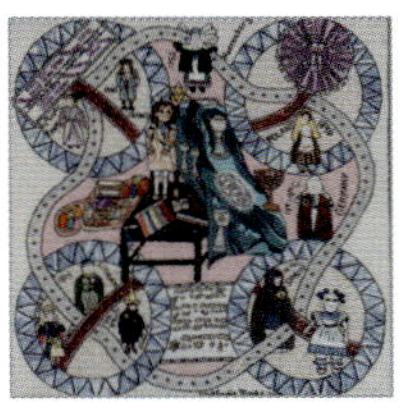

See page 85

Magical Road to Embroidery: Notes

In this spiritual portrait-of-a-life, all characters are faceless except for the dolls. Faceless characters are a rarity in the work of Trudie Strobel. Here, the faceless haunting of Trudie's personal past is echoed in tributes to her past work—work that reached into an even more distant past, the past of a people whose persecution reached its crescendo in the Holocaust. This work is another lyrical history, but this is a history rooted in the self, and at the center is Trudie's Papa Doll, with a face, who stands proudly atop the chair where Trudie sits to do her stitching every day, to create her history and the history of a people to whom she is inextricably tethered. The only other face belongs to her Mitzvah Doll, the personalized doll she makes for children of the present day to cherish.

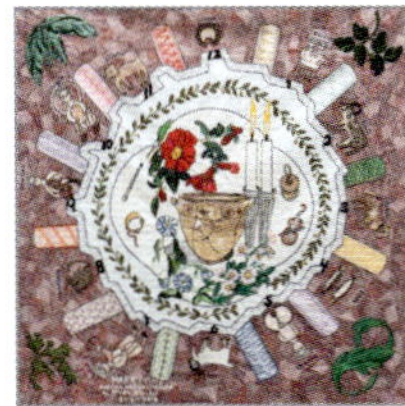

See page 170

Mark of Time: In Trudie's Words

Rabbi Grater, the former rabbi of Pasadena Jewish Temple, asked the congregation, "How do we mark time?" Others might have answered, but my mind was too busy forming thoughts and pictures. It occurred to me that Shabbas is a place in time. And I set about designing my next work in my head as I sat there in temple, suddenly inspired.

The Beit Alpha Synagogue Mosaic Pavement from the early sixth century, 517 to 518 CE, appeared to me. The synagogue's foundation and mosaic pavement were unearthed near Beit Alpha by N. Avigad and E.L. Sukenik working on behalf of the Hebrew University in 1929. From there the rest of this temporal piece evolved, first in my head, then on paper, and then in thread.

INDEX

Aleichem, Sholem 21, 163, 166, 173–174
Alyona 32, 34–36, 40–41, 44, 70
America 9, 76, 80, 86, 89, 180
Andrusyshyn, Dotnara 40
Auschwitz-Birkenau 64
"Autumn" 150
"Badges of Shame: Eleven Centuries of Degradation" 99
"Banner for Peter Kahn Library" 30, 176
"Bar Mitzvah" 124–125
Bavarian region 81
Belzec 58, 60
"Bird of Paradise" 144
"Blessings Over the Shabbas Candles" 156
Broken Grindstones 81
"Bruce Solow and Family" 179
"Cantor Ruth's tefillin bag" 145
"Challah cover" 146
Chelmno 65
Christianopoulos, Dinos 69
"Circumcision" 122–123
"Corinne and Nicole Strobel" 97
"Destroyed" 46–47
"Diaspora: 114–115
displaced-persons camp 81, 85
displacement camp 14, 75–76, 78
"Distinguished Jewish Women of Achievement" 134, 178
Dnieper River 17, 35
Dnipropetrovsk 17, 41
Dr. Solow 92, 96, 99, 109, 163
drawn work 82, 84
Egan, Leo 109
Ermershausen 81–82, 84
"European Ashkenazi History" 18, 183
Eva 34–35, 41
"Exodus from Egypt" 110–111
"Fantasy in Roses" 9
"Faye's Tallit" 108
"Final Destination" 163, 165, 187
"Flame" 46, 53
"Floating Torahs" 55, 188
"Floating Torahs Over Jerusalem" 76, 91, 188
"Flowers" 154
"Funeral" 132–133
Galeano, Eduardo 55
Gansky Labuhn, Masha 17
García Márquez, Gabriel 89
"Gate of Jerusalem" 149
ghetto 57–58, 60, 63–65, 67, 185
"Golden Age of Spain" 86, 185–186
"Golden and Dark Ages of Spain" 116–117
Gonda Foundation 105
goose 36, 70, 78–80, 82
Hazaz, Haim 81
"Heart" 52
"Hebrew Sampler" 159
"Holocaust—The Horrifying Years" 118–119
"Imprisoned" 49
"Israel" 120–121
Israel 76, 112, 114, 120–121, 171, 174–175, 177–178, 181, 185, 187
"Jewish Calendar, The" 168, 175
Jewish Federation of Greater Los Angeles, The 99
"Joseph Ariel's tallit" 17
"Joseph Ariel's tallit bag" 59
King Chaim 64
King David 112–113
kolkhoz 17, 22, 25–26, 34–35, 39, 56, 63, 70, 72, 78
"Kristallnacht" 68
Kristallnacht 82
Kristofferson, Kris 75
Krivoy Rog 22, 25, 29–30, 43
Labuhn, Vasilliy 17–44
Leala 93
"Light #2" 62, 67, 173
Łódź 56, 60, 63–65, 67, 71
Los Angeles Museum of the Holocaust 63, 92, 105–106, 169
Love in the Time of Cholera 89
Lublin 59–60
Magen David 56, 71, 99
"Magical Road to Embroidery" 85, 189
Majdanek 60
"Margarit-g-lach" 74, 174
marguerite 72, 78, 187
"Mark of Time" 170, 189
"Marriage" 128–129
Martyrs Memorial 106
"Matzoh cover" 148
"Moody Blues, The" 99
Mordechai Rumkowski, Chaim 64
"Morning Glories" 147
Museum of the Holocaust 63, 92, 105–106, 169
Naumovich Rabinovich, Solomon 163

"Negev, The" 171, 187
Neu Chortitza 22, 41, 63, 78, 86
"Numbered Like Cattle" 46, 48
"Oyfn Pripitchok" 17, 70
"Paint Her as She Is" 109
Papa Doll 26, 29, 37, 39, 41–43, 45, 56, 58–60, 67, 85, 96, 99, 162, 188
Pasadena City College 92
Poland 55–56, 58, 75, 104, 106, 183, 185
"Pomegranate" 7
"Portrait of John and Leala" 93
Rabbi Nachman of Bratslav 56
Rakivka 57
"Rozhinkesh Mit Mandlen" (Raisins and Almonds) 25, 183
Rushdie, Salman 17
"Russia 1942" 60, 162
"Sabbath" 126–127
samovar 35, 57–59
San Marino 91–92
Schoenberg, Randol 9
"Shabbas" 157, 172–173
Shoah 99, 163
"Shoah Series" 46
Siberia 26, 31–32
Soviet Union 17, 40
"Spring" 148
"Starvation" 46, 51, 65
Strobel, Corinne 92, 97
Strobel, Hans 89, 91
Strobel, John 91, 93, 173
Strobel, Nicole 92, 97
Strobel, Paul 91, 94
"Study of Paul Strobel" 94
"Summer" 149
tatting 84, 91, 103
Teresa, Tanta 89
"Three Holiday Symbols" 155
"Time Running Out" 46, 50
"Tribute to Sholem Aleichem, A" 21, 166, 173
Trudell, John 63
"Trudie's Goose" 79–80
Ukraine 17, 58, 163
Uman 56–58
USS General W.G. Haan 86
"Winter" 151
Würtzburg 81
"Yaroslavsky Tapestry" 192
Yiddish 17, 20, 70, 166, 174, 183–184
"Yom Kippur" 130–131
Zgierski, Chana 169
Zhenya 57–59
Zoller, Cheryl 105

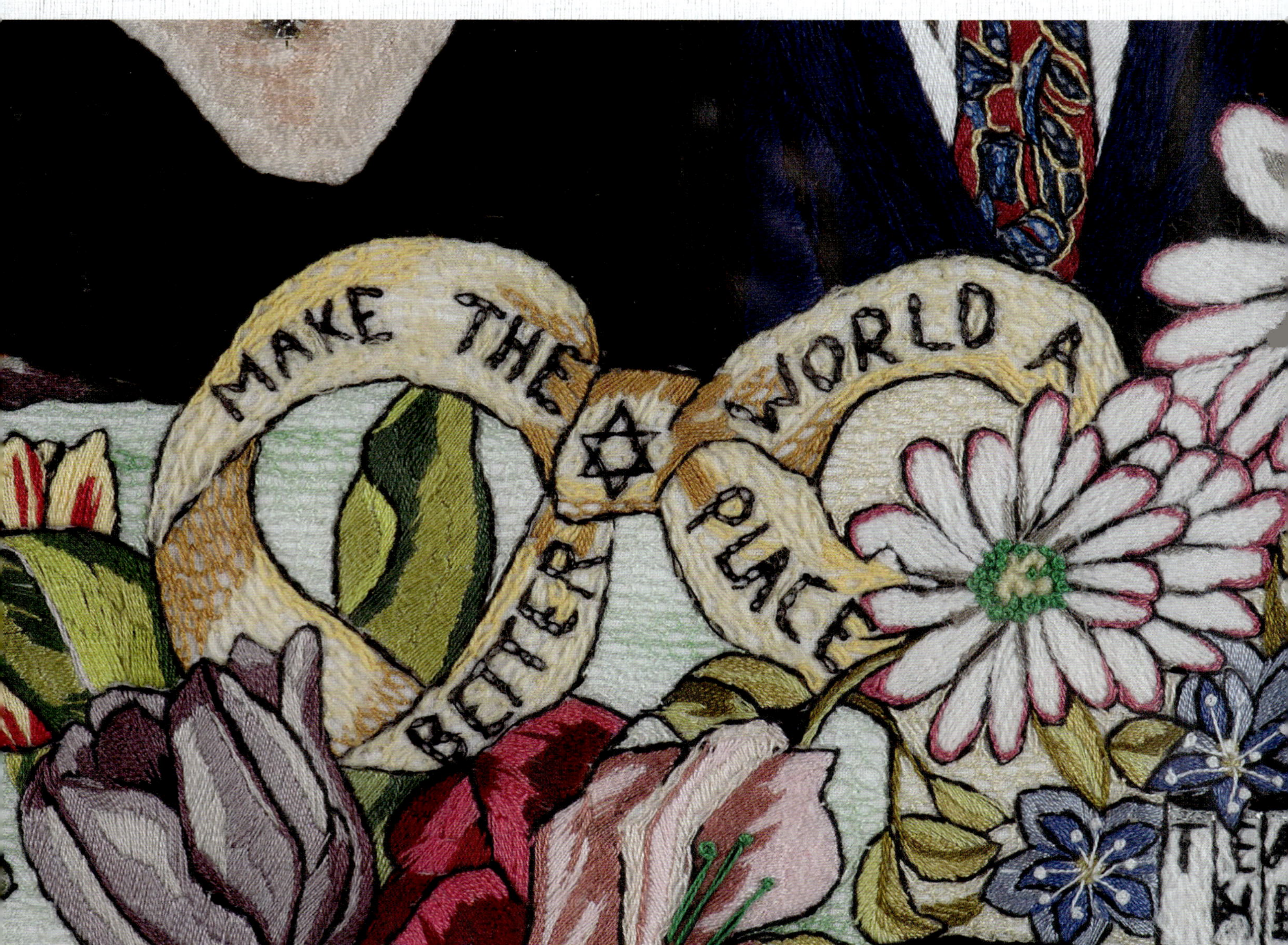

Detail from ***Yaroslavsky Tapestry*** · 2004

IN GRATITUDE

We would like to thank Colleen Dunn Bates and her amazing team at Prospect Park Books, including designer Amy Inouye, for turning a dream into a reality with vision and enthusiasm. For their love, support and heavy lifting, we would like to thank our families, Randall, Jesse and Maya Miller; Paul, John, Leala, Corinne, and Nicole Strobel; and Tom, Matthew, and Paul Soulanille. We are grateful for the insights, criticism, and encouragement of Michael Berenbaum, Lila Dworsky-Hickey, Sally Dworsky, Liora Elghanayan, Bridget Fonger, Claire Gorfinkel, Rabbi Arielle Hanien, Susan Kellie Harding, Justin Lev, John Loftus, Kathryn Edwards O'Sullivan, Alice Shulman, Cameron Slater, and Richard Thompson.

For institutional support, we thank the Memorial Foundation for Jewish Culture. Special recognition is owed to the keepers of Trudie's work: Los Angeles Museum of the Holocaust, Selma Benjamin, Ruth Bernstein, Heidi Caetano, Sam Egan, Donna Egan, Sara and Larry Freedman, Jona Goldrich, Rabbi Joshua and Francine Grater, Cantor Ruth Berman Harris, Charity Hume, Samara Hutman, Marcia Josephy, Marilyn and Martin Kirschen, Izak and Faye Langholtz, David and Masha Loen, Lisa Lommel, Micki Minovitz, Bryna Moscovitz, Pasadena Jewish Temple, Yaron S. Rabinowitz MD, Ernest and Evelyn Robinson, Shelley Rosen, Mark Rothman, Randol Schoenberg, Brian and Sharon Solow, Margaret Solow, Larry and Sharon Neumann Solow, Lee and Toni Solow, Corkey and Bruce Solow, Bernard and Phyllis Sosner, Rabbi Daniel and Chana Sperber, Edie Taylor, Barbara and Zev Yaroslavsky, and Abigail Yasger.

A foundational element of the story in these pages is the heroism of one mother, Masha Gansky Labuhn, whose memory we hope to honor with this book.

The idea for this book came only after Maya Savin Miller, then fourteen and post-bat-mitzvah, wrote a short story called *Trudie's Goose*, which was first published in *Bluefire Magazine*. It was Maya who brought Trudie into all of our lives. We therefore dedicate this book to Maya Savin Miller. In the words of Trudie Strobel, "Change starts with the vision of the young."

— Jody Savin, Ann Elliott Cutting, and Trudie Strobel

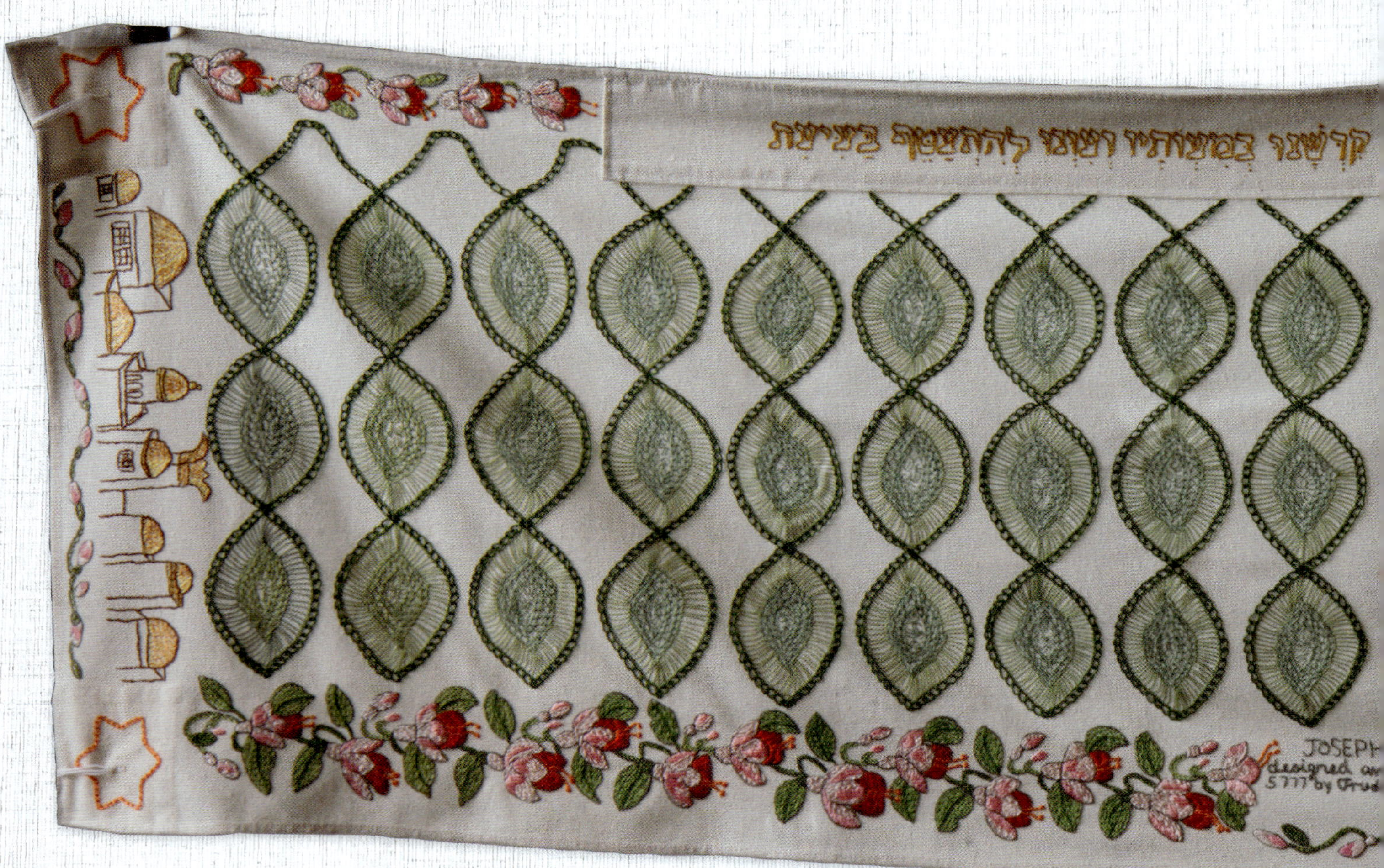

Joseph Ariel's tallit, completed 2018

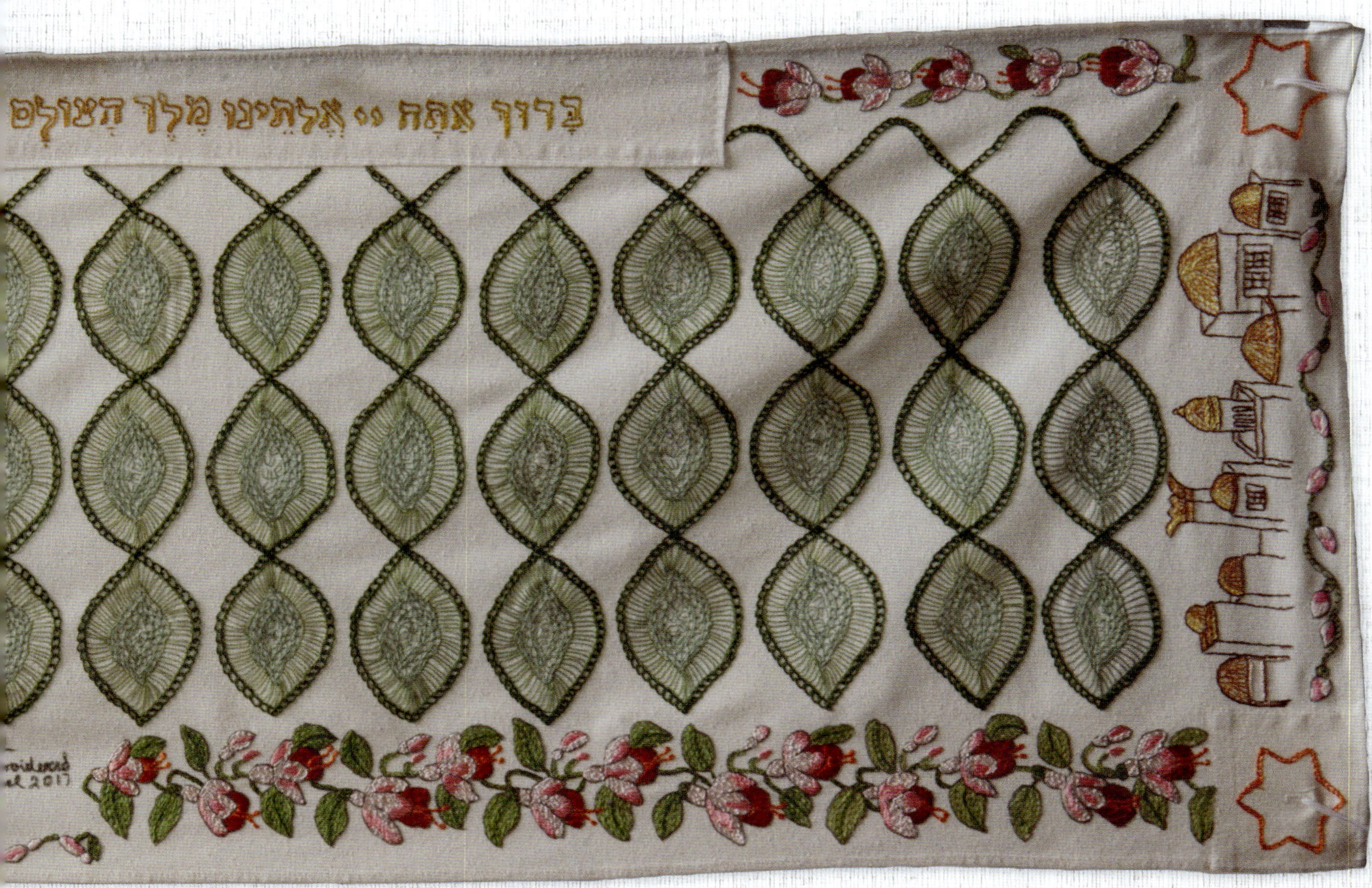
ברוך אתה אלהינו מלך העולם